THE
PROTESTANT WAY

KENNETH HAMILTON

THE
PROTESTANT
WAY

1956
ESSENTIAL BOOKS, INC.
FAIR LAWN, N.J.

PRINTED AND BOUND IN ENGLAND
FOR ESSENTIAL BOOKS, INC. BY
HAZELL WATSON AND VINEY LTD
AYLESBURY AND LONDON

TO

PROFESSOR JOHN G. McKENZIE

with affection and gratitude

PREFACE

THIS BOOK is not a practical guide to Protestantism—still less an account of Protestant history. Rather, it is an essay in interpretation, trying to do a little spade-work among the foundations of Christian theology and church-life in order to justify the claim that there is such a thing as a distinctive 'Protestant way'.

Again, although this is a book *about* theology, it is not a book *of* theology. Only occasionally have I ventured to argue a theological point. For the most part I have been content to state accepted theological positions and to evaluate them from a Protestant point of view. The implications of theological systems, rather than the systems themselves, have been my concern. For that reason, my approach to the thinkers of the past appears very largely to be made through their present-day followers and interpreters. It is the disciple who usually develops the implications of the teaching he regards as being authoritative for him, so that even his misunderstandings and exaggerations are instructive. I have chosen a few representative authors, each with a clearly defined outlook, to present divergent views on the matters dealt with here, rather than cast my net too wide; so that some names are continually recurring. This may perhaps ensure that other opinions than the ones which I personally hold shall get a fair hearing.

Part of the work of interpretation is always to break down accepted phraseology and familiar metaphors. Those who are accustomed to think of the Church as *the Body of Christ* may be distressed to find the various Christian Churches described in these pages as *parties*. Obviously, the words *the Body of Christ* tell us much more (and almost certainly something much more essential) about the Church than the word *party* tells us. Yet the latter word may tell us something about the Church which the former words do not. In the hope that the result will be worth while, I have sought to put theological thought frequently into non-theological dress. Hence the ubiquity of the term 'value' for (as John Oman has contended in his *The Natural and the Supernatural*) the quality of sacredness can be conveyed, outside the sphere of religion, only by means of the notion of absolute value. Also, at the risk of falling into the slough of jargon, I have been rash enough to seize upon some common words of everyday speech and bind them to a technical sense—or follow someone else who has done so. *Dialogue* is the chief of these thefts, but there are others which will not, I hope, cause the reader too much discomfort. As Lewis Carroll's Humpty-Dumpty believed, so far as the handling of words is concerned the end justifies the means.

I owe my thanks to the library staffs of Dalhousie University and the University of King's College, Halifax, for their patience and diligence; to Professor Hilton Page, who read the manuscript, for his help and kindly encouragement; to Mrs Merritt Grantmyre, for her assistance with typing; and to my wife, who knows my gratitude.

Elmsdale   KENNETH HAMILTON
Nova Scotia

CONTENTS

CHAPTER ONE

NAMES AND VALUES:
A PRELIMINARY INQUIRY

I. PROPER NAMES AND GROUP NAMES

THE WORD *protestant* means 'one who protests', but a *Protestant* is a member of a group of people who are distinguished from other groups. When such a word as *protestant* undergoes this metamorphosis it turns almost exclusively into a proper name. Proper names, as John Stuart Mill pointed out, serve as labels for identification and have really no meaning. But what has no descriptive meaning as a name may have all the more historical meaning as an existing entity. The dog we call 'Scottie' means much more to us than the notion of a dog in general. Every historical label (*Scottie* belongs to history just as much as *Napoleon*) conveys another kind of meaning altogether from the meaning discovered by logical definition. This meaning is at once vague and concrete. It is vague because we cannot describe it exhaustively; at the best we can give an inadequate description which may serve to convey to other people what we are talking about. And it is concrete because it refers to the realm of historical existence to which we ourselves belong.

In the case of an individual proper name we can point directly to the reality which bears the label. The name *Thomas Smith* has a meaning for us if we know Thomas Smith, or if we are told: 'There goes Thomas Smith.' There are, however, collective or generalized labels, largely proper names in that they refer directly to history, but retaining descriptive meaning. We may call these *group names*. Group names are connected to historical existence by way of an idea; we cannot point to them directly. On the other hand, their close relation to historical existence makes any purely descriptive definition impossible. Here the idea is always the essential link between a group name and its meaning, although we are seldom conscious of the fact. We speak freely of *Americans*, *Asiatics*, and *Jews*. We could hardly do without these labels, and yet when we come to ask exactly what we understand by them the ambiguity of the words at once becomes apparent. A man may be called an Asiatic because he is a Jew, and so not an American; or he may be an American although he is an

Asiatic, but not a Jew; or he may be a Jew and an American, but not an Asiatic. The various classifications depend upon whether the idea of place of birth, citizenship, racial origin, religion, language, or cultural standing is made the test of belonging to one or other of these groups.

This sort of difficulty over the right application of group names does not come merely from failing to use language with sufficient care. It comes from the complexity of historical existence. However carefully terms are defined within any particular context (as they must be if complete confusion is to be avoided), the effort to understand the world we live in entails using labels that are ambiguous and ill-defined. For instance, historians could not describe the course of European history without reference to the complex of cultural changes known as the *Renaissance*. Yet some historians believe the Renaissance to have been completed at a date when other historians would say it had not yet begun. It would be futile to abandon the insight into the history of Europe given by the generalizing label *Renaissance* until complete agreement had been reached about what the Renaissance actually was. We must accept the fact that group names are established by a method of indirect pointing which is necessarily inconclusive, and recognize that to demand absolute finality here is to demand the impossible. Our ideas may be faulty, but they are the condition of our coming to know anything at all about historical existence. And we must continue to scrutinize and redefine our labels so that they shall distort the reality they seek to make explicit less and less as the task of applying the labels proceeds.

The danger of assuming we know what we are talking about when we use labels, and so of reducing these to meaningless catchwords, is a very real one. The only remedy is a ceaseless and critical examining of the ideas which give content to the labels we use. 'When a term has become so universally sanctified as "democracy" now is', writes Mr T. S. Eliot, 'I begin to wonder whether it means anything. . . . If anybody ever attacked democracy, I might discover what the word meant.'[1] *Democracy* is a label that has been lifted out of a complex historical setting and used as though it were obvious and self-explanatory. The descriptive meaning of 'democracy', i.e. the rule of the people, says very little unless the terms are limited by some regulative idea. When the need for some idea to interpret the word by giving it content is ignored, then the word inevitably loses meaning; it ceases to point to any determinate reality that

[1] *The Idea of a Christian Society* (1939), pp. 14–15.

exists, or to an ideality that might conceivably exist, and turns into a comfortable sound which is so familiar that it lulls all critical curiosity to sleep. In the same way, *Communism* has been made into a bogy-word today for most of the Western world. It is only necessary to attach the label of *Communist* to a policy or a person to condemn either, irrespective of the worth of the policy or the integrity of the person. The fact that the words we use cease to have reliable meaning is only one result of this disastrous process. Equally, the world we live in becomes less intelligible as we deprive ourselves of the mental equipment with which to survey and analyse it.

II. FOR AND AGAINST

It is interesting that, in order to find out what 'democracy' is, Mr Eliot should wish for someone to attack it. In any scientific inquiry complete impartiality and objectivity are absolutely essential; but then science does not deal with proper names as such. Proper names (and group names are like proper names in this respect), because they belong to historical existence, carry with them value. That is, we are moved to accept or reject them. And more than that, we feel duty bound to approve or disapprove, to attack or defend them. This is very obvious indeed where individuals are concerned. Whether with good reason or not, we like some people more than others. And, whatever our personal feelings toward them may be, we know that our approval or disapproval of individuals ought to be directed to advancing right values in them or through them. We say: 'I ought to punish Billy'; 'I ought to vote for Brown'; 'I ought to write to Jones to thank him for what he did.' In all such judgements is contained an opinion about the worth of certain values, and also the claim to know something essential about the person concerned. We are for or against Billy, Brown, and Jones—or at least for or against some quality in them which we call a part of their 'character'. And an individual's character is in the most exact sense his *meaning*, the reality which is signified by his name.

Everyone knows how hard it is to estimate the true character of a person. A group name is almost as poor a guide to the real 'character' of the entity it labels as an individual's name is to him. Indeed, most group names are very like nicknames given to people on account of some particular characteristic; and, like nicknames, the original reason for the name may easily become forgotten, while the name itself has stuck. Why there are Whigs and Tories is buried in the past. No one remembers why a Teetotaller is a total abstainer from alcohol instead of a total abstainer from meat, or a total partaker of both. The plain sense of Quaker, Freemason, Republican, Democrat, and (in England) Public School is largely irrelevant. Such names as Conservative, Presbyterian, and Boy Scout preserve something of their descriptive meanings, but these alone without a social and historical context would be very misleading. Knowing what a 'congress' is will not go far toward explaining *Congress* in the U.S.A. or the *Congress Party* in India. Many labels which look so like pure abstract nouns that often they are not dignified by a capital letter reveal their identity as *mainly* proper names by their obstinate ambiguity. We have already come across *democracy* in this connexion; *liberalism* is another group name of the same sort. It looks as though a descriptive meaning could be found for these terms without invoking any of the particularities of history. This is an illusion. We need to be acquainted with both Classical and Modern Europe to become familiarized with the general sense of *liberal*, so that we can guess more or less confidently what is intended by a *liberal* education or by *Liberal* Theology. Yet, even then, we have not any definition of *liberalism*, which can assume very different forms according to place and period.

When a label has no necessary relation to what it labels, so that it can be applied to aspects of existence with quite diverse characteristics, it can be said to be meaningless. It no longer points, even indirectly, to any part of the real world. The idea behind it has been lost, and so it no longer communicates any real value. A bogus value may still cling to the name, but the value has no real existence because it is attached to a label belonging to nothing. That is why Mr Eliot believes an attack upon democracy might restore its meaning. All forms of government cannot be equally good. An attack upon any form of *democratic* government will call attention to the fact that the name stands for something determinate, and so stimulate the desire to define the meaning of *democracy* better. The idea which alone can give content to the label will thus be consciously brought under review. Just the same loss of meaning takes place when every one agrees to condemn a label, such as *Communism*. Unless some activity called *communistic* can be defended, what is bad in *Communism* cannot be known. Decrying *Communism* then becomes a purely emotional indulgence destroying the possibility of recognizing and choosing values.

Psychologists are well aware of the way in which words become charged by the associations that gather around them and touch off the emotions these associations generate, even when the words have only an accidental connexion with what causes the emotion.[2] The power of labels to attract to themselves the emotions that properly belong to the values the labels claim to represent is peculiarly impressive and partly justifies Robert Louis Stevenson's cynical saying: 'Man is a creature who lives not upon bread alone, but principally by catchwords.' The demagogue who wishes to inflame his followers uses the 'suggestive' power of words instead of trying to convey rational information. Nevertheless, the emotion that runs amok among the echoes caused by names has its proper place among those values that are of vital concern to mankind. An orator can inspire as well as bemuse, and poets increase our appreciation of the full meaning of words while exploiting their full emotional power. Everyone is obliged to make up his mind whether he is for or against the values he meets in the course of living. He has to will the good as he sees it. He is foolish (and no doubt wicked) if he makes up his mind on the strength of his emotions, but he is unlikely to come to a decision of any consequence without emotion. Emotion is the smoke which shows that the fire of will is burning somewhere—though often the thicker the smoke the less satisfactory the fire.

In social gatherings a ban is often put upon political and religious discussion in order to avoid discord. Since no two aspects of experience involve values affecting our lives more deeply, this ban is not surprising; discussion must inevitably reveal differences of value and so excite emotional tensions. Naturally too, words used in these connexions acquire a strong emotional aura and become explosive. But it is the group name—the label that has a definite and restricted social connotation—which stirs up high feelings most quickly and is probably the chief reason for the social ban. *Communism* is more often and more vehemently denounced than *totalitarianism*. It is less 'up in the air'. *Protestantism* is a safer rallying-cry than *Christianity*, though we might be reluctant to admit it. We would like to think that we are 'for' the greatest good and 'against' the blackest evils. It is not so simple as all that. The labels we are accustomed to are

---

[2] In *Psychopathology of Everyday Life* Freud gives many examples of words being forgotten, twisted, or misplaced because they call to mind other words connected with emotional experiences. He also illustrates how an underdeveloped critical sense produces the same results. Freud quotes from *Julius Caesar*, iii. 3:

CINNA. Truly my name is Cinna.
BURGHER. Tear him to pieces! He is a conspirator.
CINNA. I am Cinna the poet! not Cinna the conspirator.
BURGHER. No matter; his name is Cinna; tear the name out of his heart and let him go.

(Penguin Edition (1938), p. 82 *n*.)

between us and the values we would champion. We make the label our standard of value.

III. VALUES, INSTITUTIONS, AND PARTIES

Value is revealed conceptually in ideals, unconsciously in suppressed desires, consciously in religious faith or a 'philosophy of life', and socially in institutions—the most universal of which is a culture or civilization. The individual draws his first understanding of values from his social environment. Throughout his life, society, through its institutions, is the chief mediator of values to him. He becomes aware of value when he begins to express his personal will and finds that some of these expressions are approved of by his parents, some not. The institution of the family has made its impact upon him, for good or evil, and what he becomes afterwards will be partly (some would maintain chiefly) the fruit of that impact. As his experience widens he will gain knowledge of the wider ranges of society and become involved in the complex of institutions belonging to it, education, law, economics, religion, and so on. He will enter, of necessity and also voluntarily, into many different kinds of association with his fellows. His tastes, his habits, his beliefs, and his interests will be largely conditioned by his social experience and opportunities. He will be a man of his age, of his country, and of his social inheritance. If he rebels against his environment, the form of his revolt will reflect much of what he has revolted against.

It is very understandable, then, that social institutions should supply us with so many of our values, and that group names should bulk so large in our emotional life. Values do not appear to us abstractly, but clothed in the garb of familiar institutions we accept and respect, institutions which bring into being groups we can belong to and whose privileges we can share. University students are not the only ones to know an *Alma Mater*. There is a nursing mother in each of the social organizations within society for all of its members. Even those who are unable, or unwilling, to take advantage of the privileges society offers, or who are treated like stepchildren, are unlikely to escape from the institutions of the parent society or be unaffected by its values. The non-caste untouchables of India are an integral part of the institution of caste from which they are excluded, and conform to the over-all pattern of Hindu culture. In our own highly organized society the misfits who fail to lead a 'normal' life within the ordinary institutional set-up which their neighbours find sufficient, are sent to what are fitly called *institutions*. There they are, if possible, trained to take their place in society at large when they are able and willing to do so.

The institutions that mean most to us are those that touch our lives most closely and that supply us with groups we can join with most obvious benefit to ourselves. If there is 'no place like home' it is because the intimate relationships of family life can be found nowhere else. Yet the sense of *belonging* does not come from nearness by itself. Unity is felt most fully when values are shared in common. Thus the institutions that represent important values, even when they are more remote, may command greater loyalty than those that are closer to personal interest. A man may leave his family to defend his country, to pursue his profession, or to become a hermit. Both politics and religion have their roll of martyrs who gave themselves for the *cause*—the value that seemed supremely worth while.

Institutions are made effective by the people who run them. It is not enough for an institution to maintain itself as an organization, for it must also have the support of people who have the will to make it work. People must believe in it, which means that they must appreciate the value it embodies. An army that has lost its morale degenerates into a rabble, and an administration that has become hopelessly corrupt is ripe for overthrow. Since the men who run institutions do not necessarily share the same values, they may easily conflict in their beliefs about the form an institution should take. More fundamentally, different beliefs about values will lead to disagreement over which institutions should exist and what their interrelationship should be. Diversity of belief leads to the formation of parties.

The party is concrete, a group to which one can belong. It may be nearer or more remote; a local cell or a world-wide organization. If organized, it will be itself an institution, as a political party is. But it need not be organized. There are unofficial parties (*factions*) within parties, and there are parties made up of other parties (when official these are called *coalitions*). What counts is that men should feel that the party is the mediator of some important value to society. A party may begin as a spontaneous discovery that several people share a common interest and concern, but it tends to institutionalize itself to carry out its aims most effectively. For the party lives by creating the will of its members to advance the values it embodies by advancing the party itself. When it loses this ability it ceases to function as a party. When it has created itself into an institution, a party may find that members of the party have taken over the institution and are running it under the party name as an instrument of a new party. In spite of the continuity of name and organization, it will then be another party altogether, for parties exist solely to further certain values. They may work in opposition to established institutions, or may use these to express their own values and to further their own life, but when the values change the parties change.

Today we have seen the Party, under this name (not all parties are called parties!), alter the face of the world and the course of history. Yet the spectacular achievements of the Fascist and Communist parties are only an extreme example, made possible by modern technology, of the way power has followed and been dependent upon mass acceptance of the values advocated by a crusading party. The party may go by many names and have many different goals—from world dictatorship to reforming the alphabet—but if it kindles belief in the values it mediates, it becomes a force to be reckoned with. Because few people readily grasp values in the form of abstract ideas, the most popular embodiment of values has always been the party leader. As the Ideal Leader his personality and personal will can create the party and determine the party programme. Napoleon was a supreme example of this leadership principle. Modern dictatorship used the *Führer-prinzip*, but also the abstract system of party values as expressed in the ideology of the Party.

The values embodied in, and mediated through, a party are those contained in its policy or programme. These include the professed aims and intentions as well as those actually pursued. From the former much of the emotional appeal of the party is derived; it is pledged to do what is 'good', and so all 'good' men must come to the help of the party, pledging their loyalty to the righteous cause. But once the easy transition of emotion from the party principles to the party as an actual power group is made, the latter undeclared aims are by far the most important. The group name now represents all that the original values stood for, while the party becomes the mediator of another set of values altogether, which will continue to arouse the same intensity of emotion as the others, because both are identified with the existence of the party. Indeed, a further emotional factor emerges in the growth of party spirit. The party is seen to stand over against other parties—*we* against *they*. Even if men see that the values they cherish are not embodied as perfectly in the party as they would desire, they see them to be denied altogether in rival parties, therefore they must not relax their full support of the party if they want the values to survive at all. In the subsequent inter-party strife these values can easily be lost sight of altogether, especially if the party declares that conditions demand a temporary putting aside of its ultimate aims until they can be more fully carried out.

Modern totalitarianism shows the extreme working out of this party logic. Fascism makes the Party the embodiment of all national ideals; what it does is *ipso facto* an expression of the ultimate values immanent in the national spirit. Communism makes the dictatorship of the Party the practical equivalent of the dictatorship of the proletariat, which is the necessary precondition of the final withering away of the State. In both cases, opposition to the Party is the one intolerable evil. In both cases, the power of the Party is made secure by propaganda designed to make the Party emotionally indispensable. To the question as to whether modern political totalitarianism is to be considered a religion the answer clearly is that the Party is the mediator of both political and religious values to its followers—hence the strength of its emotional appeal.

While the totalitarian Party provides an almost clinical sample of the mechanics of party power, it is only a very obvious illustration of a universal principle. All party groups exhibit some of the same features, and all party names have tended throughout history to unleash the elemental forces that have worked so much havoc in the twentieth century. At the same time, this negative picture has its positive aspect. As party and power go together, the achievements of civilization we recognize with pride and seek to preserve are also the fruit of party endeavour. Values which are always in danger of being corrupted by the party which professes to champion them are not always totally abandoned, and what is good in them may survive. Similarly, changes in party leadership and the consequent changes in party values are not always for the worse. There may be development in values and progress in ideals that escape the debasing influence of greed for power, or that are not materially affected by it. The lessons of history do not invariably point in one direction, and that a downward one.

IV. THE PROTESTANT LABEL

Our concern in this study is with the group name *Protestant*. We are now in a position to understand some of its features. Thus, it is a proper name in so far as it refers essentially to history. It is a group label rooted in events and personalities and places, not a simple entity which can be held up for inspection and judged accordingly.

Nor is it given to us in history altogether, for no amount of historical research will reveal it. An *idea* of what Protestantism is must be used to give meaning to the term. This idea must be in turn critically considered, scrutinized, and redefined before we can form any reliable opinion about the reality the label represents.

Value is involved in any view of the term. *Protestantism* can only be known by being attacked and defended. The emotional overtones which the name evokes cannot be ignored. But neither must feelings of approval of disapproval be allowed to obscure the truth of the matter. We cannot be neutral in our judgement, yet partisanship need not lead us to falsify the evidence. A painting must be subjective in a way a photograph is not, and in spite of this it can be a truthful record. The portrait that flatters, or caricatures maliciously, loses something of the essential character of the sitter.

Although Protestantism as a whole is not a party in the strictest sense, lacking an over-all organization to turn it into an institution, its component parts (the Protestant denominations) are such parties. And to the degree to which Protestantism can be said to be a party, having its own institutional forms and using other institutions for its own ends, it shows the good and evil tendencies inherent in every party group. Here it must also be seen in relation to rival parties, whose histories have intermeshed with its own.

Turning now to the *Protestant* idea and to *Protestant* history, we shall look at each component of the group label in the light of the other. There can be no finality in such an endeavour. The final judgement must be a personal one. But if Protestantism is a live force, and not a mere name, the effort is worth while. Only by seeking to reinterpret the idea can we preserve its integrity for ourselves and for others.

CHAPTER TWO

PROTESTANT AND CATHOLIC: A RE-EXAMINATION OF TERMS

I. PROTESTANT ORIGINS

FACTS ABOUT the origins of a group name are like facts about the childhood of a person: they do not tell us what we have before us in the developed product, but they give very illuminating information which helps us to get a perspective on a life. After all, a word is a living organism almost as much as a person, and its life-history is just as unpredictable, while a group name is, in a very real sense, a corporate personality. The word *Protestant* has travelled less far from its original sense than have many other of its dictionary companions. Nevertheless, its story has some interest.

The original *Protestants* were the Lutheran members of the Imperial Diet of Spires of 1529, who made a declaration (or *Protest*) stating the claim of the reforming party to freedom of worship. Thus the name was at first quite unambiguously a party name. A *Protestant* was a party member; with the spread of Reformation churchmanship the party label spread also. When the Reformation took root in England and a national Church 'by law established' appeared there, the label crossed the English Channel. Having repudiated allegiance to the Pope and adopted a foundation of Reformed principles in the Thirty-nine Articles, the Church of England was known as a Protestant Church, the name being used to distinguish it both from the Church of Rome and also, when these appeared at a later date, from the non-conformist sects. (This is the proper meaning of the Coronation Oath when, at a service of the National Church, the British Sovereign promises to uphold the Protestant Reformed religion.)

As various Churches and sects sprang into existence in the wake of the Reformation, the name *Protestant* became a 'blanket' label to signify all of them. This widening of a regular party name into a more loosely conceived one was made easier by the common background of all the Protestant parties. The Reformation was an event in Western Europe, an event that was in effect a repudiation of institutional religion as mediated through the Western form of Christianity, the Roman Church. Rome was a religious party fully institutionalized, and the disruption of the Reformation shook it severely. It survived as an institution, however, modified by the happenings which we call the *Counter-Reformation*, but still keeping intact the continuity of the party and of the institution the party had perpetuated. On the other side, Protestantism did not found any comparable institution. It expressed itself in different forms of organization: first in national Churches, but, almost at once, also in the sects. The former institutions availed themselves of the organizations that lay to hand, infusing into the existing religious institutions the new party values, as in Luther's Germany and Cranmer's England, or creating new organizations for the party, and grafting these on the secular institutions of society, as in Calvin's Geneva and Knox's Scotland. Only such institutions as the monasteries, which were incompatible with the Reformed system of values, were discarded altogether.

It is noteworthy that the Reformation began with a challenge to the values, both theoretical and practical, of the dominant party. Luther attacked the authority of Rome by his crusade against indulgences, but equally by his theological innovations; the two were opposite sides of the same coin. Once the institutional prestige of Rome had been proved vulnerable, the field was open for alternative values to be championed. A revolutionary situation necessarily developed as a result. Under these conditions some new party might conceivably have swept into power, replacing the former supremacy of Rome. Actually, because of the condition of Europe in the sixteenth century, no one party could do so on any wider scale than that of the national State. Added to this, the values which seized men's minds in the age of the Reformation were those which worked against any re-creation of the ideals which had moulded the Medieval world. A third factor was Rome's success in meeting the crisis by positive measures to reform her practice and re-state her theory.

There is much force in Lord Eustace Percy's contention that the Reformation is misnamed, its real nature having been that of a revolution of far-reaching socio-political consequences, while the Counter-Reformation was the true reformation.[1] This is certainly a more accurate reading of the facts than the one that takes the practical abuses of Rome as the prime cause for the advent of Protestantism; only it should not be inferred from the aptness of the term 'revolution' that the Reformation was a social, economic, or political movement and not, except on the surface, a religious one.

[1] *John Knox* (1937), pp. 105-6.

The Reformation was a revolution in *religious values* from which changes in other values gained impetus, as is natural in a time of revolutionary ferment. There seems to be no other tenable reading of evidence, unless we are prepared to dismiss the importance of religious values on dogmatic grounds. In this revolutionary context, Rome carried through her own reformation. The Counter-Reformation entailed the review of values within the party institution, leading to practical reforms. A decadent clergy, indicated by the low level of the monastic establishments, was reinvigorated. Missionary activity led by the militant example of the Society of Jesus—that new force which was to achieve such far-reaching influence in the post-Reformation Church—showed that life was active again in the corporate body. At Trent a decisive formulation of theological issues was an impressive sign that fundamental values were being given their place in the party programme. The Roman Church as we know it today had Trent as its birthplace.

Among the growing forces of nationalism, the changing economic pattern, and the intellectual unrest (including the dawning of the 'scientific attitude'), Rome found the times unpropitious, in spite of the gains brought by domestic reform. 'In Catholic Europe', writes Christopher Dawson, the distinguished Roman Catholic historian, 'the Church retained its hold on society only at the cost of immense strain. It was like a besieged city under the martial law of the Inquisition and behind the ramparts of state protection.'[2] But at least the institution survived the siege and remained intact. It continued as a party against which Protestantism, with its institutional diversity, showed up as another party. A *we* and a *they* had come into existence and were to face one another through the following centuries, each representing a distinct set of values, though also holding values in common. To be a Protestant meant being a non-Roman—often an anti-Roman—and vice versa. Although the revolutionary situation which issued in the religious wars of Western Europe passed, leaving men weary of religious strife, yet the rivalry of the two parties continued. It still continues. Behind all compromise and concessions, accommodation and even co-operation and mutual respect for the other's achievements, lies a fundamental cleavage of values: and so the inevitable persistence of party spirit. Today, the Roman Church faces Protestantism in the context of a lessened, but still very real, tension.

[2] 'Religion and Life', in *Enquiries into Religion and Culture* (1933), p. 302.

II. THE PROTESTANT PROTEST

Turning from the origin of the name *Protestant* to the origin of the word, we find that the root meaning of 'protest' is the act of standing or speaking as a witness. In this sense 'to protest' used to be a verb in everyday use. Men might *protest* equally their honour or their love for their sweethearts, and this usage persisted long after the word had become accepted as a religious label. When Robert Herrick wrote, '*To Anthea, Who May Command Him Anything*'—

> *Bid me to live, and I will live,*
> *Thy Protestant to be—*

contemporary readers would at once recognize a neat play upon words; for Herrick was vicar of Dean Prior in Devonshire, a cleric of the Church of England, as well as the poet of 'cleanly wanton-ness'; and the pun identified the Churchman in him with the lover.

The positive meaning of *protest* as a declaration is still recognized by dictionaries to be the prime meaning of the word, though this sense has dropped out of common speech; for us a protest is decidedly a protest *against*. In spite of Dean Inge's forthright words, 'It is ignorance which seeks to restrict the word to the attitude of an objector',[3] the shift of meaning in *Protestant* very generally misleads people. Even so erudite and careful a person as Mr T. S. Eliot assumes that 'the life of Protestantism depends on the survival of that against which it protests'.[4]

This common mistake over the descriptive meaning of the word is partly explained by two considerations: first, that Protestantism is not self-sufficient, but looks beyond itself for its completion; and second, that it is historically derivative and has been a minority party from the start. (Even the *Protestants* at Spires presented a minority report.) Put together, these two truths can be confused and give rise to the fallacy that the Protestant protest is essentially negative.

Mr Eliot's statement is true in one sense, though not in the sense intended. If every individual non-Protestant were to be miraculously abstracted from the earth, or spontaneously converted to Protestant convictions overnight, Protestant faith and practice would have no difficulty in persisting. But the label *Protestantism* would cease to

---

[3] *Protestantism* (Revised Edition, 1935), p. 1.
[4] *Notes Towards the Definition of Culture*, p. 75: quoted in *The Catholicity of Protestantism, being a report presented to His Grace the Archbishop of Canterbury by a group of Free Churchmen* (1950), p. 15.

have meaning. This would not be because Protestantism now had nothing to protest *against*, but simply that its 'protest' would have turned into a universal characteristic instead of being a distinguishing mark, setting some over against others. We do not speak of vegetarian cows, because there are no carnivorous cows. However, as a descriptive definition, *Protestant* would still remain when it had ceased to be a party label. The Protestant Church Universal is a conception logically possible and theologically valid. The protest of *Protestantism* belongs to all times and places without exception; for where faith is, there its affirmation has value. It is upon its championing of this value that Protestantism depends for its existence. The value does not require to be in opposition to anything else. It is only the party, as a party, which must have a rival to continue in being.

Thus, though it is self-justifying and needs no other value to give it meaning, Protestantism is not self-sufficient. If everything not exclusively Protestant were to vanish from existence, there could be no more Protestantism and no more Protestants. Protestantism exists as a party within the greater party of 'all those who profess and call themselves Christians'. Its constitutive value—the protest of faith—presupposes the presence of those Christian truths which are to be protested. So far as the Protestant protest is simply a protest, it is, though positive,[5] a form without a content.

The content of the Protestant protest can only be found in historic Christianity. All true Christian faith at all times was (in the Protestant view, at least) *protestant* in the sense of being a personal witness to the Christian message.[6] But Protestantism as a party had a definite beginning in history, before which it did not, as such, exist. Moreover, this beginning would have been impossible without the prior existence of the Roman Church, out of which the new party arose by means of revolt. In the cord of historic Christianity, Protestantism is one strand among others, and it appears to have been knotted in at a particular point along the cord's length. It cannot cut itself off from what went before without severing itself from the cord. The Reformation did not abolish pre-Reformation Christianity, but produced a revised version of it (this justifies the name 'Reformation'), and in this it was indebted to the institution which had produced the

---

[5] The phrase *Protestant protest*, when used from now on, carries this positive sense. This seems the logical way of speaking, even if it has an archaic sound. This usage is not always followed, however. Paul Tillich in *The Protestant Era* (1948) always means a negative protest when he makes use of this phrase.

[6] This point will be taken up again. See Chapter 3, *infra*.

older version. Historically, it is true to say that Protestantism is inseparable from that against which it rebelled.

History made Protestantism dependent in another way as well. The revolution of values which took place at the Reformation was of necessity one which was carried out with a wary eye to the points of conflict between the old and new parties. The confessions of faith produced by the Reforming Churches specifically singled out particular areas where disagreement was sharp and so all the more in need of being defined clearly. The Thirty-nine Articles show this process (in spite of the later attempt by the Tractarians to ignore it), as do the decrees of the Council of Trent on the Roman side. But, though each party made adjustments because of the other, there can be no question about the degree of indebtedness. As a newcomer on the scene, Protestantism had no tradition to draw upon except that of the institution whose values it largely repudiated. The Reformers were able to draw attention to the changes effected in the tradition which, they claimed, showed that drastic and disastrous perversion of former original values had been gradually effected. But in their efforts to build anew the ancient altars of the faith they had to use the material bequeathed to them—and very largely the methods of building accepted at the time as the only conceivable ones; they had to decide what to reject, what to retain, and what to reclaim. Both Reformed theology and ecclesiastical polity were indebted to the systems and the presuppositions of pre-Reformation days. Whether they followed in the old tracks, or by revulsion sought studiously to avoid them, they could not avoid a dependence upon them which the passage of time might lessen but would never obliterate.

Thus we can see how the Protestant *revolt* becomes confused with the Protestant *protest*, and the historic dependency of the party be taken to be a proof of the protest's essentially negative nature; the accident of a shift in the meaning of *protest* adding to the muddle. Any real understanding of what Protestantism is in itself must spring from finding what the content of the Protestant protest really is, a task which will occupy us in later chapters. But first we must take a look at the negative side of the protest, and investigate some aspects of the Protestant revolt.

III. CATHOLIC UNIVERSALITY

Although the Reformers' revolution was against Rome, common usage makes the opposite of *Protestant* not *Roman* but *Catholic*. Protestants now and in the past have always refused to surrender this label, saying that *catholic* means *universal*, and so cannot properly be the title of one Church among others. The Roman Church does not repudiate the title *Roman*, but insists that, being the one authentic Christian Church, *Catholic* is her true and sufficient title. Other Churches (and sections of opinion within Churches) that reject outright the revolt of the Reformation, and so will have no truck with the term *Protestantism*, claim for themselves the name *Catholic*, while either admitting or disputing the claim of the Roman Church to that name.

Whatever the rights and wrongs of these claims and counter-claims, one thing is fairly clear: *Protestant* and *Catholic*, for better or worse, have grown into two near-proper names which will not easily be removed from our daily speech. The real questions to be settled are these: What lies behind the ambiguities and fluctuations of these words? What values are involved? What ideas are needed to resolve this verbal battle?

While a full answer to these questions will only be approximated to as we proceed to discover what Protestantism entails, at the moment we need to notice that the popular opposition between *Protestant* and *Catholic* represents two diametrically opposed views of what *catholic* stands for. To the Protestant it appears that the mark of the Church Catholic is the *protest* of faith rightly made; or, in the non-theological language we have been using, that the values of the Christian faith are allowed to flourish without being intolerably distorted. To the Catholic (from now on this will be used in its sense of *non-Protestant*) the mark of the Church Catholic is the existence of the organization that can prove itself to be the veritable institution founded by Christ to carry on His work upon earth; or, again in non-theological language, that the values of the institution are preserved by the continuity of the institution. In the former view, the form of Catholicity is justified by its content. In the latter view the content is guaranteed by the form.

There is a certain divergence of opinion on the Catholic side as to what constitutes the essential institution of the Christian Church. The Roman and Greek Orthodox Churches, which do not recognize one another, each believe that the visible unity of the institution and the unbroken continuity of its tradition are essential to the idea of Catholicity: the tradition can only be known from within the organization itself, so that no two separately organized institutions can be in any true sense one institution. The Church of England is in communion with the Old Catholic Church (a body which split off from Rome over the question of the infallibility of the Pope) on terms which do not demand organic unity or doctrinal agreement. Anglo-Catholics incline to the view that Catholicity, representing the essential continuity of the Church as an institution, can exist in the absence of a visible unity of organization, outwardly recognized. This does not mean that *organization* has ceased to be the mark of Catholicity, or that the continuity of the institution has become in any way 'spiritualized'. The material continuity of the institution through continuity of organization is still as crucial as ever. It means that so long as this unity in fact exists, conscious recognition of the fact is secondary. This view has given rise to what is known as the 'Branch theory' of Catholicism: one Catholic trunk supports separate Southern, Northern, and Eastern branches. The two opinions are thus, respectively, exclusive and inclusive. According to the exclusive standard you must join the right institution to be a Catholic—unless you are already in it. You will know it is the right one, because it says so and is distinct from all the rest. According to the inclusive standard, if you are already in it you will know which is the right institution to make you a Catholic. You will know it even if parts of the institution say they are distinct from the rest and deny that the rest can be Catholic.

The Catholic standard, whether exclusive or inclusive, does not omit to reckon universality as a mark of the Church Catholic; however, universality is qualified by being placed below institutional continuity. It is no longer a test of Catholicity but only an additional proof. When Catholic institutions are widespread in space and extended over a long period of time they are universal enough to qualify as Catholic—but only if they are within the right organization. Protestants, seeing in this subordination of universality to institutional exclusiveness a complete reversal of earlier Christian practice, feel that the value expressed by *catholic* has been totally lost.

On the other hand, since strict universality seems a practical impossibility to achieve in a visibly divided Christendom, there is a good deal of plausibility in the Catholic argument, particularly on the basis of the exclusive standard. In the face of differences in Christian practice and belief, the 'exclusive standard' makes universality once again into a literal concept. All the clash of self-styled 'followers of Christ' can be disregarded as beside the point. There is one Church over the world, with one teaching. If it is objected that Catholicism today does not look like the earlier organization of the Chri tian Church, the reply is that time necessarily involves change, but that continuity in time transforms unlikeness and makes it innocuous through a principle of development. This argument has proved so attractive that many seeking for assurance among the Babel of conflicting ecclesiastical voices have found the boldness of the Roman claim to exclusive Catholicity sufficient grounds for believing it to be true. Another facet of the same approach was displayed long ago. In his dispute with Donatists, Augustine taunted his opponents with being numerically fewer than the supporters of the Catholic Church. The argument by comparative size is less convincing than the one based on the 'exclusive standard', but is not altogether foreign to it.

IV. THE APPEAL TO TRADITION

There is further issue involved in the idea of Catholicity which is very relevant to the different way the word is understood by Catholics and by Protestants. This is, briefly, that the word implies universality in time as well as in space. The Catholic, by claiming exclusive right to the title, maintains against the Protestant that he belongs both to a world-wide fellowship and to a continuous tradition. Since the Reformation came as a revolution in the history of Christendom, all that derives from that revolution stands today as the product of innovation, while those who disown all that the revolution stood for are the rightful heirs of the *ancien régime*.

The illustration, used above, of the rope with a strand knotted in along its length seems to support this view. Protestantism began at the Reformation and was not heard of before. But ropes are made up of many strands, and it is quite possible to account for a continuous cord without imagining that any one strand runs the full length of it. Catholicism is not the same now as it was before the Reformers began their work. It could not be, for the nature of historical existence makes that impossible. Therefore, when speaking of the Church of Rome, we can truthfully say that Romanism was created at the Council of Trent in the middle of the sixteenth century; and we can say with equal truthfulness that the history of that Church dates back to sub-apostolic times, or—if we accept the official Roman reading of history—to the time of St Peter himself. Protestants do not dispute the Catholic claim to stand in a tradition dating from the early days of the Christian faith to the Reformation, and continuing beyond it. They do not take sides in the argument over which institution has the best claim to represent post-Reformation Catholicism. They simply dispute that the pre-Reformation tradition is an indivisible unity and that it has passed to any one heir, or limited number of heirs, of the tradition. Protestantism, on its side, claims a share in the Catholic tradition, without wishing to assert that it can prove lineal descent from a continuously dominant *élite* who guarded the catholicity of the Church down the ages. All it asserts is that such faithfulness to the Gospel as the Reformers were concerned to proclaim was never wholly absent from the Church which carried that Gospel from the days of Christ's ministry to the division of Western Christendom.

Thus the Protestant attitude to the question of how far the pre-Reformation tradition can be shared between Protestantism and Catholicism is determined by an appeal to two criteria: *History* and *valid protest*. History is an essential court of appeal here, because the universality implied in the word *catholic* is rather more closely dependent upon history than upon geography; the *when and how long?* is a more serious question than the *where and how far?* In this appeal to history, Protestantism is not an interested party, or interested only within limits. Of course it would make a great difference to Protestantism's understanding of its own position if, for example, it could be proved that St Peter was in fact the first Bishop of Rome. But Protestantism's existence is not absolutely bound up with any other historical events except those which gave rise to the substance of the Gospel and are declared in the apostolic preaching. Some historical judgements, if proven, would strengthen its cause, and others would make it revise some of its present convictions, but none would imperil its very being. It is not so with Catholicism, for the Catholic claim to represent the one and only Christian tradition— and not just one strand in historic Christendom—rests on a number of disputed readings of history. This being so, it is not surprising to find that the history of a Catholic institution, such as the Roman Church, provides us with instances of attempts made to prune history to the shape of theory by pious forgeries of the type of the 'Donation of Constantine'. The temptation to produce forced evidence for what is believed *a priori* is naturally very strong, when the only alternative is to make assertions apart from the evidence. Protestants believe that there is a real place for refusing to wait for evidence in order to hold right beliefs, but this is in the sphere of direct personal apprehension of truth[7] and not in pre-judging matters of historical fact.

The second appeal, the one to valid protest, is non-historical,

[7] See Chapter 5, Section 1, *infra*.

though it has an historical reference from being grounded in the historicity of the Incarnation. It can perhaps be explained best by an example. Writing from a Catholic and Anglican standpoint, J. V. Langmead Casserley explains how, in his view, the Catholic tradition was broken at the Reformation. He argues that the Reformers took a drastic step and founded new Churches—'called after the name of Christ indeed and dedicated to His glory but certainly not founded or contemplated by Him in the days of His flesh'—furnishing them with 'new ministries differing both in origin and principle from that of the ancient Church'.[8]

A Protestant is likely to wonder, in all reverence, whether Christ in the days of His flesh ever contemplated the Church of England any more than the Presbyterian Churches or the Church of Christ, Scientist. But the crux of the matter is plainly in the phrase *founded by Him*. An appeal to history in this connexion would take the form of investigating whether Catholic belief in the Apostolic Succession has a basis in fact and, if so, which of the conflicting opinions about where a 'valid' ministry existed were correct. An appeal to valid protest, on the other hand, might start with a historical investigation as to whether the theory of Apostolic Succession could be traced back to the apostolic period. But even were the findings here negative, it would still have to be decided whether the Reformation's ministries were new 'in principle', although ancient in origin. The only final appeal here possible is to the faith which arises out of fidelity to the foundation-charter of the Church, in the Gospel of God's Salvation through Christ. Are we so certain that we know what Christ contemplated? Do we know beyond all room for self-questioning that we know what He meant by 'sheep . . . not of this fold' (John 10_{16}) and by His prayer 'That they all may be one' (John 17_{21})? There is no way in which we can know whether our protest is truly valid, but we can at least count it important that no easy assumption of certainty makes it thoroughly invalid. Casserley falls back upon an appeal to history by citing the example of 'the ancient Church'; it is, of course, a question-begging one. It assumes that by looking to an institution in a certain historical setting, calling itself the Christian Church, we can tell at once whether the tradition has been broken, when the point at issue is what the Christian tradition really is.

Because the Catholic rates form above content, he tends to assume that the second follows from the first. Thus the well-known formula

[8] *No Faith of My Own* (1950), p. 85.

of St Vincent of Lerins, *Quod semper, quod ubique, quod ab omnibus creditur*, is sometimes quoted without its last word, as if Catholicity was something concrete and tangible instead of something *believed*. But the claim of the Catholic to possess *the* tradition makes universality of content as necessary to maintain as universality of form. Again, history presents a hurdle which, at all costs, Catholicism must surmount. Catholics who hold to the 'exclusive standard' are forced to prove that tradition has never altered, essentially, in what it has taught. This is so extremely difficult to reconcile with any historical consciousness that some version of Newman's famous theory of 'development' is required to make it plausible. Even then it is difficult to maintain consistently. The Roman Church, by now committed to a Thomistic philosophy and theology, finds such 'un-Catholic' developments as the dominant nominalism of the age just preceding the Reformation slightly embarrassing. In such cases, the line taken is that heresy was stopped 'in time'. Other discrepancies are excused by the plea that proper doctrinal terminology was 'undeveloped' at the time.

If an *inclusive* standard of Catholicism is admitted, then the course is much more simple. There is no need to hold that Catholicism speaks with one voice and proclaims a single message. The problem then arises, however, as to which of various conflicting voices speaks for the authentic tradition. Take, for example, the apparently wide divergences between the theologies of Augustine and Aquinas. Writing as a Roman Catholic, Jacques Maritain states that St Thomas is the interpreter of 'the most authentic thought' of Augustine as well as 'the echo of the whole Catholic tradition'.[9] Outside Rome, the unity of the Catholic tradition is by no means taken for granted. The Anglican E. L. Mascall gives to his book, *He Who Is*,[10] the sub-title 'A Study in Traditional Theism', and makes clear that for him personally the only tradition possible must be Thomistic. But J. V. Langmead Casserley in *The Christian in Philosophy* regards the 'perennial philosophy' of Western Europe to be Platonic-Augustinian and not Aristotelian-Thomist. After saying that Thomism is 'a

---

[9] *Three Reformers, Luther—Descartes—Rousseau* (revised ed. 1929), pp. 178–9. Maritain does not stop to note that an echo usually gives back part only of what it echoes and consigns the rest to silence. The contributors of *A Monument to Saint Augustine: Essays on Some Aspects of his thought written in Commemoration of his Fifteenth Centenary* (1945), a Roman Catholic publication, do not spare their warnings that Augustine, writing before the days of *scientific theology*, may be understood wrongly and even lead the uninformed into heresy. Much of his thought, evidently, is 'unauthentic'.

[10] 1943.

brilliant and timely interlude, a departure . . . from the general line of development', he adds that we must not exaggerate this distinction, but he also goes on to reaffirm that Aquinas departed from many of the 'basic convictions' of Augustinianism.[11] Peter Munz, in his *The Place of Hooker in the History of Thought*,[12] does not hesitate to oppose to one another in sharp contrast the Thomist tradition revived by Hooker and the Augustinian tradition which, according to Munz, can be virtually identified with the theology of the Puritans attacked by Hooker.

If Protestants feel inclined to join in these contentions about the 'main-stream of doctrine', it will be from historical interest. Finding which tradition was dominant at particular periods and how continuity of thinking runs from age to age is a help to understanding the present through the past. But the Protestant will not try to build the case for his commitment to Christianity-as-Protestant on any verdict of history. Instead, he will examine the history of thought for the supra-temporal light it can throw on the soundness of the protest he has accepted. Jeremy Taylor could say in his day that Augustine taught a *Protestant* doctrine of the Lord's Supper. He could say it, because it meant plainly that Augustine's teaching was like the Anglican and unlike the Roman doctrine as he knew them. A modern Protestant would not so easily say that, because it would so easily carry misleading historical implications—the kind of misreading of history which occurs today when Cromwell is casually labelled a 'dictator' or Sir Thomas More's *Utopia* is said to advocate 'Communism'. Instead of believing that they are right because they follow a particular tradition, Protestants find themselves appreciating a tradition because it illuminates for them what lies beyond all tradition and gives to them that which makes them worth preserving.

In the middle of the seventeenth century Archbishop Tillotson wrote:

They would have us to show them a society of Christians that in all ages has preserved itself free from all such errors and corruptions as we charge them withal, or else we deny the perpetual visibility of the catholic Church. No such matter. . . . And tho' we were not out of the catholic Church before, yet since our reformation from the errors and corruptions of Rome we are in it upon much better terms and are a much sounder part of it; and I hope, by the mercy and goodness of God, we shall for ever continue so.[13]

---

[11] (1949) pp. 50–1.   [12] 1952.
[13] Quoted in *The Golden Book of Tillotson*, edited by James Moffatt (1926), p. 76.

Just as Tillotson contended against Romanists in his day, so for our own times comes a very similar statement addressed to non-Roman Catholics by the eminent champion of the ecumenical movement, Visser 't Hooft:

If there is any continuity in the life of the Christian and in the life of the Church, it is not a continuity in time and space but a continuity of God's creative action. Sometimes God's continuity will seem to us an interruption in the human development. To Protestants the event of the Reformation is a strong case in point. They cannot see the action of Luther as an arbitrary break-away from a sacred tradition, for to them it represents the restoration of a deeper and invisible continuity in faith.[14]

This goes to the heart of the Protestant view of what a *Catholic tradition* really is. It is one determined by content and not by form, and its continuity depends upon faithfulness.

V. PROTESTANT *versus* CATHOLIC

What makes the two terms we have been considering into labels which have shed most of their descriptive meaning, and then passed into the realm of proper names, is that the Protestant-Catholic situation appears as an 'either-or'. Several points of view have to be severally explained, but to grasp the difference between *we* and *they* almost any identifying mark is enough. Paired names of all sorts and conditions multiply about us—Cowboys and Indians, Roundheads and Cavaliers, Guelphs and Ghibellines, Yankees and Dodgers, White Livers and Yellow Bellies—and once we come to connect them together we do not care very much how, or why, they came by their names. Juliet's dismay over Romeo's name was not at all because it happened to be Montagu, but because hers happened also to be Capulet.

Since nearly all of us in the West have grown up under one or other of the opposing labels, the words *Catholic* and *Protestant* awaken in us feelings of loyalty and hostility. Encouraged by our education to adopt certain attitudes toward them, we fence them about with memories drawn from personal experience, and identify them with the ideals we most value. This 'either-or' situation, seen largely in terms of *we* and *they* is, of course, fruitful ground for the wildest prejudices and the most futile misconceptions. It calls for scrupulous honesty and the ability to be self-critical, as well as the

---

[14] *Anglo-Catholicism and Orthodoxy* (1933), p. 172, quoted in *The Nature of Catholicity* (1942) by Daniel T. Jenkins, p. 76. Jenkins has argued the Protestant case very lucidly in this book, which owes much to Barth's rediscovery of Reformation principles.

will to examine facts without rancour. We must be prepared to alter our presuppositions if we become aware, through contact with an alien point of view, of values we had previously ignored. But this does not mean that we need to bring ourselves into a neutral position in order to be fair to both. A right understanding of the issues involved can come only when these are regarded as important enough to be the cause of decisions dividing men over what they believe to be right or good. And unless we cherish stable beliefs of our own we shall not see the issues as they really are. Of course, it does not follow that either *we* or *they* must be right, or that the division of party is an ultimate and inescapable one wholly dependent upon a conflict of basic values.

The 'either-or' situation must be accepted as, in part, inevitable. If divisions exist, they will bend names to fit them. *Evangelical* is a word that is free from some of the ambiguities of *Protestant*, because it has no negative suggestion. Yet, at least from the time when it was exported from Europe to Britain, an Evangelical Protestant has been known as the kind of person likely to be most particularly anti-Catholic. In Europe and America, having grown into a recognized denominational name, *Evangelical* has become a formal variation of *Protestant*.

Protestant-Catholic opposition is most intense when the alignment of *we* and *they* is carried on through different levels of everyday life by the party spirit working through the major institutions of society: politics, law, economics, and education. Religion concerns the basic ways of man's thinking about the whole organization of life, and so his religious beliefs are bound to permeate, directly or indirectly, these institutions. It does not follow, however, that a religious party must use social institutions for party ends, because the area of direct influence of religious values upon social values may be deliberately restricted. Social values, like religious values, are embodied in institutions and championed by parties; and parties and institutions equally fail to express these values unequivocally. Therefore, though religious values (being more fundamental than social ones) govern the social values to be cherished, they do not dictate the institutional form these values will take, nor the party that most fully champions them. Thus two men with the same religious beliefs may be party members of opposing political groups or other social organizations with a party programme, seeking in this way to establish similar (not necessarily identical) values in the society they belong to. They can do this only under certain conditions. The conditions are that they distinguish between: (a) the interests of their religious party as the vehicle of religious values, and (b) the interests of their religious party as an institution. If they are not willing to make this conscious distinction they will necessarily be forced by their religious allegiance to promote those social organizations, and only those, that are best adapted to further the interests of their religious party, and that carry the approval of their religious leaders.

Different beliefs about the way religion enters into the affairs of daily life are among the things which divide Catholics and Protestants. Protestants tend to stress the desirability of withdrawing the religious party spirit from social institutions, while Catholics tend to stress the need to retain religion's rule over the way society is organized. Though the division is by no means absolute—especially on the surface—since some Protestant bodies claim State recognition and support in various degrees—nevertheless it represents a cleavage in outlook that goes very deep.[15] It is perhaps more important than the practical issues on which Protestant and Catholic opinions frequently find themselves in head-on collision, such as the provision of separate denominational schools, or the appointment of national diplomatic representatives to the Vatican, or public education concerning birth-control.

At its widest extent, the subordination of social institutions to a religious party is reached where the nation is identified as a whole with a particular religious faith. This is a much more far-reaching matter even than State recognition of a religious party's claim for preferential treatment. The latter recognition is *political* and may be withdrawn when a change of government takes place. But when a people and a culture are made one with a religious party a revolution in *ideas* is required, a revolution which is never brought about without endangering the whole fabric of society. The representatives of religion in this situation become the leaders of reaction, denouncing all social change as a revolt against the soul of the nation as such. Mustapha Kemal created modern Turkey by his determined assault upon the idea of the Muslim state in his revolution. Spain, after the bitterness of ideological conflict in her civil war of the nineteen-thirties, has returned to the ideal of one State, one Church. In the People's Democracies (Yugoslavia being a partial exception) the Communist Party is virtually State and Church combined. There is no parallel situation in any Protestant country, even where there are national Churches. In Canada the Church-State ideal of the old

[15] See Chapter 7, *infra*.

French colonial policy, which triumphed over an earlier more liberal one, has survived as a cultural ideal. French Protestants have to combat the notion that French-Canadian culture is essentially French-Catholic in its social expression.

VI. PROTESTANTISM *versus* CATHOLICISM

Once words have become labels for opposing parties they are readily extended from the parties themselves to what the parties stand for. *Protestantism* may refer to the whole party viewed from a historical standpoint. The judgement, 'Protestantism in North America encouraged a national temper of sturdy independence', is a historical judgement. On the other hand, *Protestantism* may refer to the idea behind the party. The judgement, 'Protestantism is hostile to the arts', is a generalization about the essential nature of the Protestant party, alleged to hold true in any historical setting. Yet it is clear that both the opinions quoted are really much the same in being both abstractions from historical existence, the only difference being that the second is carried farther away from history. If the idea behind the party name can be taken out of the actual setting of the party's life for better definition, it is because the party name contained this idea from the first. That is why every 'ism' is neither wholly abstract nor wholly a datum of history. *Protestantism* cannot be defined by adding up the total achievements of all Protestants. In the same way, it is quite insufficient to have a clear conception of what *Protestantism* stands for without any reference to any Protestants, past or present.

Since every party exists for the sake of some value, there can be no party which is immune from the generalizing label of the 'ism'. The little church that wrote above its door, 'No Modernism here—or any other Ism', was unduly self-complacent for, by its own admission, it stood for anti-Modernism. All that can be granted is that some parties emphasize their *being in being* more than their desire to exist in order to advance a cause. The *Kiwanis* are less single-minded in their aims and objects than the *Society for the Prevention of Cruelty to Animals*, though, no doubt, equally believers in humanitarianism. Where a party exists in order to carry out a single, easily identifiable purpose, as does the S.P.C.A., then its 'ism' can be stated with some degree of confidence; but such cases are few. How seldom, for instance, does a movement growing out of some ideal sponsored by an individual remain a reliable guide to the teaching of its founder. Was Nestorius a Nestorian, Augustine an Augustinian, Wesley a Wesleyan, or Marx a Marxist? Historians concerned with the history of ideas have constantly to show how 'ism' grows out of a distortion of one man's system of ideas by his immediate followers who seize on some leading notion to the exclusion of the rest, resulting in subsequent fissions within the 'orthodox' party when other aspects of his thought are rediscovered. Nothing is more elusive than the 'essence' of a party that gives it its status as a party and, probably, its name.

When Catholics and Protestants face one another over some particular issue splitting them into two rival parties, the difference between them seems plain. But what separates Protestantism from Catholicism? Some apologists of the Church of England claim that their Communion is both Protestant and Catholic. By this they imply that there are two distinct elements, corresponding to the two names, which are blended in the Anglican 'middle way'. The difficulty is in finding out what these elements are. Certainly the Church of England preserves much that characterized the Church of pre-Reformation days and that has been discarded or radically altered in other Protestant bodies. Yet there is no Protestant body which is without some element, however tenuous, linking it to the Roman Church. All that can be said is that the Church of England 'looks' Catholic in its liturgical forms, its church government and its doctrinal emphases in a way many Protestant Churches do not. None of these things in itself is decisive, for each may be duplicated in individual Churches of unmistakably Protestant character, but taken together they appear to 'add up to something', as we say. On the other hand, the Church of England was undoubtedly affected by the Reformation and introduced in its early history as a National Church certain doctrines and practices common to most of the Reformed Churches. Its historically recognized title has been *Protestant*. Is it then Protestant in the sense that it embodies the basic convictions of the Protestant Reformation? Or does the fact that it is not in communion with most of the leading Reformed Churches mean that it is essentially Catholic? Or is it possible for a Church to be both truly Protestant and Catholic while standing over against the professed representatives of each? The difficulty of answering these questions is increased because no clear answer can be secured from within Anglicanism itself, where the widest divergence of opinion exists and (to some extent) has always existed.

Instead of finding in the Church of England a clue to the meaning of *Protestantism* and *Catholicism*, we seem to have only added another problem to our list, namely: granted the existence of a party called

Anglican which—it is said—embraces both *Protestantism* and *Catholicism*, what is the idea represented by the complex called *Anglicanism*? In order to get any farther we have to come back to the *parties* within Anglicanism. Here we find the Catholic insistence, which we have noted before, upon the form of the institution of the Church as its essential quality[16] based upon considerations which in the Protestant-Anglican view are the constructions of a 'fantastic and unhistorical theory',[17] while a mediating party, like Sir Roger de Coverley, sees much to be said for both sides.[18] While Catholics and Protestants continue to face one another across a barrier of unresolved differences, so will Catholicism and Protestantism. Those who band themselves under one label may not read into it identical values. But any attempt to discover the meaning of a party label apart from the party as a living force is self-defeating. The label's meaning will then become progressively vaguer as it is divorced from the parties who champion it, or else the meaning will be attached in an arbitrary fashion and cease to represent values which are actually cherished by any one. And yet the continued existence of a value depends upon the efforts of people who believe in it to understand it. Protestants and Catholics can only serve their party responsibly by seeking to discover the meaning of *Protestantism* and *Catholicism*. Unthinking loyalty to a party name is, in the end, a poor form of devotion.

VII. HISTORY AND IDEAS

In our effort to penetrate the meaning of *Protestant* and *Catholic* the root cause of our difficulties lies in the uneasy balance between history and ideas which characterizes the group name. This comes to a head in the ambivalence of the 'ism' that can be either a concrete or an abstract universal, according to whether it points to historical or conceptual existence. Our use of group names is inevitably conditioned by our total understanding of the world—including the world of history. Interpretation by way of ideas is a necessity of our nature, and words are the indispensable instruments of our ideas.

Without the medium of ideas history would be a meaningless

[16] See *The Apostolic Ministry, Essays on the History and Doctrine of Episcopacy*, edited by Kenneth E. Kirk (1946).

[17] W. R. Inge, *Protestantism*, p. 104.

[18] 'Both these emphases are part of the truth. They do not contradict but supplement each other. There will always be those who grasp most fully one side of the truth, and they need to be continually corrected by those who stress the other side'—*The Fullness of Christ: The Church's growth into Catholicity, being a Report presented to His Grace the Archbishop of Canterbury* (1950), p. 71. (A companion volume to *Catholicity* and *The Catholicity of Protestantism*.)

succession of unrelated events, each unique and mysterious. History remains, for all our efforts, the field of unique events and thus essentially mysterious. We cannot explain history, we can only accept it. (The Universe which Carlyle advised Margaret Fuller to accept was the Universe of History.) But by means of human interests, human values, and human ideas we are able to understand something of the past and present, and even able to adapt ourselves to the future. 'The historian is concerned,' says Ralph Barton Perry, 'not with mere aggregates of unique and humanly important events, but complex unities which endure through time.'[19] Those unities must come within his intellectual grasp to be meaningful. That is why it is often stressed that all history is contemporary history.[20] Unless we attempt to organize our knowledge of past events and subject our knowledge to the values we believe in, history becomes impossible—'bunk', as Henry Ford is said to have thought all history to be. A Philosophy of History is a necessary ideal, though in fact there can only be philosophies of history, as personal and varied as metaphysical systems have proved to be. Group names are the product of men's thinking about history, and their changing meanings reflect the philosophy of history of those who use them.

In Henry Fielding's *Tom Jones* the Reverend Mr Thwackum remarked: 'When I mention religion I mean the Christian religion; and not only the Christian religion, but the Protestant religion; and not only the Protestant religion, but the Church of England.' This eighteenth-century character's method was sound enough, though his application of it left much to be desired. Party bias had led to an imperfect grasp of historical reality, resulting in a too arbitrary handling of accepted usage of the word. Yet every one who states an opinion or argues a case is likely to strain the ordinary meanings of words to some extent, imposing his own definitions upon them. When Alexander Pope tells us that 'true Wit is Nature to advantage dressed', we learn something about the current meaning of *wit* in the eighteenth century, but also something about Alexander Pope. The dictionary itself is only the distillation of the way men do their thinking with words, and any adequate dictionary must be historical, recording the changing meanings brought about by the living interplay between word and idea. There is a great deal in the saying of Lord Balfour: 'One need never define one's terms; for, if one em-

[19] *Realms of Value* (1954), p. 383.
[20] See, for instance, R. G. Collingwood, *The Idea of History* (1946), *passim*, and Arnold J. Toynbee, *A Study of History*, X (1954), p. 232.

ploys words sufficiently often, everyone will understand what one means.'[21] Even where an author defines his terms with care, he is so seldom likely to be entirely consistent in his use of them that Balfour's method has to be used in every case. Very often consistency is obtained only at the expense of inadequacy—as in the case of the redoubtable Thwackum. A general cogency in exposition is usually more desirable than formal definition in all but severely technical subjects.

Whenever a group name is removed too far from its setting in history, however convincingly its connexion with an idea is argued, we are left with a feeling that violence has been done to it. In his book, *Protestanism*, Dean Inge declares Protestantism to be an element inherent in all religion—not alone in Christianity—standing over against the equally universal element of religious Conservatism; the latter emphasizes the institutional side of religion and adapts itself to current popular beliefs, while the former stresses ethical integrity, personal commitment and loyalty to particular truths of faith. We may agree with this analysis, and yet not feel entirely happy over such statements as 'The prophets were the Protestants of the Hebrew religion'[22] or 'Christ taught a very radical Protestantism'.[23] A group name without its historical reference is like a fish out of water; unless put back into its natural environment it must die. Paul Tillich distinguishes between the Protestant *principle* and the Protestant *reality*. Protestant reality is 'a special historical embodiment' of the 'universally significant' Protestant principle, which is an 'eternal and a permanent criterion of everything temporal'. This principle is 'indicated' in all the great religions, pronounced by the prophets, and manifest in Christ; it judges Protestant reality, which may pass away, to be re-born through the principle.[24] In spite of his care in separating the idea from the party name, Tillich does not escape from the consequences of misappropriating a name. The Protestant principle stands for the idea of Protestantism in its purity, i.e. for the values Protestantism strives to embody. But values are not found disembodied; they wear historical forms. To call the pure idea

[21] Quoted in *Alethetropic Logic, A Posthumous Work*, by Sir Almroth E. Wright, p. 169. To Sir Almroth Wright's scientifically trained mind—he was a great medical man—Balfour's attitude seemed almost wholly perverse. He preferred the saying of another friend (unnamed): 'If you don't define your words you are depriving yourself of the very great advantage of knowing what you are talking about' (ibid., p. 167). This was evidently Mr Thwackum's view also.

[22] op. cit., p. 5.

[23] ibid., p. 9.

[24] *The Protestant Era*, Author's Introduction, pp. xi–xii.

Protestant is necessarily to connect it to time and to identify it—however remotely—with a party. The Protestant principle as an objective criterion remains veiled for us in the subjectivities of historical interpretation.

An opposite confusion of language comes from using a word which is primarily abstract and descriptive as though it were an easily recognized historical label. *Orthodoxy* is sometimes used as an equivalent for *Catholicism*, the link between the two words being the idea that true doctrine belongs to the Universal Church and no other. The Greek *Orthodox* Church is by the same token *Catholic*. *Orthodoxy* thus carries the implication of being a party set over against *Sectarianism*. J. V. Langmead Casserley writes persuasively in this vein:

> Real orthodoxy is not closed but cumulative, not static but continuous, a dialectical way of thinking which sifts the gold from the dross in the confused intellectualism of the passing age, and incorporates what it finds of value there into its own majestically expanding tradition.

He is careful to insist:

> Of course, the orthodoxy we have in mind here is the authentic, dialectical, living, growing and expanding orthodoxy of Christian history, and not the closed and static orthodoxy of its feebler defenders and less discerning critics.[25]

The sentiments here are admirable as general principles but, if *orthodoxy* is not simply the idea at its most exalted but also the idea visibly expressed in Christian history, we are left uncomfortably poised on an idea which claims to be a historical label but has no historical party to attach itself to. The same writer refers to 'the Catholic criticism' of 'doctrinaire and life-denying puritanism'.[26] Is the *puritanism* referred to here intended to mean the Protestant puritanism of the sixteenth and seventeenth centuries, and the *Catholic criticism* supposed to point to the objections raised by churchmen in Catholic denominations to Protestant social teaching and practice during those centuries? Or is this the criticism by 'real' orthodoxy of the puritan ideal: *puritanism* being the name for the vision of a religion free from all external aids and every compromise with worldly values—the universal principle called by Charles Williams 'the way of the rejection of images'?[27] The danger about this kind of ambiguity in the use of labels is that we easily allow party

[25] *Morals and Man in the Social Sciences* (1951), p. 177.
[26] ibid., p. 183.
[27] *The Descent of the Dove: A Short History of the Holy Spirit in the Church* (1939), *passim*. The phrase derives from the theology of mysticism, but Williams uses it in a much wider sense.

prejudices to pre-judge what is really a matter of general principles. We make up our minds on the strength of an appeal to party allegiance and imagine we have made a decision 'on principle'.

Short of the extreme measure of giving up all words which are partly proper names and partly descriptive words there is no safe high-road to the realm of unambiguous meaning. Nor can we insist that all party labels shall be restricted to a limited historical context. It is a counsel of despair that would eschew all interpretation of debatable words, because interpretation is partial and personal. The chapters which follow attempt the task of interpreting Protestantism as something that has a meaning in history and beyond it. This approach avoids making history an affair of proper names, unique and useless as the source of general lessons about universal human concerns. It also seeks to avoid an *a priori* method of reading history as though it existed solely to embody certain eternal principles laid down before Creation and destined to continue until the Heavens are rolled back like a scroll. Protestantism is the human attempt to express certain values within a party. To understand these values we have to explore the forms under which Protestantism has attempted to give values an historic existence, and at the same time to reach beyond the purely temporal to the eternal.

CHAPTER THREE

PROTESTANT BELIEF:
I. 'NO OTHER FOUNDATION'

I. THE GOSPEL

IF A Protestant is someone who 'protests' his faith, there is no reason why a Roman Catholic—or for that matter a Muslim or a Buddhist—should not be called a *Protestant*. The Protestant protest, however, differs from the Catholic in other ways than in declaring allegiance to articles of faith which the other would repudiate. (Indeed, 'orthodox' Protestantism in its claim to maintain the *catholic faith* need not, at least in theory, diverge from Catholicism in the substance of its articles of belief.) It is both the centrality of the protest and the relation of the protest-ants to it which give the Protestant section of Christendom its distinctive character, so that the label of *Protestant* is not simply a historical accident and still keeps its descriptive significance.

Two other names prominent in Protestant history indicate this particular feature. They are *Evangelical* and *Confessional*. While these names have been adopted as denominational titles, they stand for much more than any sectional interest, for they speak of the primacy of the Gospel of Jesus Christ as the content of belief and of witness to faith in the Gospel as the form of belief. We might say that Protestantism stands for a certain attitude toward belief even more conspicuously than it stands for certain beliefs. The Protestant Churches are not roughly similar because their beliefs are more or less identical. There is, in fact, a very substantial agreement between them on major points of doctrine. Sometimes this approaches to virtual identity; sometimes there are sharp differences of opinion on secondary issues. There is also a conspicuous agreement on what are crucial beliefs and what are secondary, though important. (Bodies, such as the Jehovah's Witnesses and Christian Science, which are not agreed about the 'fundamentals' have no good reason to be called *Protestant* and are usually quite explicit in their repudiation of fellowship with the other Christian groups.) Over all other considerations, the conviction among Protestants of all kinds is that fidelity to the Gospel is something that is obligatory for all Christians, even at the expense of divisions among Christians.

This basic attitude is, of course, relevant to the denominational fragmentation of Protestantism, and we shall return to consider it more than once again in that context. What needs to be noticed at the moment is that this conviction is not just recognition of the claims of conscience. The right to follow conscience is recognized in Catholicism also. The Roman Church admits the possibility of a man being saved if he follows the light of truth as it appears to him, even if his vision leads him away from the Church. It is true that the Catholic conception of authority makes it hard for non-conforming minorities in a Catholic community to put liberty of conscience into practice. But the widespread notion that Protestantism exists to safeguard the right of the individual to follow his personal beliefs is at the best an overworked half-truth. It has arisen chiefly because of the historical development in Protestant countries of the 'open society' where religious orthodoxy is no concern of the State. Protestant insistence upon fidelity to the Gospel is, first and last, an expression of an understanding of the meaning of faith.

Faith, for the Protestant, is conceived as a personal response to the acts of God as revealed in history, and supremely in the historic event of the Incarnation. The Gospel is the Good News of the Word made flesh and dwelling among us (John 1_{14}), so that belief in Him should give everlasting life (John 3_{16}). This view of faith as personal and called into being by decisive acts of God is the foundation of all Protestant witness. As well as having a profound influence upon Protestant practice in the area of church life, it has had an equally far-reaching effect upon Protestant theology. And it was the theology which preceded—both historically and logically—the church life. It is no accident that when Protestants look back to the beginnings of Protestantism as a historic movement they look back to a theologian, Martin Luther, whether or no they follow that teacher's formulation of the Gospel or belong to the church party he originated. Luther was not absolutely the first Protestant, but he was so striking an exemplar of Protestantism, as well as being so decisively the leader of the first successful revolt against Roman Christianity that he has become the symbol of the Protestant spirit.

II. CONFESSIONAL THEOLOGY

Luther was a professional teacher by accident, being made a Doctor as the by-product of his monastic vocation. He was a Christian thinker by necessity, feeling the utmost constraint in his soul to find the truth of the Gospel in personal terms. The experience of the forgiveness of Christ bestowing eternal life came to him, after he had long sought for it in vain, simultaneously with his discovery of what it meant when expressed in theological terms. The supreme value he had found was mediated in words by means of which he was able to communicate that value to others. His work as a Reformer began in his theology. *Justification by faith alone* spread Protestantism over Europe.

Protestant theology has had its system-builders and its scholastics. It can sometimes be abstruse, since loyalty to truth may lead into difficult paths; and sometimes arid, since a living awareness of important themes may degenerate into a juggling with verbal symbols which have lost contact with reality. But its connexion with the life of piety and the ordinary church member has always been remarkably close. Dogmatics has never been simply a university subject, being very much a concern of the pulpit and the pew. So Protestant theology, as with Luther, has always been a *confessional* theology, a statement of the faith as it touches the life of Christian believers. Theological language can become dated, even if it is drawn directly from the Bible, because all words (including Biblical words) do not continue to be the bearers of the same values for ever. But as one aspect of the Gospel becomes obscured by its becoming identified with a theological interpretation that is wearing out of the hearts and minds of men, other aspects come forward with new meaning. While the Gospel reaches its hearers, it will find words and ideas to convey its message.

Because the Gospel can be approached from many angles while retaining its unity, it has often happened that Protestant theology has grown up from a single Biblical root. *Justification by Faith alone* with Luther, *the Sovereignty of God* with Calvin, *Christian Perfection* with Wesley, *the Kingdom of God* with Ritschl, and, in our own day, *the Word of God* with Barth: each has brought a renewal of the Gospel to those who confess the faith. This theology of the single root does not mean that one isolated Scriptural phrase has been exploited to the neglect of all the rest, for its intention has always been to understand the whole Gospel by first making sure that a part is correctly interpreted. Inevitably, this has meant a particular emphasis, and as such has led to a reaction attempting to restore the balance by a succeeding theology, itself destined to be superseded. But the process has been dialectical—a reaching out toward the truth in the manner unavoidable for the human mind. If Orthodoxy can ever be justly opposed to Sectarianism, it would be in this context. Orthodoxy, living and dialectical (and, for that reason, never possessing the perfection of finality), is that protest which contains as much of the Gospel as human minds can grasp at one particular point in history, having learnt the lessons taught by the orthodoxies of previous ages. Sectarianism, by contrast, is the protest which assumes that it declares the Gospel so truly that its theology cannot be argued *against*, except by the wicked or the stupid. Thus Sectarianism denies the possibility of a valid counter-protest, which dialectical theology by its nature expects and requires, while Orthodoxy must continually overcome the temptation to think that its present formulation of the Gospel is the final one.

It will be seen that this view of Orthodoxy is quite at variance with the Catholic conception of doctrinal purity guaranteed by continuity of the Church as an institution. But it is in so far as they *protest* that they alone are orthodox that the Catholic Churches can most fully be called 'sectarian' in the sense indicated above. It is in their demand that men become *orthodox* by accepting a churchly theology, or else be branded as heretics, that the Catholic Churches show the sectarian character of their protest, just as the Protestant sects prove their sectarianism by protesting that they alone proclaim a 'pure' Gospel. Sectarianism is a matter of cherishing a certain type of theology and not a matter of organization and size. Orthodoxy, too, depends on the fidelity to the truth of the Gospel of the theological system followed. Orthodoxy is not to be judged by declaring that a particular protest is, or is not, the final truth about the Gospel; it is to be judged by its readiness to follow Gospel truth to the extent of admitting its former protest incomplete or even mistaken.

Protestant theology has believed the theology of the single biblical root to be a trustworthy guide to the Gospel because of its trust in Scripture as the primary witness to the Gospel message. The protest of individual men and of individual Churches may well be distorted presentations of the Gospel, however sincerely these have confessed their faith when they have presented it in what seemed to them to be adequate theological forms. But the protest of the Bible itself is primary, because it is given to us in the historical revelation which the Bible records.[1] Even the Bible itself, however, cannot be taken to

---

[1] 'It being thus manifest that God, foreseeing the inefficiency of his image imprinted on the fair form of the universe, has given the assistance of his Word to all whom he has ever been pleased to instruct effectually, we, too, must pursue this straight path, if we aspire in earnest to a genuine contemplation of God;—we must go, I say, to the Word, where the character of God, drawn from his works, is described accurately and to the life; these works being estimated, not by our depraved judgement, but by the standard of eternal truth.' Calvin, *Institutes of the Christian Religion*, Bk. I, Chap. VI, 3 (translation by Henry Beveridge, 1949).

be the Gospel pure and simple. To think so is to cherish Bibliolatry. The Bible is the most authoritative presentation of the Gospel; it speaks the Word of God to men, but it is not God speaking with His own authority, because it remains a human presentation of that Word. Remembering the fallibility of Scripture as a man-made record, confessional theology still asserts that men will not know the Gospel if they neglect its witness or prefer their own conception of the Gospel message to the one to be found there. Historically, Protestantism has declared its belief in the trustworthiness of the Biblical record by the Reformation principles of the *clarity* and the *sufficiency* of Scripture: the Gospel will reach men's understanding clearly enough if it is heeded earnestly enough; and, Scripture being the best interpreter of Scripture, the Gospel will be sufficiently known when one part of the Biblical record is truthfully read in the light of the whole.

Confessional theology is a theology for believers. It arises out of the Word of God speaking to men. Theologians are not a class of specially enlightened persons who expound Christian truths to inform ignorant, though otherwise satisfactory, Christians. The Catholic phrase 'Christ and His Doctors' strikes strangely upon the Protestant ear. Teachers were, of course, a distinct class of people in New Testament times (Acts 13$_1$, 1 Cor. 12$_{28}$, Eph. 4$_{11}$, etc.) and are needed in every community, not excepting the religious community. Theologians may be learned folk, leaders in the university, and scholars with the esoteric knowledge proper to specialists. But whatever their special function may be, theologians have no privileges before the Gospel. They are Christian disciples, seeking no more than to carry out in one particular station in society the duty laid upon every Christian disciple, to 'preach the Gospel to every creature' (Mark 16$_{15}$). Kierkegaard was voicing a fundamental Protestant view when he poured scorn upon those who 'were Professors in the fact that Christ died'.[2] The Church needs its historians and its philosophers, its Professors of Biblical, and Historical, and Systematic Theology. But its theology is essentially the faith that is a reality for all its members and expressed in the life of the Church as a community of believers.

Nevertheless, theology is the*logy*, an interpretation of the faith that is consciously held by those who share a common tradition of belief and worship. And Protestantism, as Tillich reminds us, is a

[2] Walter Lowrie has collected a number of Kierkegaard's caustic references to the 'Professor' as a 'second Judas' in his *Kierkegaard* (1938), pp. 506 ff.

highly intellectualized religion. 'The minister's gown of today', he writes, 'is the professor's gown of the Middle Ages, symbolizing the fact that the theological faculties as the interpreters of the Bible became the ultimate authority in the Protestant Churches.'[3] In reaction to this intellectualist tradition there arose within Protestantism a counter-tradition of pietism, emphasizing the experiential element in Christian discipleship at the expense of its formal expression in conceptual terms. When the 'orthodox' theology of Protestantism ceased to carry spontaneous conviction, an alternative was sought, not in a new formulation of the Gospel message, but in the immediacy of emotional conviction. The danger here was that emotion by itself is a less stable vehicle of conviction than even the intellect by itself. Pietism, if it is to be more than a passing mood, generally clings on to some remnants of a once-meaningful theology. The emotionally powerful preaching missions of the last three centuries are fittingly called 'revivals'. Without a memory of a faith that was compelling to the whole of human experience, any predominantly emotional appeal must be without effect. Confessional theology should not be 'coldly intellectual' any more than it should be 'mindlessly sentimental'. Protestantism, suffering both from an over-intellectualism and from over-emotionalism that have made its witness less effective than it might have been, has learnt that it is not only the content of theology that is beyond its powers to express adequately, but also its form. To hope to find all that is required of a believer by less than a total dedication of the self to the Gospel is an illusion.

III. THE LIMITATIONS OF THEOLOGY

Because of the intimate connexions between confessional faith as a living experience and confessional theology as a believing expression of that faith, theology among Protestants is not the same clearly marked area of human activity that it has become in Catholicism, more especially in the Roman Church. In the system of Thomas Aquinas, theology is a science: an activity whose end is knowledge. It has its prescribed field of operation. Natural Theology, which is a part of Philosophy, treats of divine things in so far as they are accessible to the reason; and Revealed Theology (which is theology proper) expounds the truths of the Christian faith as they are known in the Catholic Church.

Protestant theology has no comparable charter. It seeks to express

[3] *The Protestant Era*, p. 227.

the truth of the Gospel, but from the start it cannot hope to encompass that truth. For the fullness of all things is Christ and the Gospel is His, not to be fully revealed until the end of time. We can know what the Gospel is to the degree that God illuminates our hearts and minds, but *all* that it is we can never know. When theology is evangelical it is centred upon God's revelation of Himself through Christ. When it is confessional it remembers that it stands under its Lord to witness to that revelation. It is not empowered to undertake any other task. Such knowledge as it can impart is not knowledge that has any compelling power upon the intellect apart from the presence of faith. It is, of course, clear that, in trying to state truthfully the Gospel message and to draw out the implications of Christian faith, confessional theology will tread upon ground covered by other systems of belief, philosophical as well as theological. It will have to point out when fidelity to the Gospel is incompatible with these beliefs. It will have to take into account all knowledge, or claims to knowledge, in other fields; but it will not assert any opinion of its own to be *scientific*, i.e. the object of certain knowledge, since it can judge only in the light of its protest of faith what it can accept and what it must reject. Instead of saying, 'This is true and that is false', confident that an objective judgement has been made, it must answer from a personal view-point 'Yes' and 'No', expressing a conviction it believes to be in accordance with the mind of Christ.

Writing about Roman Catholic theology, Mr F. J. Sheed informs those he feels he has a duty to teach ('all who know less theology than I') what a *Catholic intellect* means:

This means that when we look out upon the universe we see the same universe that the Church sees; and the enormous advantage of this is that the universe the Church sees is the real universe, because She is the Church of God. Seeing what She sees means seeing what is there.[4]

Confessional theology has no such enormous advantage to boast of. It has no confidence that it can sweep away ignorance and error entirely from the intellect. Its confidence is in Christ who is Himself the truth. The Holy Spirit, which leads men to all truth, is His gift. Certainly the Church is guided by the Holy Spirit and, in so far as it is faithful to its Lord, is able to communicate saving truth. But the Church itself walks by faith and not by sight. It does not see all things with the eyes of God and communicate that vision to the intelligence of the believer. Although it guides him so that he shall know the truth, this truth is the truth of Christ (2 Cor. 11_{10}), the

[4] *Theology and Sanity* (1947), p. 3.

truth that makes free (John 8₃₂), and by no means necessarily a knowledge unmixed with error.

The Catholic idea that God *does not allow* the Church to teach error[5] is not one which has any foundation in Scripture or which makes much sense historically. Paul found Peter and James blameworthy over their teaching concerning circumcision, and this teaching was apparently current in the Church until the apostles agreed to change it (Gal. 2₁₁ f). This has been the pattern of Church History through the ages: errors and abuses tolerated or enforced, until reformed by the efforts of those who interpreted the Gospel more faithfully than others. All that the Church can claim is that by its witness Christ has been preached; and if this is the Church's glory—without which it would cease to be the Church—its shame is that so often Christ has been preached in the context of envy and strife (Phil. 1₁₅). Controversial bitterness has disfigured the witness of the Church and its theology until the *odium theologicum* has made Christian love a thing to mock at, and men have turned their backs upon the Church in order to learn how to live peaceably with their fellows.

If theology attempts to declare the wholeness of the Gospel, and at the same time knows that every attempt it makes will fall short of that wholeness, humility should be theology's first characteristic. The theologian is the servant of the Word, and the 'Queen of the Sciences' must be, like her Master, among men as one that serves (Luke 22₂₇). The pre-eminence of theology's task is that it is to proclaim Christ's rule and to lead men to His Cross. Thus theology's business is not really *scientific* or concerned with knowledge, but *missionary* or concerned with carrying out the commission entrusted to it. Faith is its object, as the Gospel is its subject, and the knowledge it seeks to bring is the knowledge of faith.

It is not that factual knowledge is something indifferent to it but that no such knowledge is primary in its operation. A professional theologian may be well-informed about his subject; he may have the historical information and the training in conceptual thinking which make him competent to guide others in this field; but he can never confidently assert that he knows more theology than another less fully equipped than he is with knowledge or dialectical skill. His knowledge *about* theology does not necessarily guarantee insight *into* theology. The theological teacher, whose business it is to see that others have the necessary technical equipment they need for

⁵ Sheed, op. cit., p. 211.

approaching theology with some understanding of what they are about, does not consider himself on account of his office and qualifications fit to instruct his fellow-Christians in their faith. His standing in the institution of the Church has no necessary relation to his grasp of the essential Christian values. Therefore he may venture on the strength of his knowledge and his Christian concern 'to throw a pinch of spice into the theological pot' (as Barth described his own contribution to contemporary thinking), yet he himself cannot judge whether the addition is healthful or noxious. Paul used another metaphor to the same effect when he said of the building of the Church: 'But let every man take heed how he buildeth thereupon. For other foundation can no man lay than that is laid, which is Jesus Christ. . . . Every man's work shall be made manifest: for the day shall declare it, because it shall be revealed by fire; and the fire shall try every man's work of what sort it is' (1 Cor. $3_{10b, 11, 13}$). Theology is no different from every other work of the Church. It must be built by faith upon the foundation of the Gospel of Christ, and judged not by man's judgement but by God's.

There are two observations which should be made about the limitation of theology in the Protestant view. The first is that, by a necessary inference, the humility of theology supposes its aggressiveness. If no Christian can say with pride that he knows more theology than any other Christian, no Christian will allow the claim of another to a higher knowledge by virtue of a special qualification not possessed by others. Of course this aggressiveness has nothing to do with an individual claim to know as much as anybody else without qualification, which would be mere self-conceit and the antithesis of humility. Rather it is the recognition that when a protest is made, and made in all humility and without self-righteousness, it cannot be abandoned. This aggressiveness appears in a conscious, half-humorous light in what Paul calls his 'folly' and 'boasting' (2 Cor. 11). It appears without any *ad hoc* defence and entirely without self-consciousness when Paul claims to be doing God's work under the guidance of the Spirit: 'According to the grace of God which is given unto me, as a wise master-builder, I have laid the foundation, and another buildeth thereon' (1 Cor. 3_{10}). So long as the foundation is Jesus Christ, the work is beyond man's judgement. In this confidence, self-assertiveness is deprived of its egoism. 'But when Peter was come to Antioch, I withstood him to the face, because he was to be blamed' (Gal. 2_{11}). It is on this basis of the protest of faith that the Protestant 'protest' (in the negative sense) is justified. There is no external authority that can validate a theology. But a theology which is based upon the Gospel and held confessionally can admit its imperfection and yet say a decisive 'No!' to another theology which is seen to contradict the Gospel message.

The other observation about the Protestant limitation of theology concerns a common Protestant misapprehension of what the limitation means. Because theology is not made valid by its intellectual cogency as a system or capable of being proved true or false, it is often assumed that formal theology, the theology that goes with the university gown either in college or pulpit, is an optional extra and that 'real' theology is a *theology of experience*—which in practice means a theology of emotional experience. This reaction to the Catholic tradition (which regards theology as scientific) and to Protestant scholasticism (which codified particular Protestant theologies as though they were a new Mosaic Law) is justified only as a protest against a self-sufficient theology. It is not justified as a positive protest for, as we have seen, when faith gives up the effort to understand itself it fails to win a total allegiance of the whole personality and also tends to live upon an out-worn 'formal' theology whose intellectual expression is no longer capable of commanding allegiance. Unless a theology of experience is a theology of *total* experience its impact, however striking, will be ephemeral. The Protestant protest has been traditionally kept vital by the pulpit. But behind the pulpit with its power to stir the feelings lay the thorough theological discipline of the ministry and the instructional religious discipline of home and Church. Faith cannot be kept alive by a pulpit which advocates Phillips Brooks's dictum 'Truth through personality' but subordinates truth to exalt personality. P. T. Forsyth wrote in the heyday of the popular preacher and the depreciation of theology: 'The non-theological Christ is popular; he wins votes; but he is not mighty; he does not win souls; he does not break men into small pieces and create them anew.' [6]

IV. FAITH, THE CHURCH, AND THE SACRAMENTS

Theology, being the expression of a faith valued as an ultimate value, can have no meaning or existence apart from that faith. But is faith the final and the only value? Protestantism holds that it is, and in a double sense. The Christian faith is the Gospel, the Good News of Jesus Christ. The Christian faith is also the faith of Christians, the believing and trusting response by which men are brought into

[6] *The Taste of Death and the Life of Grace* (1901), p. 65.

communion with Him; for the Gospel is not simply news *about* Jesus the Christ, but essentially the living Christ Himself. Catholics can admit only the first sense—and then with a difference. For them the Christian faith is certainly the 'Catholic' faith, i.e. those things which are held to be essential to a right knowledge of what the Christian religion means. But this knowledge must come through accepting those truths which the Church guarantees to be true. This knowledge-by-agreeing-that-the-Church-alone-knows is faith, and the only way of coming into communion with Christ and knowing His benefits. To partake of the life of Christ means to belong to the Church, His mystical Body, and to partake of the Sacraments of the Church whereby His life is mediated to the members of the Body. Any other approach can only be by the special grace of God whose will is inscrutable and beyond the understanding of men, and yet who has made His will clear beyond contention to those who have been brought into knowledge of Christ through His Church. Recent Papal pronouncements about the danger of allowing laymen to teach theology shows how jealously the position of the Church in its status of guardian of doctrine is upheld in Roman Catholicism.

Catholic theology is thus unmistakably a knowing of what there is to be known, because God has made it possible for men to know it. There are two kinds of knowledge because there are two kinds of revelation. To the minds of all men equally God has made clear the truths of reason. To the Church He has made known the truths of the Catholic faith, a revelation of mysteries beyond the reach of mere reason, though not incompatible with its knowledge. To know is good; but for man, as a composite creature of intellect and will, to knowledge must be added love so that he cleaves to the truth through loving obedience to God in His Church.

It is true that the above summary applies to *one* theological outlook—the Thomistic view officially adopted by the Roman Church—and is by no means the only theology compatible with Catholicism. But while the position of Thomism is in part a historical accident (equally, of course, in the Christian view, an act of Providence), it represents a working out of the inner logic of Catholicism, and any other theology makes more difficulties for Catholic convictions to surmount than exist in the marvellous clarity of the Angelic Doctor's balancing of faith and reason. If faith is to mean assent to the teaching of the Church, as Catholic tradition demands, no better foundation for that assent can be found than Thomist natural theology, which claims to be nothing but the product of unimpeded rationality. When in the seventeenth century Richard Hooker wished to justify the Established Church, he did so by reviving the structure of Thomist theology, even though at the same time he had to uphold the Protestant account of faith which had been accepted by the Church of England from the Continental Reformers.

Protestantism has no comparable architectonic system representing the logic of its position which it can substitute for Thomism. Protestant Scholasticism of the late Reformation period and German nineteenth-century systematic theologians have tried in vain to fill the gap. True, Calvin's *Institutes of the Christian Religion* was a great formative influence behind the new faith. It was one of the few books to earn fully a right to the epithet of 'epoch-making', for it brought about a new age and determined the course of Protestantism over a large part of the globe for generations. But its real importance was historical. To-day even Calvin's heirs do not consider themselves bound to follow Calvin's methodology. For any real Protestant equivalent to the *Summa* of Aquinas one must turn not to another theological system but to a theological insight: the *justification by faith alone.*

It was Luther's *sola fide*, derived from his reading of *The Epistle to the Romans*,[7] that began the Reformation. Luther's conception of Justification was turned by orthodox Lutheranism into the keystone of a theology. It became the *material principle* of the Protestant protest, with Scripture serving as the *formal principle*. Today there is a widespread re-appraisal of Luther's message by Protestant thinkers outside Lutheranism who are anxious to discover once again the full meaning of their Protestant heritage. Also, by a strange turn in things ecclesiastical, Catholic theologians of the Anglican communion have become aware of Luther as a significant theological force. The Swedish Church, with its vigorous independent Lutheran tradition, is by virtue of its episcopal 'regularity' in communion with the Church of England, so that Swedish theology has attracted those who otherwise might not be inclined to take Luther seriously.[8] A not altogether dissimilar state of affairs exists in connexion with the widespread contemporary influence of the Danish author Kierkegaard. Kierkegaard's writings on the religious conditions in his day were, in fact, a criticism of orthodox Lutheranism in the Danish Church in the nineteenth century from the standpoint of a re-

---

[7] 'Therefore we conclude that a man is justified by faith without the deeds of the law' (Rom. 3_{28}). For emphasis Luther added 'alone' to 'by faith'.

[8] See, for instance, A. G. Hebert's introduction to his translation of *Eucharistic Faith and Practice, Evangelical and Catholic,* by Yngve Brilioth (1953).

statement of Luther's own theology. Kierkegaard's literary and philosophic abilities make his work seem personal and original, but there can be no doubt that his thought moved entirely within a Lutheran orbit. Karl Barth has confessed that his spiritual ancestry runs through Kierkegaard to Luther; there are many others who stop short at Kierkegaard, as though he were a theological Melchisedek without spiritual parentage.[9] Luther's importance cannot be limited to those theologies that have been constructed from his teachings, or even to the achievement of his personal teaching. Whether Justification remains a decisive theological conception or no, Luther's making central the protest of faith lighted once for all time the guiding principle of Protestant theology.

By faith alone . . . the protest becomes the essential mark of Christian religious affiliation. The all-sufficiency of faith, as Luther proclaimed it, was not intended to exclude other truths but to point to the most essential truth. The *sola fide* is sometimes thought to make the Church and the Sacraments unnecessary, to teach that good works are superfluous—or impossible—for the Christian, and to make mere feeling the criterion of truth.[10] 'These ought ye to have done, and not to leave the other undone', said Jesus to the Pharisees over their misunderstanding of the Law (Matt. 23_{23}). Luther found in the acceptance of Christ's revelation of the God of forgiveness the one thing needful. Without faith in Christ there was no knowledge of God that was not idolatry, no service of God that was not disobedience, and no worship that was not blasphemy. With faith came all that enabled us to live 'in Christ', and nothing needed to be added to faith to make men Christians. 'Believe on the Lord Jesus Christ, and thou shalt be saved' (Acts 16_{31}). 'Whosoever believeth in him should not perish, but have everlasting life' (John 3_{16}). Faith was the receiving of the Word of God by men, a believing trust that brought men into a personal relationship with the living God. Such faith could stand alone because it was the movement of the whole personality into relationship with God, so that nothing was, in principle, left to be added.

[9] In the Index to J. V. Langmead Casserley's *The Christian in Philosophy*, Kierkegaard, Aquinas, and Augustine have the most frequent mention. Luther does not even find a place.

[10] See, for instance, the expression of Luther in the Anglo-Catholic statement, *Catholicity, a Study in the Conflict of Christian Traditions in the West being a Report presented to His Grace the Archbishop of Canterbury* (1947), criticized at length in *The Catholicity of Protestantism*. Within modern Protestantism Luther is very imperfectly understood also: see *The Heritage of the Reformation*, by Wilhelm Pauck (1950), Chap. 1.

This faith was, of course, a very different matter from the faith which is conceived as mental assent to certain propositions as being objectively correct or historically accurate, the kind of faith parodied in the schoolboy's definition that 'faith is believing what you know isn't true'. St James very understandably objected to this latter kind of faith 'alone' without any of the accompanying marks to show it to be genuine. Demons, he said know about God and that *faith* makes them bristle with fear. Luther too often quoted 'so faith, if it have not works, is dead in itself' (Ja. 2$_{17}$)—his well-known verdict about the *Epistle of straw* was not his final word on James—but he pointed out that if Satan were really to believe that Christ were Saviour *for him* he would cease to be the devil. That is why he contended against the Catholic-Scholastic conception of a faith that needed to be 'informed by love':

If they called this formed or furnished faith, the true faith which the Scripture teacheth, this their gloss would not offend me, for then faith should not be separated from charity, but from the vain opinion of faith.[11]

Luther's main contention against 'them' (the Schoolmen) was that faith in its Scriptural sense is no abstraction but the whole of man's relationship with God. It does not need charity to complete it, because it is not separate from charity. In exactly the same way, *faith alone* does not ignore the Church and the Sacraments, because it is not faith apart from them.

Just as the Bible declares the Gospel without itself being the Gospel, so the Church and the Sacraments mediate the Gospel to men by faith. According to Luther, men can know nothing of a 'naked God': God appears to them through 'veils' which in revealing Him also conceal Him. In the terminology we have been using, values are not found except embodied in parties, institutions, and organizations in so far as they are concretely known; while conceptually values are realized in ideas which must always be personal judgements and never objective facts. If we identify a value with any of its external manifestations we distort it; and though we must make a personal judgement our final authority, we must never identify it with objective truth. Now faith is distinguished from personal belief in that it brings in another authority besides a purely human one: namely, divine revelation. And the Church and the

[11] *A Commentary on St Paul's Epistle to the Galatians*, ed. by J. P. Fallowes, p. 157. For a full discussion of the Reformation conception of faith as *fiducia* (trust) contrasted with Scholastic *assensus* (assent to doctrine) see J. S. Whale's *The Protestant Tradition. An Essay in Interpretation* (1955), Chapters II and III, especially pp. 68 ff.

Sacraments as institutions rest upon the authority of the revelation. The value made known by Christian revelation is Jesus Christ.

Thus Protestants know no 'naked God' or value pure and simple. They know God through Christ the Mediator who said: 'He that hath seen me hath seen the Father' (John 14₉). And the Mediator Himself is not known directly. He is known by participation in the Church and through the Sacraments. Yet neither Church nor Sacraments give us the Mediator *by themselves*. The Catholic doctrine of the Church and the Catholic 'objective' theory of the Sacraments assume that this is the case. The Protestant view is that while Christ is not known apart from the institutions which mediate Him to believers, He is not known even there except by faith. Divine revelation itself must be known through its personal apprehension.

Protestant belief, the belief that the personal appropriation of truth can be more than a mere opinion because it can respond to God's revelation in Christ, finds its typical expression (though not its only expression, for this can take many forms) in Luther's Justification by faith alone. We must now turn to the implications of the Protestant belief in faith as the essential condition of understanding revelation which underlies the whole development of Protestant theology.

CHAPTER FOUR

PROTESTANT BELIEF:
II. OBEDIENCE TO FAITH

I. GOD AND MAN

THE COMMON Catholic view of the Reformation is that it broke the integrity of the Catholic faith, and in so doing put man in the place of God. Christopher Dawson writes:

Thus it is no accident that the loss of Christian unity in the sixteenth century was accompanied by the loss of the unity of Christian life. The attempt of the Reformers to spiritualize religion ended in the secularization of society and of civilization. The Reformation is a classical example of the blunder of emptying out the baby with the bath.[1]

It is sometimes contended also that the process was less the ill consequence of a disastrous but well-meant blunder than the devil's harvest of a disguised but deliberate self-aggrandisement. Jacques Maritain has declared:

The Reformation unbridled the human self in the spiritual and religious order, as the Renaissance (I mean the hidden spirit of the Renaissance) unbridled the human self in the order of natural and sensible activities.[2]

In this picture of demonic spiritual pride, Luther takes chief place. Maritain quotes Moehler in this connexion:

Luther's self was in his opinion the centre round which all humanity should gravitate; he made himself the universal man in whom all should find their model. Let us make no bones about it, he put himself in the place of Jesus Christ.[3]

Now Luther's *sola fide* was taught in company with its twin principle of *soli Deo gloria*; for him the glory of God was the necessary presupposition of faith. A recent study of Luther by Philip S. Watson has taken as its central theme the *theocentric* character of Luther's theology as contrasted with the *egocentricity* of Catholic theology.[4] Here two theological outlooks clash decisively. Protestantism and

---

[1] *Enquiries*, p. 301.   [2] *Three Reformers*, p. 14.   [3] ibid., p. 15.
[4] *Let God be God! An Interpretation of the Theology of Martin Luther* (1947). The theocentric-egocentric theme is a dominant one in Anders Nygren's *Agape and Eros*. (Watson, who has translated this work, see p. 89, *infra*, is clearly indebted to Nygren). In giving the Protestant view of theocentricity in terms of Luther's theology I have followed the general lines of Watson's exposition.

Catholicism both claim to stand for the glory of God; each sees the other as mistaking self for God.

Clearly, neither side will convince the other merely by an appeal to history. The issues are too involved and the opportunities for special pleading (by introducing party values) too obvious. Were the Middle Ages, those 'ages of faith', more Christian than the modern world which, since the Reformation, seems to be drifting away from Christianity into irreligion? Possibly; but then why has Catholicism not stopped the rot? It has been always numerically the stronger party over against Protestantism and has had virtually a free hand in many parts of the world.[5] Possibly not, since the presence of a culture based on religion and ecclesiastical control over society does not necessarily imply the rule of faith over the hearts of men. Was the Reformation the dawn of a new hope for inward faith, freed from ancient error and the bondage of priestcraft and superstition? Possibly; yet the Middle Ages, for all their half-Christianized barbarism may have been the fore-promise of a really Christian world— a fragile bastion against the pagan forces which came flooding in when the ideal of Christendom, one and Catholic, was thrown violently aside in the Reformation. Possibly not; has not the modern world grown more demonic and more destructive with each new effort to achieve an illusive 'freedom'? But then, is it Protestantism that is to blame for the anarchy of the world of to-day, or is it not that Catholicism is reaping the reward of its pretensions to power in the multiplying of power-madness? So the debate must go on endlessly, unless there can be some agreement about principles of interpretation. History illustrates values, but only when we are clear about the values we are looking for and how they are to be recognized.

A clash of theologies is evidence of a fundamental disagreement about values. Indeed, there can be no surer proof of such disagreement. Every thorough attempt to understand existence, when it comes up against a choice of ultimate values to live by, turns inevitably into theology whether or not the name of God actually appears in the position which is upheld.[6] Equally, every theology rests, in the last resort, upon a conception of God which is not in the least made un-

---

[5] Wilhelm Pauck has argued along these lines. *The Heritage of the Reformation*, pp. 184–5.

[6] J. V. Langmead Casserley justly draws attention to the far-reaching effects of 'theomorphism' (i.e. interpreting nature and man in terms of what we make our God), illustrating his contention by the 'depersonalizing' tendencies seen at work in different spheres of modern life consequent upon adopting the 'scientific attitude', which (in fact) equates God with nature conceived as impersonal order (*The Christian in Philosophy*, p. 34).

equivocal because the name of God is invoked. The cause of the
clash between the Catholic and Protestant views on egocentricity
and theocentricity lies in the fact that, in looking for assurance about
the nature of God, they look in different places.

Luther raised the issue of theological thought as being first and
last dependent upon faithful witnessing to the Gospel. Do we present
the Gospel as it is given to us, even if we present it faultily, or do we
assume that we know the categories into which it must be fitted? Are
we willing for God to be God, or do we insist that He conform to the
mould we have made for him? Theology may connive at idolatry:

It is not enough to say or think: 'I am doing it to God's glory; I mean it
for the true God; I will serve the only God.' All idolators say and intend that.[7]

Catholicism senses idolatry in the 'single root' theology of Justification. Thus Maritain asks:

Why does the doctrine of salvation absorb all the Lutherian theology, if it
be not because the human self has become in actual fact the chief preoccupation of that theology?[8]

And he answers it with a quotation from Denifle:

For him, then, there could only be question of soteriology, and that in this
sense, that *man remained its central point*. To-day, Protestant theologians
take pleasure in the thought that Christ is the centre of Luther's 'system'.
Nothing is more untrue, and nothing more in contradiction to the conclusions of a psychological inquiry into the process of his evolution.
*Although it speaks often of Christ, the centre of Luther's theology is not
Christ, but man.*[9]

These are confident assertions. To the question of whether an appeal
to psychology to confirm the theological judgement is worth very
much we will return later.[10] First it might be worth while to examine
the Protestant case.

Protestant theology does not seek theocentricity (the value in
question) in any other way than Scripture displays it, searching there
for an understanding of what God has to say to men. The Bible is a
book about God, but it is clearly also a book about men. It begins
with God—yet God is shown only as already creating the world
where man is to be set. After man's creation comes his fall, and from
then until the time of his redemption by the Second Adam is the
story of God's dealing with His people and of the great cloud of wit-

---

[7] Quoted by Watson, op. cit., p. 91.
[8] op. cit., p. 17.
[9] ibid., p. 190 (italics as Maritain quotes them).
[10] See Section 2, esp. pp. 65–6.

nesses who respond to God's call to His people by faith. The history
of the reception of Christ's Gospel by the men of the New Covenant
follows after the account of Christ's sojourning among men and of
His atoning death on their behalf, leading to the conquest of death,
man's last enemy. The Bible ends when the first heaven and earth
have passed away and the redeemed glorify God in the Eternal City.
God is not seen apart from man; and when man knows God it is as
his Creator, *his* Judge, and *his* Redeemer. When the prophet of God
has a vision of God in His majesty, it is so that he can respond to
God's command to witness to His will for Israel; the vision issues in
the personal answer: 'Here am I; send me' (Isa. 6$_8$). Though Paul
has known visions and revelations (2 Cor. 12$_1$), he is determined to
know nothing among the Churches but Christ crucified (1 Cor. 2$_2$),
and this knowledge becomes '*my* Gospel' (Rom. 2$_{16}$). From the beginning to end, God is portrayed in Scripture as He who is active in
the history of His people. The whole record of Scripture is nothing
but the record of His activity for the salvation of men. The New
Testament itself centres round the Crucifixion of the Son of God,
who was also the Son of Man.

There appears to be, therefore, a strong *prima facie* case for taking
soteriology as the leading theological issue arising out of a Scriptural
reading of the Gospel. To the accusation that it 'absorbs' all theology
in the doctrine of salvation, Protestantism can reply that God's redemptive act in Christ reflects the whole of God's revelation of Himself. If Christ be not God's truth, where is God's truth to be found?
The first preaching of the Gospel was to elicit the right response
from men: 'Repent ye, and believe the gospel' (Mark 1$_{15}$), and 'Repent ye therefore, and be converted, that your sins may be blotted
out' (Acts 3$_{19}$). The Gospel was carried by 'the servants of the most
high God, which shew unto us the way of salvation' (Acts 16$_{17}$).[11] The
fact that man appears together with God in the theological approach
to the Gospel does not in the least mean that man is made *the central
point* in doctrine. Egocentricity must be read into this theology; it
cannot be deduced from it.

II. THE RECEPTION OF THE GOSPEL

The doctrine of salvation does not appear to have a centre at all (at
least in so far as basic form is concerned), but only two poles: God
and man. To make the doctrine into an egocentric one it must be

---

[11] The source of this statement was 'a spirit of divination', afterwards exorcized
by Paul. In the New Testament, the spirits are recorded as being truthful witnesses;
they recognize Jesus as the Son of God (Mark 5$_7$).

assumed that one pole is subordinated to the other and thought to be
dependent on it, so that God exists for the sake of man. Because salvation has man for its object, there is a sense in which salvation exists
'for the sake of' man. It can thus be argued that the *doctrine* of salvation is willed by man so that he can be the receiving party. But the
argument is plainly weak unless it can be assumed that no other
motive than brash egoism can be considered. Those who, like Maritain (and his favourite authorities, Grisar and Denifle), try to discredit Lutheran theology are at pains to show that Luther himself
was utterly self-centred, either from animal passions or from spiritual
pride. If it is not assumed from the first that the doctrine of salvation is
cherished from psychological reasons it seems reasonable to suppose
that the Reformers counted it supremely important, because faithfulness to the Gospel demanded that it be taken altogether seriously.

God and man together form the axis of the doctrine of salvation.
But this axis is given meaning only when the whole doctrine is seen
to exist in order to reveal the activity of God condescending to man.
For Luther the Glory of God is the origin and the end of faith. If
we are to believe Maritain, this theocentricity is only *'theoretically
and according to Luther'*, not *'actually and according to Truth'*. 'For
since we are no longer sharers in the divine nature, we can produce
no vital act of our own, no essentially personal act which comes from
God vivifying us supernaturally [12]. In this estimate the proof that
Luther's axis of glory-faith is irredeemably egocentric is that Luther
denies to man an independent centre *of his own*, whereby his personal
act can bring life. A strange proof! True, the Catholic statement of
the case does not sever man and God; man's own personal act still
'comes from God'. The paradox of an act having two authentic
sources—man's will and God's will—is retained in this statement of
'truth'. Yet it is not clear why it must be preferred to Luther's paradox of the sinner who is justified by the righteousness of God—
simul justus et peccator. Surely Luther's presentation, as well as standing much closer to Scripture ('while we were yet sinners, Christ died
for us') (Rom. 5₈), preserves intact the primacy of God's act over our
receiving it. Indeed, the theocentric natures of the glory-faith axis is
unchallenged, for what links together the two poles is the grace of
God; and grace is identical with God's glory revealed to men. It is
unconditioned grace, acting without any requirement that the other
pole, man, must produce some 'vital act' of its own.

Nor can the grace of God in Luther's theology be impersonal in its

[12] *Three Reformers*, p. 168 (Note 4). The italics are Maritain's.

operation. The reason why no 'personal act' is required of the human object of grace in its own right is that grace is always personal in *its* own right. Grace is the gracious God acting and bringing salvation. When faith is conceived as a personal relationship originating in grace, then God's glory is of necessity the governing factor in the relationship. Man receives, but he receives because God gives. The glory-faith axis is theocentric because grace makes it an axis—there is no independent centre at the receiving end.

While Catholic theory demands a personal act to show that men share decisively in the Divine nature, Catholics often deplore any signs of a personal reception of the Gospel. E. L. Mascall considers it to be a point against the Protestant conception of revelation that it speaks through distinctive and lively (vital) persons. He quotes Professor Gilson's remarks about Barth:

God speaks, says Karl Barth, and man listens and repeats what God has said. But unfortunately, as is inevitable as soon as a man makes himself God's interpreter, God speaks and the Barthian listens and repeats what Barth has said.[13]

But it is surely no evidence that a man is not God's interpreter because men can identify a voice belonging to a particular man and are moved by his personality and his phrases. The prophets were most decidedly 'individuals' and even eccentrics. The New Testament itself is a study in distinctive styles, which are different enough to furnish a basis for biblical textual criticism. When we hear the Gospel record we cannot help hearing also John and Paul—to take two conspicuous examples only—whose individual accents, far from keeping the authentic note of the Gospel from us, help us to take it to ourselves. Augustine, Luther, Wesley, Barth, and countless others point us to Christ; and the better they do a work not their own, the less we are likely to overlook the men themselves. Those who are concerned to show the glory of God, and lose themselves in their witness, find themselves. The One who came to do His Father's will is the one individual man whose *personality* has most fascinated the world.

The interpreter, witness, and protestant (the three words vary only slightly in meaning) stand for nothing in themselves and everything in their message. Like theology itself, the theologians who seek to make the Gospel known to men must be humble. This humility has its complement in audacity which often looks like demonic pride. Not only Christian disciples, but also their Lord, have been accused of

[13] *He Who Is: A Study in Traditional Theism*, p. 28 (Note 1). Mascall also prints a similar statement by Maritain.

egocentric arrogance. Sensitive humanitarians outside the Christian tradition, such as C. S. Montefiore the Liberal Jewish thinker, have been full of admiration for the figure of Jesus—except for His apparent lack of charity toward those who disagreed with Him. From the view-point of a tolerant humanism Albert Guérard writes: 'Beside the gentle Jesus stands the rebel who denounced evil-doers and called woe upon them. . . . This yielding to anger was perhaps the inner flaw that made Jesus so human and so tragic.'[14] Guérard thinks that the humility and defiance are to be explained psychologically as love of the oppressed turned to hatred of the oppressor, but compatibility of the two can also be explained as being divergent expressions of the same principle. A loyalty possessing the whole personality can only too easily be thought to be personal aggressiveness. Thus Paul can speak of 'my' Gospel and insist on his authority as an apostle, because he can say: 'I live; yet not I, but Christ liveth in me' (Gal. 2_{20}). Those who wish to discredit the integrity of the witnesses will, of course, stress the likelihood of loyalty being a mere mask for egotism.

The psychological approach is an easy one to turn to destructive purposes, since it can make every reason into a rationalization and every idea into an ideology, leaving no possible defence open except the unsatisfactory one of the *tu quoque*. Techniques of destruction by psychological inference are varied. One such technique may be seen in mild moral objections to the personalities of those holding certain beliefs. L. Harold de Wolf, who champions the place of reason in religious thinking, censures certain 'irrationalists', such as Kierkegaard and Barth, for showing a displeasing arrogance.[15] Then there is the appeal to psychology to confirm an unfavourable verdict already held on other grounds, as in Denifle's view of Luther's theology, quoted above.[16] There is also the psycho-socio-historical approach which sweeps up persons, and social changes, and even the course of history itself in one psychological generalization. According to Erich Fromm, not only did Luther and Calvin show themselves to be in 'the ranks of the greatest haters among the leading figures of history', but the brand of hatred they sponsored was the repressed hatred of the middle classes of their age for the upper classes; this being shown in the moral indignation 'which has invariably been characteristic for the lower middle class from Luther's time to Hitler's'.[17] To

[14] *Bottle in the Sea* (1954), pp. 129–30.
[15] *The Religious Revolt against Reason* (1949), pp. 116–17.
[16] See p. 61, *supra*.
[17] *Escape from Freedom* (1941), pp. 95–6. Note the linking of the names Luther and Hitler. Guilt by association is still the most effective as well as the simplest of methods to discredit any one without needing to supply any real evidence.

all these attempts to prove ideas false by suggesting that the bearers of the idea are contemptible there can be only one course: to refuse to be side-tracked by personalities where principles are at issue. A man may be in the right although he is unpleasant, or although his motives are low ones, or although others with the same opinions are self-deceived. The fact that totalitarianism uses moral indignation to blind its dupes tells us nothing about the moral indignation of those who, on moral grounds, oppose totalitarianism. This is not to say that the evidence made available by psychology is valueless, but only that it must be kept within its own proper limits and subjected to more inclusive values.

When the issues are faced squarely and apart from tendentious claims that one side can offer only *theory* while the other stands for *truth*, it seems that Catholicism distrusts Protestant theocentricity because it appears defective in its doctrine of man. In giving no place for a purely human will to goodness that can co-operate with grace, such a theology as Luther's to Catholic minds seems to have built an impassable barrier between man and God; thus the claim to give God the glory will inevitably turn into its opposite and result in the demonic human will setting itself up in the place of God. The Protestant rejoinder is that the Protestant doctrine of man seems inadequate only when judged in terms of the Catholic doctrine of God and grace.

That compromise between Catholic and Protestant views is not altogether impossible is shown by the fact that representatives of both faiths were able to agree over the issue of Justification at the Conference of Regensburg in 1541. But plainly agreement cannot be consolidated unless there is some common ground granted by both theological standpoints. The question of the reception of the Gospel is one of the main points at issue where theocentricity is concerned. Granted that God gives and man receives: what does man receive and how does he receive it? When the Protestant says that man receives justifying faith and receives it as a free gift of grace, he finds that the Catholic does not consider this a sufficient answer, and he is presented with another answer in a wholly different set of terms. Protestantism finds Catholicism's terms difficult to accept because they express values which appear to be foreign to the Gospel as well as being given in language remote from Scripture.

III. POSSESSING THE TRUTH

Particularly strange to the Protestant are the Catholic values as set forth in Thomism. Interpreting the Thomist view of theocentricity, Maritain writes:

Catholic theology is ordered to God, and it is, by that very fact, a science chiefly speculative. Lutheran theology is for the creature; that is why it aims above all at the practical end to be attained. Luther . . . makes the science of divine things revolve round human corruption.[18]

We have seen the Protestant answer to the charge of egocentricity: Grace is indeed only known by the creature it rescues from corruption, and the theology which seeks to interpret grace can do so only in terms of man's reception of salvation. Catholic theocentricity, as Maritain expounds it, is evidently proved by the fact of theology being a science able to show what Lutheran theology cannot do, namely that man can 'produce a substantially supernatural act'. It would thus appear that Catholic theology is also for the creature; not indeed to bring him the practical assurance of forgiving grace, but to give him the speculative knowledge of divine things. To the Protestant view, this looks very little theocentric. Theology exists less to tell the Catholic what God does for him than what he can know about God and what he can do for himself.

Next, the Protestant notes that Catholicism, in its Thomist form, claims finality as well as authority for its theology; not finality in the things necessary for a Christian to believe (for new dogmas are now declared to be *de fide* by Rome which were not so in St Thomas's time), but the finality of absolute certainty concerning all articles of faith taught by the Church. If the Church declares that unaided human reason can prove the existence of God, then reason can do just that. Any one who says he uses his reason and comes to a different conclusion must be unreasoning or unreasonable, or both. Only if we see what the Church sees do we see what *is*. Protestantism claims authority for its theology—the authority of the Word and the Spirit—but not finality. In one way, the way of extension, Protestant theology asserts finality as Catholicism does not; for it does not expect to add to the number of things a Christian must believe in. Doubtless, 'The Lord hath more light and truth yet, to break forth out of His holy Word',[19] but this concerns the Spirit's illumination rather than any information about God's mighty acts in Christ

---

[18] op. cit., p. 17.
[19] Attributed to Pastor Robinson on the occasion of the sailing of the Pilgrim Fathers.

necessary for our salvation. The finality that is alien from Protestant-ism is the finality of a statement, as a statement and apart from a right apprehension of it. Justification by faith itself, *as a doctrine*, can be made the cause of idolatry as readily as other truth held apart from God's gift of a right understanding of it. 'The letter killeth, but the spirit giveth life' (2 Cor. 3₆) is surely not adequately interpreted as a directive to read parts of Scripture allegorically instead of literally (which was Augustine's view), and is better understood as a warning that all propositional statement in general is fallible unless the Spirit of Truth conveys its meaning to our total understanding.

Catholicism's understanding of theology may be pictured as a box, open at one end for future extension, but for the rest of its length securely enclosed, so that what is inside and what is outside cannot be doubted. The nearest image appropriate for Protestant theology would be a locked door, with a key beside it. Catholicism sees theology as objective and complete in itself, to be accepted or rejected. For Protestantism theology has no meaning apart from its use. It is men who are outside or inside the sphere of revelation.

In this connexion it is instructive to see how a technical term of Catholic theology such as 'infused grace' is a metaphor chosen from the sub-personal realm. That would be no great matter if the meta-phor were kept alive in the poetic ambivalence of common speech. The Bible speaks of being 'full of grace' (John 1₁₄), and 'full of good works' (Acts 9₃₆), as well as 'full of leprosy' (Luke 5₁₂). But once the metaphor has been killed in the interest of 'scientific' usage it has very real dangers. Catholic theology speaks of grace as something a man may have in his own right once God has *infused* it into him, and so, in effect, severs *grace* from God *gracious*. The primary meaning of an operation involving a liquid has come to the fore. The biblical metaphors which were pivotal in Reformation theology—*justification* —*redemption*—*adoption*—are drawn from the field of personal rela-tionships. And Protestant theology has been concerned to interpret the key words of faith, such as *faith*, *grace*, *repentance*, and *truth*, in their Biblical personal context. It is illuminating that under Catholic-ism the inward motion of the soul indicated by *repentance* should have been transformed into the outward observance of *penance* through the use of the Latin *poenitentia* to translate the Greek *metanoia*, while *saints* have become a separate class of particularly notable devout persons instead of the ordinary name for a Christian disciple. (The last word, by long usage, has become too definite a label now to revert to its original descriptive meaning.)

The personal reference of the terms of Scripture, depersonalized in Catholic theology in order to make theology 'scientific', was essential to the task of pointing man to God, or at least, so it seems to the Protestant mind. Catholicism feels itself free to construct its own categories. The promises of God can be presented as propositions. The Word of God that confronts men with unconditional authority becomes a series of statements, correctly phrased according to a standard agreed to by the Church, and these statements themselves become the necessary object of unconditional assent. Catholics claim to possess the truth, because the Church teaches only what is true. Values, in this interpretation, are completely and correctly expressed in party doctrine, just as they are fully and finally embodied in a party organized as an institution. Only in so far as the Church Militant is separated from the Church Triumphant does the institution materially organized fail to embody the full value of the faith, but in essence there remains the need for completion alone and certainly not for correction or re-expression. The certainty of truth which man may possess for himself on earth by membership of the right institution will be perfected by his attaining the Beatific Vision in heaven, where his degree of bliss will depend upon his degree of intrinsic merit. What man can know, and what man can have, and what man must do is the continual refrain of Catholic theology.

IV. PERSONAL RESPONSE AND OBJECTIVITY

An objection to the way of interpreting religious truth in personal terms is that it lacks all objectivity and reduces the certainty of belief to the vagaries of 'religious experience'. The reply to this must be, 'How is objectivity to be proved in matters of belief?' Either the truths of religion substantiate themselves, or they are confirmed by some other authority.

God's revelation can hardly be referred to any authority superior to itself. If God speaks, that is objective fact. The only question to be resolved is how one recognizes revelation: how do we know that God is *speaking* and that it is really God who speaks? If the answer is given that revelation is known in the Church by the inspiration of the Holy Spirit, we still want to know the limits of the Church and how we recognize it. Do we know when the Holy Spirit's inspiration is active by knowing where the Church is? Or do we know by the Holy Spirit's inspiration how to recognize the Church?

The first answer is generally to be inferred whenever the 'objective' view is championed, while the second alternative implies an

individualistic answer appealing to 'religious experience'. Both
views are questionable. The 'objective' view rests on the assumption
that there is knowledge apart from faith that is beyond dispute, and
so must postulate an authority more certain than revelation. The
'subjective' view allows no authority outside the individual conscience that can be known at all. Catholicism favours objectivity.
Subjectivity is seldom found pure, but is present in most of the
efforts to found a 'religion of humanity'. A recent defence of almost
consistent subjectivism in religion has been given by J. H. Badley,
who contends:

Our real religion—that which matters most in every age and in each individual—is whatever we feel to be most worth while in life, the dominant
object of our reverence and aspiration, and the response that this provokes
in the conduct of our lives.[20]

The Protestant understanding of the way God's revelation of
Himself is established rejects both the 'objective' and the 'subjective'
ways. It believes that God speaks to men in the Church and through
the Church, so that the individual conscience is not the final court of
appeal. It also believes that where the Holy Spirit is, there the
Church is, so that the existence of an institution claiming to be the
Church is not proof of the Holy Spirit's presence. It claims that
objectivity belongs to God's Word alone, and both the Church as a
visible organization and the believer as an individual make subjective
claims to stand for the truth, except inasmuch as they actually
respond to what is objectively given.

This third view sees subjectivity as the essential character of the
other two. The 'objective' view has no justification for its assurance
that certitude can be turned into certainty by the act of turning to
certain external marks to prove the truth of its contention; it merely
succeeds in creating a false absolute supported by a party. The
absolute is false because, being set beyond criticism, it has become a
mere ideology, in the strict sense of that much-abused word. It is no
objective reality but a claim to possess the means of judging truth by
dogmas which cannot themselves be questioned. By contrast the
'subjective' view is frank in seeing that what we claim to know we
claim to know for ourselves only. Banding together to make a collective certitude is no way out of the subjective impasse; better far to
trust to individual intuitions, says the subjectivist, and make our
indubitable values (they are at least *ours*, if we are honest with ourselves) the measure of all things. What subjectivism does not face up

[20] *Form and Spirit* (1951), p. 24.

to is that a pure individualism in religious standards leads inevitably to a meaningless relativity. The absence of meaning is usually covered up by quietly dropping all specifically religious reference and finding the 'real' purpose of religion in making men happy.[21] Standing between a false absolutism and an anarchic relativism, the Protestant way appears dogmatic to the subjectivist and subversive to the objectivist.

The subjectivist interprets the work of the Reformation as a stirring of true religious consciousness still holding on to the old forms of religion because hardly aware of the revolution it has brought about.[22] The objectivist agrees with the diagnosis and reverses the values: the Reformers, rebelling against the true faith, ushered in an epoch of religious apostasy they had not intended. These opposite valuations draw a confident conclusion from their own premises concerning the rightful place of religion in society—which is why they produce historical judgements so readily. Protestantism must view its own history with less simple explanations of its development. In the practical world of affairs, where some workable compromise between ideologies must often take precedence over any consistent policy of putting one's own beliefs into practice, the Reformers had to choose between two paths, one of which held to the old tried way of authoritarianism, while the other led to new ground by way of belief in human development freed from the restrictions of formerly powerful institutions and dogmas. At first, endeavouring to put new wine into old bottles, the Reformers copied the methods of the objectivists, but finally allied themselves with the subjectivists. They had no wish to make the world safe for subjectivism, but they helped to make the attitude of mind which finds it intolerable that objectivists shall legislate universally in the light of their own absolutes. We shall follow this process in the next three chapters.

Yet Protestantism, though it has not gone back upon its decision to collaborate with subjectivism, has never been entirely at home with

[21] 'Here, then, communion with the Unseen and with our fellows is at one, in a worship showing itself not in acts of homage to a Heavenly King but in all that can help to establish a Kingdom of Heaven upon earth'—Badley, ibid., p. 222. In other words, worship is of some use when it ceases to be worship and becomes social welfare. Michael Polanyi has pointed out how Bentham's principles, if consistently carried out, would have led to the Nihilism of Russia and Central Europe; but Bentham in fact relied upon traditional beliefs about what makes man happy. (*The Logic of Liberty* (1951), p. 104.) Bentham's philosophy is a secular counterpart of subjectivist religion. Both live unconsciously by the dogmas they consciously reject.

[22] Badley asserts: 'The Reformation, in its religious aspect, was essentially a demand for freedom of thought and conscience' (ibid., p. 115). The demand was a social implication of the Reformation faith, perhaps, but it was never its *religious* expression. 'Religion' used in so loose a sense loses all meaning.

this partner. All attempts to identify it with modern individualism, like those seeking to show it to be the disguised spirit of capitalism, or nationalism, or middle-class interests, are grotesque over-simplifications. Where Protestant theology has become 'liberal' (an exceedingly vague label used to cover different movements during the past century-and-a-half which tried to make a working synthesis between contemporary knowledge—particularly the natural and historical sciences—and Christian faith),[23] it has always aroused a strong 'orthodox' reaction when it compromised the Protestant protest over-much. In its confessional theology it cherished the biblical doctrine of salvation, with its two poles of God and man, and set over against subjectivism—as against objectivism—its third way, which we may call from its image of the God-man axis, the way of 'dialogue'.[24]

Because of the strength of the Catholic theological tradition, Protestantism at the Reformation was not fully aware of the essential cleavage between objectivism and the way of dialogue. There were—and are—frequent attempts to set up Protestantism as another objective theology, based on the finality of the Bible as a divinely guaranteed book or on confessional statements as final expressions of truth. At the same time there have been counter-movements to keep alive a truly dialectical theology by re-interpreting the way of dialogue within Protestantism. One of the most fruitful of these for our times has been the existentialist teaching of Søren Kierkegaard.

Kierkegaard's original contribution to a rediscovery of Protestant values is shown in his rescuing the term *subjectivity* from the usual *subjective-objective* antithesis. Instead of the context of a private world more likely than not to be illusory because it was not the public world, Kierkegaard used *subjective* to indicate personal and inward knowledge over against an impersonal view of the world. Kierkegaard was concerned to establish the difference between knowing about God and knowing God. In line with the Protestant theology based on dialogue, he considered only the latter the concern of Christians, so, to stress the irrelevance of 'objective' knowledge about God, he spoke of subjectivity being the dimension of religion:

[23] *Catholicity* has presented 'liberal religion' as though it were a compact body of theological opinion that can be set over against 'orthodox Protestantism' as the one half of a 'divided' Catholicism—divided at the Reformation (p. 42). The confusions of this view are pointed out in the *Catholicity of Protestantism* (pp. 38-9).

[24] In contemporary theology this way is often called *the Divine-Human Encounter* (Emil Brunner's book with this title appeared in English translation in 1944). I have chosen Martin Buber's metaphor of *dialogue* (see Chap. 5, Section 2, *infra*), however, because it can be used also to describe man's encounter with his neighbour.

The existing individual who chooses to pursue the objective way enters upon the entire approximation-process by which it is proposed to bring God to light objectively. But this is in all eternity impossible, because God is a subject, and therefore exists only for subjectivity in inwardness.[25]

The restatement of the fundamental principles of Biblical and Protestant thought has been immensely influential in stimulating a fully conscious awareness of what confessional theology is about. In particular it has helped to banish the assumption that faith, the personal response to God's revelation is bound to individual caprice which can only be banished by an objective, and therefore conceptual, statement of authoritative articles of belief.

V. SPECULATION AND DOGMA

Kierkegaard's existentialism brought again into prominence the attack upon the self-sufficiency of human reason which had been a prominent feature of Reformation theology. Just as Protestant rejection of 'objectivity' is often taken to mean a plunge into mere feeling, so Protestant criticism of reason is often supposed to imply advocating irrationalism.[26] This misunderstanding springs from the belief that reason itself is attacked, when the criticism is actually directed at a misuse of reason through failure to recognize its proper limits. In particular, the exaltation of reason in theology, to the extent that God's revelation is considered to be unnecessary for part of theology's proper work, is vehemently rejected by Protestantism. It is its view of the function of reason that underlies Protestantism's dissatisfaction with the objective-subjective categories, and this view in turn rests on its understanding of faith. Faith is not to be explained in terms of intellectual perception and assent to rational proof. So, while reason has its necessary place in theology in so far as all our understanding of every realm of experience must be communicated by rational discourse, obedience to faith does not imply the independent authority of reason. Reason in its role of speculation

---

[25] *Concluding Unscientific Postscript* (translated by David F. Swenson (1941), p. 178).

[26] *Catholicity* asserts: 'Among large sections of orthodox Protestants, a dislike of rational thought, for fear of rationalism, has become traditional' (p. 24). As *The Catholicity of Protestantism* replies, this alleged tradition is incompatible with the actual *bulk* of Protestant theology (p. 56).

In *The Religious Revolt Against Reason*, L. Harold de Wolf considers various criticisms of reason by Protestant theologians whom he labels 'irrationalists'. But, in attempting to refute the 'irrationalists', he never faces the question of how far 'rationalism' is admissible in religion, with the result that his answers are, on the whole, indecisive. His plea for the use of reason *along with* faith tends to be a limitation of faith to rational goals: for example in his rejection of the use of paradox, unless it can be subjected to some synthesis.

cannot declare what faith is and what it is not. Faith is independent of reason. That is not to say that we need not trouble ourselves to be reasonable in matters of faith, but only that reason is the means of expressing supra-rational truth and never the final judge of its truthfulness.

If reason is supposed to have authority in the sphere of religion, speculation will be believed to give meaning to a revelation incomplete and incomprehensible without it. The argument that God's Word can be correctly heard only when the hearer gives intellectual assent to a particular metaphysical system follows from the presupposition that reason has such authority. This presupposition limits faith in revelation, for it prescribes that revelation can never go against reason; but equally it limits reason also, because the reason alone able to be finally authoritative must be no mere instrument for approximating to truth but very Truth itself, shining by its own light. Reason is thus equated with one particular set of speculative findings which are declared to be objectively true. It is hardly surprising that Protestantism finds that the rationalism involved in the argument that faith is established by reason is intellectually suspect, as well as contrary to the protest of the Gospel as self-authenticating.

Protestant objection to self-sufficient reason is confirmed by the methods used by Catholics to show that the biblical record is compatible with an independently developed metaphysical system. Here is how Etienne Gilson deals with 'the method of biblical revelation' in a prominent instance:

In order to know what God is, Moses turns to God. He asks His name, and straightway comes the answer: *Ego sum qui sum, Ait: sic dices filiis Israel; qui est misit me ad vos* (Ex. 3$_{14}$). No hint of metaphysics, but God speaks, *causa finita est*, and Exodus lays down the principle from which henceforth the whole of Christian philosophy will be suspended. From this moment it is understood once and for all that the proper name of God is Being and that, according to the word of St. Ephrem, taken up again later by St. Bonaventure, this name denotes His very essence.[27]

'Once and for all' sounds final enough; and the principle here discovered in Exodus is taken to be clear beyond all doubt:

When God says that He is being, and if what He says is to have any intelligible meaning for our minds, it can only mean this: that He is the pure act of existing.[28]

Yet it is quite evident that the assumed finality exists only when appeal is made to one tradition and to one theory of intelligibility.

[27] *The Spirit of Mediæval Philosophy* (1936, reprinted 1950), p. 51.
[28] ibid., p. 52.

Much more than 'a hint' of metaphysics, a whole system is invoked. In a footnote, M. Gilson argues that the evidence supplied by A. Lods concerning the meaning of the name *Jahve* shows 'that the patristic-mediæval philosophy is a correct development of this text'.[29] This conclusion entails denying Lods's own view of the matter, and there is no mention at all that the medieval exegesis of the Mosaic text has for a long time now been set aside by Hebrew scholars.[30] We are given, in fact, a fully developed Thomistic metaphysics of Being and Existence based on a verbal similarity—which may well be nothing more than verbal—between the terminology of that metaphysics and a Biblical text standing alone without further Scriptural support. On this single point M. Gilson is prepared to build a great inverted pyramid of speculation ('all the studies that here follow will be merely studies of its results').[31] Obviously the 'principle' is not deduced from the text but read into it, and the 'meaning' of the text is judged solely on the grounds that Thomism is the only rational system of philosophy.

The Protestant view that theology is first and foremost *dogmatics*, the teaching of the Revealed Word apart from speculative developments about its implications, is therefore no rejection of reason, but rather the plea that reason shall not be prematurely identified with any metaphysical system. The authority of dogmatic theology is not in the theology of any theologian (for all teachers, however faithful and enlightened by the Word, are fallible) but in the events that each theology proclaims. Speculative theology may be 'ordered towards God', but it is founded in man's view of what *is*, and whatever is built upon this terrestrial foundation is as likely to fall short of its goal as was the equally ambitious tower of Babel, which also aspired to reach to heaven from earth.

'Canst thou by searching find out God?' asks Zophar the Naamathite of Job (Job 11₇); Job does not cease to question, but he finds an answer only when God speaks directly to him. The tension of reason and faith can be resolved by believing that faith is, as least in part, nothing but faith in reason and that reason has no need of faith. Protestantism finds that this dogma goes against its protest that the

---

[29] ibid., p. 434.
[30] 'In Heb. writing of the historical period the name is connected with Heb. *hayah*, 'to be', in the imperf. Now with regard to this verb, *first*, it does not mean 'to be' essentially or ontologically, but phenomenally; and *secondly*, the impf. has not the sense of a present ('am') but of a fut. ('will be'). A. B. Davidson, *A Dictionary of the Bible*, edited by James Hastings (Sixth impression, 1905), Vol. II, Article 'God', iii.3.e. (p. 199).
[31] op. cit., p. 51.

sole reliable dogma is grounded in God's revelation. It is no answer to say that reason is a gift of God and so not to be despised, for the question at issue is how this gift of God is to be fitly used.

VI. NATURAL AND REVEALED THEOLOGY

In the classical Thomistic tradition, Catholicism claims for reason a delimited but specific place which is known as Natural Theology. Natural Theology is part of theology, so that its conclusions are authoritative, and also an authentic part of philosophy completely divorced from the truths of revelation, so that its conclusions are rational and binding on all rational men. Protestant theology has no such commission to give to reason, and is willing to let philosophers argue out matters in their own terms, without telling them, from the vantage-point of 'objective' truth, when they are being irrational. It leaves the critique of reason to Christian philosophers. Theology is vitally concerned with philosophy, but this concern is born of the realization that Christian thinking is not to be carried out in watertight compartments and embraces every aspect of existence. This concern means that while Protestant theologians find that the subject-matter of Natural Theology is primarily something for philosophy to appropriate, they are bound to examine the consequences of separating theology into 'natural' and 'revealed'. In this connexion, their principal question is the effect of the division upon the conception of revelation.

Protestants consider that revelation is the necessary starting-point for all Christian thinking. Nothing can be known that is wholly apart from revelation. The background of Catholic thought is that grace presupposes nature and faith presupposes natural knowledge, while the background of Reformation thought is that nature is meaningless without grace and that knowledge without faith is sophistry. Of course, Protestantism is not saying that we know nothing about the world or the self apart from the specific teachings of Biblical truth. What it affirms is that in all that we know (or think we know) we are dependent upon God's revelation, and that the only sure knowledge of spiritual truth is through God's revelation in Christ.

For Plato the Sophist was the person who made distorted images of the truth, and this analogy is very close to the Protestant way of thinking. Even a distorted image must rest on some dim appreciation of the reality it distorts. So instead of a division into two levels (a level of nature which is complete in itself but is perfected by grace, and a level of grace which can be added to nature), Protestantism sees knowledge to be made possible by man's appropriation of God's revelation in different degrees. There is considerable divergence of opinion in 'orthodox' Protestant thought about the place of 'natural' knowledge outside the specific revelation given in the Incarnation. This fact has been given prominence in our own day by Brunner's guarded recognition of a 'general revelation' in his *Nature and Grace* and Barth's emphatic reply *No!*[32] When Catholics criticize what they take to be the Protestant denial of the sphere of the *natural* they usually like to quote Barth, whose declaration that there is no 'point of contact' between God and man is taken as evidence that Protestant theology makes a complete separation between nature and grace.[33] This separation comes from assuming the Catholic background of thought and ignoring the Protestant one. The Reformation doctrine of 'total depravity' in Catholic eyes cuts man off from God altogether, since God's grace is assumed to be effective only when man has some goodness *of his own*. To the Protestant mind it is the only statement which takes seriously enough both the gravity and ubiquity of sin and the grace and omnipotence of God. Apart from grace, man distorts the good even while he seeks to achieve it, and apart from faith he distorts the truth even while he seeks to comprehend it. God gives man the grace and the faith alike by which man, the sinner, is saved from the vain attempt to possess either goodness or truth, which are the gifts of grace and never merits *of his own*.

To the Catholic, 'revelation itself needs rational justification . . . before he can accept anything upon the authority of God, he must first of all have been convinced that there is a God and that God has spoken'.[34] To the Protestant, no man who is a man can fail to know that there is a God, though he may fail to admit the fact: the Christian does not argue from some 'natural' promise to reach the conclusion that God exists, for the existence of God is not an inference from evidence, but a matter of the response of faith in the believer. Reason may be used to 'prove' the fact that there is a God and that there is not a God, and who shall say that one proof only is rational? The believer will say that sin has perverted reason, and the unbeliever will say that faith has overruled reason, so in the end we are

---

[32] *Natural Theology* (1946), with an Introduction by John Baillie. See also, John Baillie, *Our Knowledge of God* (1939).

[33] See *Catholicity*, pp. 22–3, and the answer to the charge in *The Catholicity of Protestantism*, Chapter 3, 'The Creation of Man and His Fall', and Chapter 4, 'The Theology of the Natural', in which the teaching of Luther and Calvin is expounded. Mascall (*He Who Is*, pp. 23 ff.) makes substantially the same charge against Protestant theology as does *Catholicity*.

[34] Mascall, op. cit., pp. 26–7.

left with dogmatic assertions.[35] For Protestants the terms 'atheist' and 'theist' are convenient labels, indicating what theological opinions men profess but telling us little about their actual faith, while for Catholics they represent essential stages in mankind's spiritual condition. Over against the Protestant Justification by Faith stands a Catholic Justification by Reason: only in the latter it is not man who is justified in the sight of God, but God whose Word is justified in the sight of men. Having discovered by a correct use of reason that God *is*, a 'necessary base' has been constructed upon which revelation can be 'erected'.[36]

The conception of reason as the mediator of revelation is quite unscriptural. The assertion that Catholic 'natural law' is the clue to the first chapter of Romans[37] overlooks the fact that the knowledge of God spoken there is not said to enable men to make correct statements about God, or to prepare them to receive the Christian Gospel, but *to render them without excuse*. The context of the statement by Paul about the existence of a 'general revelation', far from being concerned with the rational basis of supernatural truth, is wholly centred around saving faith and damning disobedience. The argument is directed to the conscience, where man stands before God either listening to His voice or refusing to hear it, and there is not a trace of the thought that man must first consult a process of rational enquiry to know that it is God who demands his obedience. It is perhaps relevant in this context to note that when Milton speaks of justifying 'the ways of God to man' his 'great argument' is the story of the Fall and the Incarnation. Paul's witness to the authoritativeness of God's Word is, likewise, an appeal to the authority of God's mighty acts in history and of His direct confrontation of men in creation. It is a direct echo of the Old Testament witness that the fool says in his heart that there is no God (Ps. 14_1, 53_1, Rom. 1_{22}). The Catholic reading of the witness, making the fool's folly lie in defective logic,[38] is so patently mistaken that only an ingrained habit

---

[35] A similar situation exists in regard to the so-called ontological argument of the existence of God. St Thomas, rejecting it, says that accepting a direct certainty of God's being is the result of thinking the faith we have been brought up in is self-evident. Mascall dismisses Baillie's reasoning in *Our Knowledge of God* (1939) on the same grounds (op. cit., p. 93). But the charge of confusing logic with psychological certitude can be brought equally against those who believe the cosmological argument to be valid, as St Thomas and Mascall do.

[36] Mascall, op. cit., p. 24.

[37] J. V. Langmead Casserley, *Morals and Man in the Social Sciences*, pp. 60–1. In *The Christian in Philosophy*, Casserley suggests that Paul was referring to the current Stoic 'proofs' of God's existence (p. 21).

[38] Sheed, *Theology and Sanity*, pp. 26–7.

of thinking of truth in terms of correct speculation can explain it.
The Biblical fool's defect is always moral and spiritual. When Jesus
used the term 'fool', He applied it to the man who (presumably
aware of the fact of human mortality and its natural implications)
failed to know his duty to God in the use of his riches (Luke 12_{20});
or He applied it to His disciples who had failed in the matter of insight into the meaning of Scripture, though they were quite convinced
that it was authoritative for them (Luke 24_{25}). As the Bible knows nothing of *proving* the authority of divine commands, so Jesus would
give no sign to vindicate His status, except the call to repentance,
the works of God that were manifest in Him, and the testimony of
the Scriptures (Mark 1_{15}, Matt. 12_{39}, 16_4, Luke 11_{20}, John 5_{39}). Yet
St Thomas tells us that Christ's divinity and supernatural mission are
fully proven through prophecy and miracle.

Protestantism finds the Catholic separation of the natural from the
supernatural particularly misleading when it seeks to build the
authority of revelation on the certainty of the natural knowledge of
God. Faith then becomes an additional dimension of knowledge,
received on authority while the former is received on direct proof.
The 'theist' simply becomes a 'Christian theist' by way of addition.
Protestantism divides men into 'disciples' and 'idolators'. Men can
only know that God has spoken by responding to His Word to them.
If they respond, they become Christians. If they reject it, they choose
some other God of their own making. Luther said that in the
practical syllogism of belief men universally recognized the major
premise (that there is a God) and erred in the minor (*this* is God).[39]
Instead of starting with certain knowledge and going on to build on

---

[39] Watson, *Let God Be God*, p. 81. The importance of this distinction of Luther's
in connexion with the theistic 'proofs' is often overlooked. If, as Aquinas argues,
reason leads us to posit a Being such as 'all men agree in calling God', two separate
questions arise. *First:* has this Being really been proved to exist—was the argument
valid? *Second:* has this Being, created to supply a metaphysical value, any religious
value—was the argument about *God*? The first is a philosophical question and the
second a theological one. And, while the dispute over the validity of the proofs has
mainly centred about the first question, Luther characteristically saw that the
theological question must be the crucial one for the Christian; for, if this is answered
in the negative, the other falls to the ground. Kant was led to refute the theistic
'proofs' as part of his attack upon natural theology and in order to open the way for
faith. The God whom he affirmed was the living God who speaks to the individual
in dialogue (though Kant restricted dialogue to the subjective apprehension of the
moral law), not the consequence of an intellectually valid statement, but the presupposition of all valid experience. Kant's essentially Protestant outlook was taken
up in Ritschl's opposition of *value judgements* and *theoretical judgements*, but in
Ritschl and his successors this led to a dualism where religious 'truth' and philosophic 'truth' went their own ways. Kierkegaard re-stated the fundamental Lutheran insight when he said bluntly that a Christianity which tries to prove itself is
paganism.

that knowledge the infallible knowledge of faith, we stand all the time under the judgement of the Living God who speaks to us through Christ. Either men receive God's revelation in believing faith, or they substitute their own vision of the Universe and of God Himself instead.

VII. SAVING KNOWLEDGE

The egocentric-theocentric issue for theology thus appears finally as an issue between the authority of faith and the authority of human reason. Both theological views regard God as the source of all truth, but the first measures truth against God's Word, and the second against the findings of reason. The first finds reason trustworthy only in so far as it is illuminated by God's Word, and the second finds God's Word acceptable when it has passed the scrutiny of reason; indeed, revelation takes the form of truths which are guaranteed to be as certain *as though* reason had established them. In Thomism, Catholic theology has enthroned the metaphysical priority of reason —deriving from Aristotle's estimate of the place of the active intellect—so that the living relationship of faith has become a mental exercise in harmonizing speculative and theological propositions. E. L. Mascall has spoken of St Thomas's very human sympathy with the ordinary man and woman too busy with their daily affairs to bother themselves with matters of divinity.[40] But the condescension which declares that those who are not able to understand, by using their own brains, may accept truths, by believing them on authority, betrays under its paternalism a fundamental contempt for the worker as against the thinker; it is the voice of Greek aristocratic self-sufficiency. Certainly, it debases the notion of belief intolerably to make it a poor substitute for knowledge.

Assured knowledge for confessional theology is the knowledge of salvation (Luke 1_{77}); 'I know whom I have believed' (2 Tim. 1_{12}) is the response of faith to God's revelation of Himself in Christ, and any other knowledge is necessarily uncertain and partial knowledge, because we are both creatures and sinners. This saving knowledge is truth we can rely on, not propositional knowledge we can possess. It is personal knowledge to which we personally respond: we receive the Word of God through Christ, for we 'know surely' that He is from God (John 17_8). Whatever other knowledge we have is reflected, directly or indirectly, from this personal authority: directly, as when Paul knew that no good thing lay in him (Rom. 7_{18}), or

[40] op. cit., p. 27, n. 2.

indirectly (by way of 'religious experience') as when Peter knew that God had delivered him from Herod's prison (Acts 12_{11}). There is no independent criterion of truth lying here within the natural order and available for man apart from revelation. This theology has a single centre in the God who makes Himself known to men.

What to the Catholic is the sphere of the natural, capable of being known apart from revelation, to the Protestant is God's creation, which cannot be known adequately while its Creator remains estranged from those who seek to understand His works. Luther used to maintain that reason was a reliable instrument when dealing with the things *below* it, but incapable of aspiring to the things *above* it. This distinction partly does away with the Catholic division between nature and grace and yet perhaps still tries to draw too definite a line between the sacred and the secular in human experience. Obviously, some aspects of the 'natural' are much more closely dependent upon Christian understanding than are others. For instance, insight into physics depends almost wholly upon a rational grasp of the facts given 'objectively' in the material universe; we do not expect a Christian physicist to differ very widely in his findings from a non-Christian physicist.[41] In the case of history, the picture is very different. The Christian historian will look at history with altogether different presuppositions and draw altogether different conclusions from the non-Christian. And so with every sphere of knowledge: revelation will have a lesser or greater part to play, but will never be unnecessary. There is no realm of knowledge from logic to psychology where *reason* can be found entirely separated from *belief*.

It is the question about the status of knowledge which is not directly and specifically a response to God's revelation in Christ which is a disputed question in Protestant theology today. Where God is not known specifically by His Word spoken in the Incarnation how truly is He known? And what are the implications of a 'general revelation' or its denial for knowledge in general? These questions are important for Christian philosophy, and important also for confessional theology, because they involve the way in which God's revelation is mediated to men.[42] But for confessional theology they are not

[41] Yet while the particular findings of physics are independent of faith, the existence of the discipline we call physics today is not. A. N. Whitehead finds the genesis of modern science in the medieval theological tradition—and also in the revolt from Scholastic rationalism and the rise of Naturalistic philosophies (*Science in the Modern World*, Chap. 1, esp. pp. 10 ff.).

[42] See Baillie, op. cit. Baillie's conclusion that Revelation is 'a mediated immediacy' (pp. 178 ff.) is a theological expression of the contention argued above (p. 57) that values are found embodied but are directly known.

central, because the revelation in Christ has been given. We can ask what we might have known apart from it and what knowledge those possess who have not received it, but we cannot pretend it has not been given and that it is not decisive for us. The Protestant protest is a declaration that God has given the knowledge that saves. All else is secondary and peripheral.

All truth is of God. Protestantism does not belittle the good that philosophy—Christian and non-Christian—may do in clearing our minds of crippling confusions and preparing the way for the reception of the truth which is in Christ. But it denies that speculation by itself gives us knowledge that is wholly reliable or that can take the place of faith. This is not *a priori* dogmatism, though it is properly a *dogmatic* statement, i.e. one deriving its authority from the Word of God in Christ. It is a declaration of loyalty to biblical and confessional truth. And, quite evidently, the contrary view results in a radical departure from the knowledge to be found in Scripture. To limit grace, whether it be in the name of reason or authoritative tradition, leads inevitably to a legalism where man is accepted by God only when he acquires merit, to a rationalism that interprets God's Word in categories of its own choosing, and to an authoritarianism that declares its own edicts infallible and so stands in the place of God. Reason cannot bestow the gift of knowledge in its own right.

When Luther called reason the 'whore', he echoed the language of the prophets to whom departure from obedience to God's Word was an idolatry which represented wilful unfaithfulness to God's Covenant with His people. He saw in the misuse of reason that fatal perversion of theology which had resulted in the Babylonian Captivity of the Church under Rome. Protestant theology counts obedience to faith and faithfulness to God's Word the essential elements of Christian discipleship. It has insisted that to put God in the centre of our thinking is an act of obedience, while to declare that we possess the objective truth about God is to attempt to make Him a prisoner of our self-centred system of truth. Parallel with its exaltation of faith alone as the way to know God, Protestantism has insisted— though less consistently, for the temptation to dogmatize is persistent—that human knowledge in every other relation must be kept open to doubt. Protestant doubt is the other face of Protestant belief. Trust in saving knowledge implies a relative scepticism about all knowledge that lies outside the sphere of faith. To this Protestant critique of human knowledge we must now turn our attention.

CHAPTER FIVE

PROTESTANT DOUBT

I. CERTAINTY, PSYCHOLOGICAL CERTITUDE, AND FAITH

IN THE sphere of religion, *doubt* stands in opposition to *faith*. 'O thou of little faith, wherefore didst thou doubt?' said Jesus to Peter sinking in the waves (Matt. 14$_{31}$), and Tennyson's mild paradox is familiar:

> *There lives more faith in honest doubt,*
> *Believe me, than in half the creeds.*

But *doubt* is no more univocal than is *faith*. Since in its everyday sense *doubt* is contrasted with *certainty*, we may begin in this context to examine its meaning.

Experience teaches us soon enough that a belief, however firmly believed, may be a mistaken one. On the other hand, it may be established as a fact—and then it is no longer a belief. Certitude (*feeling* sure) is not certainty (*knowing* for sure). Certainty is an ideal state of affairs we only discover under limited conditions. The axioms of Euclidean geometry are certain, because they have been made so; and the conclusion of a syllogism follows certainty from its premise—so long as we are agreed on the system of logic used. Usually we allow certainty to be measured by a practical test, as when Dr Johnson (according to Boswell) answered Bishop Berkeley by 'striking his foot with mighty force against a large stone, till he rebounded from it', and thus demonstrated that matter certainly existed. Such limited certainties, however, all fall short of the ideal. Either their certainty is purely formal (as in the case of axioms and syllogisms), or they are metaphysical claims which must stand subject to the counter-claims of other metaphysical systems. Boswell realized well enough that his hero had not refuted Berkeley's Idealism at all when he kicked the stone, but instead had demonstrated his belief in the common-sense philosophy of Reid and Beattie; and he himself agreed with Dr Johnson's gesture—although he knew it established nothing—saying that we must accept first principles in metaphysics, even though we cannot justify them, just as we accept axioms in mathematics. Today Positivism claims to establish certainty apart from metaphysics. It does so by accepting the methods of the natural sciences to be the proven way of achieving certainty—much as Dr Johnson accepted the evidence of his senses as infallible. Those who differ from the Positivists are quick to point out that a claim to certain knowledge does not cease to be metaphysical by sheltering behind the prestige of modern science. Positivism is one philosophical party among others, and its pretension to a special status is like that of a religious sect which proclaims itself to be 'not just another denomination'.

The distinction between *certainty* and *certitude* is not ordinarily observed in everyday speech, *certainty* being used to carry both meanings. 'This table is certainly circular', is a statement which refers to an agreed standard of truth, while a purely individual expression of belief is implied in, 'I am certain that this is the table I left my book on'. The objective and subjective uses of the word merge because both types of 'certainty' depend upon subjective (and thus *uncertain*) interpretation. The man who believed the table to be circular may be convinced subsequently that it really was oval—an illusion caused by his angle of vision having misled him. The man who thought he had left his book on the table may learn that, in fact, he had put it straight back on the shelf. Both judgements thus proved to be mistaken *certitudes*; both were *uncertain* where they were thought to be *certain*. That is why the same word can be used to cover both cases. But they are different because in the first case the man was only mistaken about his individual vision of the table, and his idea of circularity and of when tables conform to it did not have to be altered; while in the second case the whole notion of a table being related to a book was proved mistaken. *Certainty*, at least ideally, can be distinguished from *certitude*.

We have seen how Catholic and Protestant theology respectively approach the question of certainty. Catholic theology claims to be certain on the grounds of holding the sole true metaphysics, so that its claim is entirely objective and free from all taint of subjectivity. At the same time, rational certainty is backed by another claim: the claim to a certainty in the sphere of religious knowledge inaccessible to metaphysics. Where metaphysical certainty is proved by internal coherence and completeness, infallibly recognized by the reason, religious certainty is proved by external marks of authority, infallibly validated by the character of the religious truths themselves. Protestant theology makes no claim to certainty either for a Protestant metaphysics or for a Protestant religious knowledge. It claims that certainty alone exists in the religious truths which are given by religious means, but not that this certainty is passed on to any embodiment of these truths so that it can be itself authoritative and infallible.

The two approaches are so dissimilar that they hardly cover any common ground. When a Catholic theologian looks at any Protestant principle he too often reads it in Catholic terms, and carries over the assumptions of his own standpoint into a region where they do not apply. Here is E. L. Mascall making the effort to suppose that Catholic natural theology as the sphere of rational certainty is not the final word:

Belief that there is a God may be acquired, not in the way in which we deduce from the principles of Euclidean geometry that the angles at the base of an isosceles triangle are equal, but rather in the way—whatever that may be—in which a man is convinced that his wife is faithful to him, that the beer which he is just going to drink is not poisoned, or that there is such a place as Australia.[1]

The underlying presupposition of this is that belief ought to be demonstrable—*certitudes* turned into *certainties*—if not with the formal precision of geometrical propositions (though this is the only really satisfactory method) at least with the probability which is a reasonably safe guide in practice. Certitude in matters of marital fidelity, the non-toxic condition of beverages, and the existence of distant territories is obviously not always enough, for there exist private detectives, chemical analysts, and explorers whose work it is to verify beliefs in these fields. The fact that these specialists are called in only occasionally witnesses to the widespread reliance upon probability-judgements. There is nothing mysterious in this. Normal living would be impossible if we could not rely on what may be called 'psychological certitude'. We do not test the strength of every chair before we sit down, because we think it likely that it has already been tested. But if for some reason we begin to question its sturdiness, we shall certainly put it to the test.

I have called the probability-judgement giving rise to certitude 'psychological certitude', because the decisive issue in this kind of situation does not rest upon the certainty or uncertainty of the evidence available, but upon the psychological balance of the person who makes a judgement on the evidence. One man will cheerfully flop down in the most wobbly of chairs, while another will hardly trust himself to sit down anywhere. In *Othello*, the evidence of the

[1] *He Who Is*, p. 29.

handkerchief did not *prove* Othello's certitude about his wife's unfaithfulness. When Mr Mascall suggests that psychological certitude
may be an alternative to rational proof of God's existence he has not
really changed the ground of proof in the least, but merely suggested
that some people will not wish to trouble themselves with proof,
and will take proof for granted.

Protestant theology asserts that there is a much more important
way in which certitude is related to certainty than in the subjectivism
of psychological certitude. To take the example of *Othello* again, if
that play had been written to show how people come to subjective
conclusions about matters of fact we should value it for its psychological insight; people, we should say, often do behave like that.[2]
There seems to be more in *Othello*, however, than this takes into
account. We find ourselves making moral judgements about the
characters. Othello, we say, indeed loved 'not wisely but too well';
he ought to have trusted Desdemona in spite of the evidence and
Iago's psychological offensive. We might mean that he ought to have
balanced Iago's calumnies against all the other available evidence,
including perhaps his own 'intuitions'. But in that case Othello's
error was still no more than a psychological misfortune, and a very
understandable one when we remember the Elizabethan fear of:

> *The plain-song cuckoo gray,*
> *Whose note full many a man doth mark*
> *And dare not answer nay.*

But, if we do not think that Othello was the helpless victim of his own
temperament plus an unhappy combination of chances engineered
by Iago's malignity, we are bound to mean that Othello should have
trusted Desdemona *against* the evidence. What makes *Othello* a
tragedy, and not just a pathetic tale, is Shakespeare's power to convince us that Othello's love was a love which might have believed
where it did not see. The heart of the tragedy lies in the breakdown of
trust that followed from Iago's success in rousing Othello to jealousy.

Shakespeare's play makes clear that, while psychological certitude
is our only avenue to certainty in the way of knowledge, there exist
other certainties which cannot be proved but which are independent

---

[2] Psychological certitude seems anarchic and wholly individual, the most subjective of subjectivities. But, actually, it yields itself readily to objective analysis.
Modern psychology here has only refined the knowledge long possessed by ob-
servers of human nature. Subjectivity which moves within the orbit of objectivity
is quite other than the subjectivity of inwardness, which is not to be explained by
laws, for 'the spirit breatheth where it listeth' (John 3₈).

of the evidence by which we normally seek to pass from certitude to certainty. *Othello* escapes being the record of the triumph of evil, not because Iago's plotting is unmasked and the true facts come to light, but because through the deaths of Othello and Desdemona we learn the reality of their love. It would be possible to write a cynical epilogue to the play in which we learn that Desdemona had, unknown to Iago, committed adultery with Cassio. Such a development would not be inherently incredible, but it would make nonsense of Shakespeare's *Othello*, because Shakespeare has constructed it around the certainty of the love between his hero and heroine. This certainty is known, like all certainty, through certitude. But the certitude is more than psychological certitude, it is the certitude of personal encounter—dialogue—trust—love. All these names indicate the transcendence of the subjective-objective categories which Protestant theology knows as faith.

II. LOVE AS THE KEY TO FAITH AND DOUBT

When love is a personal relationship in 'dialogue', its reality can be known only to those experiencing the relationship. This knowledge of reality does not consist, however, in the infallible witness of the self to a condition of its own internal state, but in the belief that the reality exists. Because this knowledge appears as a personal belief, and nothing external to it can establish its objectivity, it is a certitude which cannot be proved to be a certainty. Yet, stated as a certitude, it is not information about a psychological state, and so is not a psychological certitude. Love, of course, has its psychological aspect, where it appears as a subjective state dependent upon emotional drives which themselves represent biological or other functions of the psyche. But unless we are committed to interpreting human life in sub-personal terms we shall not suppose the psychological element to be the ruling one. If the moral and spiritual values expressed in personal existence are real, then love is the expression of their reality; love is a certainty, objectively existing, which can be known only as a certitude. It is, in Kierkegaard's terminology, subjectivity held in passionate inwardness.

Although love cannot be proved, it finds external evidence which witnesses to the reality it believes in. Conjugal love, for instance, is witnessed to by fidelity in sex relations, and it is supported by an emotional attachment which forms the basis of family solidarity. Yet conjugal love is not necessarily disproved by infidelity, and it does not depend upon the emotional vagaries of those who share it.

Because the certitude upon which it is built is not a psychological certitude, love does violence to itself when it ceases to regard external signs as pointers to its own reality and begins to imagine these to be proofs, or when the psychological element usurps the leading place. This violence of love to its own nature is what Shakespeare shows us in *Othello*, where sexual jealousy has for the time the government of Othello's love, so that he is driven by his trust in false evidence to the 'unnatural' deed 'that kills for loving'. Trust in the certainty of the uncertain (i.e. objectively unproved) is the essence of love and gives to love its 'essential' certitude.

The certitude of love which cannot be proved has been expressed by Martin Buber in terms of dialogue between the 'I' and the 'Thou': 'When *Thou* is spoken, the speaker has no *thing*; he has indeed nothing. But he takes his stand in relation'.[3] The absence of objectivity, the having of a *thing*, means that certitude and certainty within the dimension of relation become one. Buber makes clear that the relation of dialogue has a human and a divine aspect. The 'I' stands over against the 'Thou' when the 'Thou' is another with whom I have to do 'essentially', that is, in such a way that he is no longer a phenomenon of my 'I' as well as when the 'Thou' is God.[4] Human love which must be accepted in faith is thus the key to faith in God, or more accurately, faith created by God's grace makes it possible for us to experience the reality of human love. Buber points out the double form of the Great Commandment given by Jesus, that of loving God and our neighbour (Mark 12_{29-31}): 'By connecting the two Jesus brings to light the Old Testament truth that God and man are not rivals.'[5] Similarly, neither are faith and love rivals; there is no love without faith, and no faith without love. In the realm of personal relationships, where certainty is not expected, we learn to trust the certainty of love by discovering that faith is just the trust which love demands.

Catholic theology, because of intellectualizing faith into belief that is objectively certain, has had to insist that faith needs to be completed by adding love. Protestant theology has been founded on the insight that faith includes love; but traditionally it has developed the concept of love very inadequately. Instead of gladly appropriating for love the attributes of faith and showing the two words to be different aspects of the same reality it has been over preoccupied with its

[3] *I and Thou* (translated by Ronald Gregor Smith, 1937), p. 4.
[4] *Between Man and Man* (1947), pp. 50-1.
[5] ibid., p. 51.

efforts to prove mistaken the Catholic conception of love as a meritorious act going beyond faith. For Luther the Scholastic doctrine of
charity as 'the form and perfection of faith' is one which 'utterly
overthroweth the doctrine of faith, and carrieth a man away from
Christ the Mediator', so that he can 'rest in moral doing'.[6] Luther
himself had a much more profound conception of love than mere
'moral doing', since for him the life which opens to the Christian believer is the new life of the Spirit which makes him free of all and
servant to all through love.[7] The contrast between the Law and the
Gospel in Luther's thought is one which, by its repudiation of legalism, opens the way for a profound understanding of that dimension
of love which the New Testament calls *agapē* and which is love interpreted in terms of grace. This is the thesis which Anders Nygren
expounds with great thoroughness in his impressive work, *Agape and
Eros*.[8] But Nygren, like Luther, is so concerned to show that *agapē* is
not 'moral doing' that the way in which *agapē* is to be related to moral
goodness and human affection is very insufficiently developed.

Reinhold Niebuhr has criticized Nygren's 'idea of an absolute
contradiction between *Agape* and *Eros*' as 'the error of a too rigorous
separation of the realm of grace and realm of nature'.[9] Since the
whole weight of Luther's theology is directed against the existence of
any mutually exclusive realms of nature and grace, the objection
seems unfortunately expressed,[10] but it is founded on an undeniable
historical fact: namely, that Lutheranism has signally failed to show
a prophetic realism in regard to social (as distinct from personal)
righteousness. Believing the Law to be preparatory to the Gospel,
Lutheran theology, in its opposition to mere moralism and legalistic
formulations of goodness, has failed to see the need for a dialectical
interplay between grace and law, and so between love and justice.
Niebuhr points out, very justly, that the redeemed man who, according to Luther is *justus et peccator simul*, does not live continually and
perfectly by the 'pull' of grace and needs also the 'push' of duty.[11]

[6] *A Commentary on Galatians*, p. 158.
[7] 'The Freedom of a Christian' in *Reformation Writings of Martin Luther*, I
(translated by Bertram Lee Woolf, 1952), p. 357.
[8] First issued in two parts, Part I (1932), Part II (1938). Revised one-vol. edn.
translated by Philip S. Watson (1953).
[9] 'Love and Law in Protestantism and Catholicism', Chapter 10 in *Christian
Realism and Political Problems* (1953), p. 163. In *Love, Power, and Justice* (1954)
Paul Tillich argues that love must be taken as one, and that *agapē* and *erōs* are only
two among various qualifications of love, not distinct types of love (pp. 5, 27–8).
[10] The criticism is so Catholic in its phrasing it is not surprising to learn that it
follows criticism of Nygren contained in M. C. D'Arcy's *The Mind and Heart of
Love: A Study in Eros and Agape* (1945).
[11] *Christian Realism and Political Problems*, p. 152.

Further, Niebuhr notes two different outcomes of the Lutheran conception of the life of love. The first is a restriction of the ideal of love to the personal dimension in the family and friendship, advocated today by Brunner;[12] and the second is a refusal to admit that the Christian call to love our neighbour has anything to do with our intimate personal relationships, such as we find in Kierkegaard.[13]

This latter defect in Kierkegaard's outlook provided the context of Buber's remark, quoted above, that 'God and man are not rivals'. Kierkegaard contended that the category of the Single One (The 'I' in relation to the 'Thou') had to do *essentially* only with God, and in this Buber found an inconsistency: dialogue admits the inclusiveness of love to man as well as the exclusiveness of love to God.[14] If the Protestant doctrine of love is to be more than a protest against legalism, it must see in human love a reflection of the Divine *agapē*, corrupted by sin and not to be understood unless seen in the light of believing response to the grace of God, yet nevertheless a creation of God and not simply an idolatry which refuses to give God the glory. Nygren's case is at its weakest when he maintains that Scripture itself, in the Johannine books, has been adulterated by a false *erōs* philosophy.[15] Is it not rather that *agapē* illuminates and transforms love in its other—and to unredeemed man its most familiar—manifestations?

Though Luther's doctrine of love is incomplete, it is full of creative power (witness his unsatisfactory but infinitely suggestive conception of the Wrath of God, and of destructive and retributive forces as the 'strange works of love'); by contrast Calvin's seems lacking in depth. Having explained that love is the perfection of Christian life, Calvin mostly takes the mention of the word *love* as an occasion to explain why the Scholastics have mistaken its relation to faith.[16] Niebuhr says that Luther's insight into the life lived by grace is absent in Calvin's thinking, since the latter's ethic is one of obedience to the divine law.[17] Yet, although Calvin's teaching has a

---

[12] *Christian Realism and Political Problems*, pp. 158, 167. This view is perhaps not fully appreciative of Brunner's contention that Luther's personalistic ethic leads to every sphere of existence and is corrupted when it is restricted to individualistic and pietistic morality—one of the leading themes of Brunner's *The Divine Imperative*.

[13] ibid., p. 158.

[14] *Between Man and Man*, pp. 51-2.

[15] *Agape and Eros*, pp. 150 ff.

[16] *Institutes*, Bk. III, Chap. XVIII, 8; Bk. II, Chap. VIII, 54; Bk. III, Chap. II, 41. Erich Fromm's statement that Calvin's repudiation of the priority of love to faith, as the Scholastics expounded it, was 'in blatant contradiction to the New Testament' (*Escape from Freedom*, p. 88) is both inaccurate and misleading. It is more in the nature of a 'smear' than a serious comment.

[17] op. cit., p. 151. For a defence of Calvin against the charge of legalism, see Brunner, *The Divine Imperative* (1937), p. 100.

legalistic dress, it is saved from a total surrender to legalism by the conviction which Calvin shares with Luther that faith is an inner response to grace. The Lawgiver to whom Calvin appeals is known by His mercy, and the Scriptural commands which he holds so uncompromisingly before our eyes are not made the whole of the lesson he would teach us. His continual reference to the gift of the Spirit by which we may be assured of the promises of Scripture is one of the outstanding features of Calvin's theology.

In spite of the inadequate way in which orthodox Protestantism has regarded love in its human aspects as an illustration of faith, the relation of love, where certainty is not expected and where 'essential' certitude replaces psychological certitude, is undoubtedly the presupposition of the Protestant understanding of faith. And the question of doubt can only be understood against this background of faith conceived in the dimension of loving dialogue. The certitude of faith then becomes the region where doubt has least place, psychological certitude is seen to be the meeting-place where faith and doubt mingle, and objective certainty takes on the appearance of a pseudo-reality which is the proper object of doubt.

III. IDEOLOGY AS CERTAINTY

Nothing less than certainty absolutely excludes doubt, and since human beings in their search for certainty never experience anything but certitude, doubt is a universal experience, both for individuals and social groups. We have already seen how doubt is banished 'by agreement'. When we adopt some standard of certainty we do so by an appeal to authority, and in this way achieve a practical victory over doubt. Such a practical victory is also a partial defeat, for its completeness is limited to the extent alone that the chosen authority succeeds in maintaining itself. Authority may be external (society, its institutions and its leaders), or be internal (religious and metaphysical belief) but no authority has ever been completely successful in persuading 'all of the people all of the time' to abandon doubt.

In a society largely governed by tradition, doubt is not a prominent feature, because custom is an adequate authority for public and private affairs alike, and inherited certitude meets all the questions that its members are accustomed to ask. Yet the fact that even the most stable societies are subject to social change shows that doubt cannot be suppressed altogether. The rational curiosity which seeks to challenge external authority by making internal personal judgements is an important factor in social change. Personal judgements bring about change by giving currency to new values. Traditional values embodied in accepted institutions are criticized in the light of newly perceived values, and soon the old institutions are re-moulded or replaced in order to accommodate the values which have begun to rouse men's enthusiasm. With new values come new developments of authority.

Today we are familiar with the term 'ideology'. We owe the term to the Marxists, and because of its currency as a piece of political jargon it is loosely used to stand for any system of ideas; but the Marxists' own conception of the meaning of ideology has much interest and clearly shows that the connexion between ideology and the desire to overcome doubt is very strong. Marxism teaches that history is shaped by economic development which determines class-structure. Class interests, however, are disguised by the formation of systems of rationalization, or ideologies, which disguise economic realities as philosophies, religions and the like. Of course, Marxists take the Marxist analysis of history to be the truth, and not just another ideology. But we note that it is 'indoctrinization'—i.e. the conscious suppression of doubt concerning Marxist ideology— which has actually been instrumental in bringing about, or in keeping in being, the acceptance of Marxist economic and political policies: because when the ideology is accepted doubt vanishes and certainty is guaranteed by authority. An ideology is, in effect, a set of values accepted as certain by a party intent on establishing these values as an internal authority and on making the party itself into an external authority.

Religion cannot accurately be called an ideology, and yet every religion has a strong ideological content, for religion everywhere appears as an activity which seeks to conquer doubt and to support authority, external as well as internal. This is true whether the religion takes the form of an ecstatic cult, such as the orgiastic mystery cult of Dionysus, or a sober ethical code, such as Confucianism. The *Bacchae* of Euripides shows the fate meted out to the non-conforming individualist by believers who find their faith scorned; and Confucius, who had little to say about the gods and lived by the guidance of reasonableness, would omit neither the customary sacrifices nor even the traditional linen cap which was the prescribed wear for ceremonial occasions. Yet to identify religion with social conservatism or the prescription of individual thought is to miss out half the picture. For religion is also the source of the most violent social upheavals and the inspiration of the lone prophet challenging the entire society he belongs to and denouncing its values.

Religion is most ideological when it insists most on establishing certainty through the internal authority of doctrine and the external authority of religious leadership. The heretic who presumes to doubt the official creeds and the schismatic who breaks away from the official church are the most culpable offenders in the view of ideological religion. Modern totalitarianisms show themselves to be ideological religions most clearly in their heresy-hunting and their persecution of the non-conformist. Catholicism tends to have a large ideological content, because it both identifies certainty with orthodoxy and estimates the well-being of religion with the prosperity of the Church as an organized institution. Protestantism has, internally, a lesser temptation to make religion ideological, because its theology is not conceived in terms of certainty and that certainty put under the control of a party claiming absolute authority. Yet Protestantism is not less free from ideological taint, because its very freedom from ecclesiastical authoritarianism makes it externally susceptible to pressure from other ideologies, which may infiltrate into its religious life and cause the certitudes of faith to be interpreted in terms of the certainties declared by these ideologies. This process can be seen in the way some Protestant Churches which were also National Churches became subservient to nationalism, and equally in the excessive rationalism of some developments of liberal Protestantism during the last century. Protestantism has not always remembered to be confessional before all, but has on occasion trimmed the Gospel to suit current beliefs about the Divine Right of Kings, national destiny, evolutionary progress, *laissez-faire* economics, or some other dogma that temporarily extinguished doubt among its followers.[18] Nor has Protestantism always been faithful to its confessional principle even in its attitude to theology but has attempted to copy Catholicism in establishing doctrinal and institutional certainty. Trusting either in the Bible as an infallible book, or in some Church

---

[18] J. V. Langmead Casserley (*Morals and Man in the Social Sciences*, pp. 176–7) draws attention to the value of 'orthodoxy', by virtue of its growth out of a long tradition, in preventing thought being engulfed by the ideologies of the moment. Undoubtedly, a long-standing tradition is a bulwark against the tide of ideological fashions which an intellect unfortified by tradition finds it hard to resist. Casserley underestimates, however, the ideological tendency in every system of thought (and hence in every tradition of 'orthodoxy') which considers that it has found certainty. Casserley considers that, on the whole, only men in groups demand ideologies, while individuals can pursue 'pure truth'. But the drive to make the party line a substitute for truth, which is the motive for ideological thinking, is present in individuals as well as in groups. I would dissent from Casserley's admirable analysis of ideology only in believing he has not sufficiently considered ideology's demand for certainty. *Ideology always claims to be an orthodoxy; and the claim to represent orthodoxy is very often ideological.*

order and statement of faith as final, it has preached an ideological message of certainty to be found by joining that party which alone possesses the wholeness of Protestant truth. What we call today *ideology* is very plainly what in Biblical and Reformation language is called *idolatry*: human constructions are mistaken for the living God.

IV. FAITH *versus* RADICAL DOUBT

Religion is not wholly ideological because it can never be entirely subordinated to authority vested in one party. Every orthodoxy breeds heresy within its bosom. The heretic is the enemy of orthodoxy, but that is not the same thing as being the enemy of religion as such, for the issue here is one of 'true' religion against 'false' and what authority shall decide which is true is precisely the debated question. The schismatic withdraws from the orthodoxy party—but it is for the purpose of founding a new orthodoxy. This process keeps doubt alive and saves it from being extinguished by a certainty which would destroy it in the name of authority.

Doubt is an implicate of faith[19] just as it is the negation of certainty, for the certitude of faith admits the constant possibility that certitude and certainty do not coincide. There is, however, a limit to doubt. If the certitude of faith is considered impossible, doubt dies with faith. Religion implies the acceptance for oneself of values which are believed to be universally binding. A radical doubt which would refuse every claim of religion cannot properly be called *doubt*, since the word implies a context of faith to which the disbelief of doubt is subordinated. Radical doubt in its fullest sense is virtually impossible. That is why religion, though it may be used for ideological purposes or become organized to function as an ideology, is essential for all men at all times. The logical conclusion of a thorough-going atheism is, as Dostoevsky argued in the *Brothers Karamazov*, suicide. In consequence, irreligion is usually mixed with a good dose of unconscious religion. Modern atheistic existentialism as popularized by Sartre, for instance, contains strong overtones of Christian theology.[20]

Paul Tillich has analysed the essence of religion in terms of belief in relation to its opposite, despair. He defines despair as the human

---

[19] I take the phrase from Geddes MacGregor's valuable study *Christian Doubt* (1951). Although I cannot follow many of his conclusions (see pp. 100–4, 129–31 *infra.*), I am much indebted to MacGregor's book.

[20] Casserley (*Morals and Man*, pp. 219–20) points out that Sartre's category of the uniqueness of human persons is founded on the doctrine of Redemption. Sartre's emphasis on choice, giving freedom from guilt, points the same way.

dimension of fear—fear being a psychological phenomenon and despair an ontological category. The despair which can find no value in existence can only be countered by the courage of religious faith, which affirms the reality of value in the universe in face of life's apparent meaninglessness.[21] *Despair* here is what I have called *radical doubt*. When doubt does not serve its purpose of driving belief to validate itself but becomes autonomous, then nothing is left but to despair of life itself. Bertrand Russell's well-known words about 'building on the foundation of unyielding despair' serve to show how impossible it is to banish religion from our thinking, for if any positive meaning is implied in despair being called *unyielding* some religious affirmation is made. The Stoic choosing suicide shows despair indeed concerning the worth of historical existence, yet his despairing act is a gesture of unyielding faith in the rightness of human volition, and vindicates the rationality of the universe; while the 'meaningless' choice of the Sartrean existentialist, who glories in the irrationality of the universe, unyieldingly proclaims that the freedom of the individual *creates* meaning in meaninglessness. Scepticism can be completely unyielding, and at the same time completely atheistic, only if it admits that despair is quite as futile as every other human attitude.

In the *Book of Job*, Satan who requests the opportunity to test Job's faith is among the sons of God (Job 1_6). Doubt cannot destroy faith, unless it turns into despair, or radical doubt. We are well aware of what it is to revise our beliefs, for certitude is not certainty and, until faith becomes sight, doubt will be always present. Whenever certitude is disturbed, however, there is a possibility that we shall relapse into radical doubt instead of going forward to a more enlightened certitude. If we find that our certitude has been only psychological we may be inclined to look for psychological comfort. Avoiding the healthful questioning of doubt, we may hope to restore our shaken complacency by accepting the authority which promises certainty. By refusing to give a place to doubt for fear of falling into meaninglessness, we make our beliefs into ideologies which protect us from doubt—at the cost of idolatry. While we hold to certitude we believe we are right and those who differ from us wrong, but since we hold our beliefs in doubt we are ready to subject our own convictions and those of others to God's truth. When we hold our beliefs to be certainties on assured authority, then others are made fools or knaves by the very fact of their differing from us. Fanaticism

[21] *The Courage to Be* (1952). See especially Chapters 2 and 3.

is born of making ourselves into gods and removing our ideas from the possibility of criticism. Oliver Cromwell's 'I beseech you, in the bowels of Christ, think it possible that you may be mistaken', is one of the great affirmations of history.

Though doubt can never be silenced, there are certitudes which no doubt can remove. We are driven back by criticism of our beliefs upon beliefs which we cannot dismiss as psychological. Reality confronts us directly and personally, and we can only respond to it. Halting between two opinions when the issue of an ultimate allegiance is at stake is, as Elijah reminded his people at Carmel, the great apostasy (1 Kings 18$_{21}$). At such times Luther's, 'Here stand I, I can do no other' is the inevitable form of the response. Even though the confession of faith is made with the clearest understanding of a reality apart from the self and with a concern for that reality to the forgetfulness of self, the 'I' must have a place in the confession. The nature of faith demands that the 'Thou' be met in relation to the 'I'. So it was that Kierkegaard formulated his theology in terms of the individual, subjectivity, and inwardness:

Faith is precisely the contradiction between the infinite passion of the individual's inwardness and the objective uncertainty. If I am capable of grasping God objectively, I do not believe, but precisely because I cannot do this I must believe. If I wish to preserve myself in faith I must constantly be intent upon holding fast the objective uncertainty, so as to remain out upon the deep over seventy thousand fathoms of water, still preserving my faith.[22]

Faith can never forget that its sole avenue to truth is certitude—no plain path, as Kierkegaard reminds us, but a venturing out into the deep. When we reason syllogistically nothing is added by putting before the conclusion, 'I think', even though the certainty of our reasoning depends upon the truth of the system of logic we are using and we have no objective assurance that our reasoning corresponds to truth. But in the witness of faith the 'I believe' is an integral part of the witness.

In spite of its revolt against 'objectivity', Protestant theology has traditionally held that those who believe may know for certain that they are saved. Catholics find this claim presumptuous and, in face of the denial that there can be any prior knowledge of God's existence, almost blasphemous. Now no theology, unless hopelessly egocentric, would ever place the creature before the Creator so crudely as

[22] *Concluding Unscientific Postscript*, p. 182.

to say that man's destiny comes before God's being.[23] No such thing is, of course, implied in the Protestant doctrine of the assurance of salvation, which is a witness to the unity of faith and grace. The priority it denies is the priority of what man knows about God over what God reveals to man.[24] We do not first learn through our own powers that there is a God, and afterwards find out from a reliable source that He is gracious. God has willed that we should find Him in His saving work. It is the unfathomable love of God reaching out to save us through the Cross of Christ that reveals the Creator of the universe. We do not know God as He is unless we know Him by His forgiveness in His redemptive work.

So while the Catholic can only hope for salvation, unless indeed he has received a special revelation, the Protestant finds the only certainty possible here, in the certitude of faith made possible by the Word of God. All revelation is, in this sense, special revelation, since it is revelation to men as *individuals*. This is neither pride nor individualism. It is not pride for, as we have seen, faith is not faith unless it is received as the free gift of grace apart from any merit in the one who receives. It is not individualism, for though faith is an 'I' confronted by a 'Thou' the personal relation does not exclude community, but in fact makes it possible. The command to love our neighbour is 'second' to the command to the individual to love God above all, and yet the Great Commandment is a single commandment. We can love our neighbour all the time only as we learn to love God all the time. Although grace is received individually, it is not received apart from the Church, and in the community of faith the individual 'I' is most fully itself without being independent of others.[25] The individual certitude in this relation is founded in the only objectivity faith knows: the trustworthiness of God's Word. Doubt in this relation would be despair, the radical doubt which

[23] This order of man's destiny establishing God's being is, however, exactly what the 'theology' of atheistical Existentialism declares. Theistic philosophies of an Evolutionary God, such as Whitehead's *Religion in the Making*, seek rather to show that man and God together share a common destiny in the progressive realization of being, and even here man's progress depends upon God 'going before' and making progress possible (see pp. 168-9 *infra*).

[24] 'But, they say, it is rash and presumptuous to pretend to an undoubted knowledge of the divine will. I would grant this, did we hold that we were able to subject the incomprehensible counsel of God to our feeble intellect. But when we simply say with Paul, "We have received not the spirit of the world, but the Spirit which is of God; that we might know the things that are freely given to us of God" (1 Cor. 2₁₂), what can they oppose to this, without offering insult to the Spirit of God'— Calvin, *Institutes*, Bk. III, Chapter II. 39.

[25] See also the further discussion of the relation of the *person* and the *individual* (Chapter VI, Section 5, *infra*).

denies that God can speak to us and that what He reveals to us can be certain and not merely subjective illusion.

The lives of the great religious figures give ample illustration of the conflict between faith and despair. Augustine did not find the Word of God for himself until he responded to the '*Tolle, lege*' which spoke to him as an individual. Luther has recorded the many temptations that came to him over the validity of his faith. He regarded them as direct assaults of Satan, the one whom the New Testament calls the father of lies (John 8_{44}). Protestantism holds that the greatest lies are not to be found in the realm of conceptual thought, but are those which oppose the operation of faith in the soul. The fool who says that there is no God is he who snares his own soul and destroys it (Prov. 18_7). The doubt that probes our certitude, asking whether our beliefs may not prevent us from receiving God's Word, is a doubt appealing to faith. But the doubt which asks for more than the assurance of faith that God has spoken to us is a doubt appealing to the wisdom of the world which knows not God (1 Cor. 1_{21}).

Jesus spoke of the unforgivable sin being the sin against the Holy Spirit (Mark 3_{29}); we must remain for ever unforgiven if we will not accept the free forgiveness of grace, denying the Spirit by refusing to recognize His activity within us. Protestant theology recognizes this by the central place of Redemption in its thinking. Justification makes the possibility of forgiveness depend (from the human side) upon the acceptance of forgiveness as the ultimate fact of faith, while (from the side of God) God who forgives also gives the faith, making acceptance possible. All may be doubted except the goodness of God as revealed in Christ. Where this is believed, a thousand doubts may remain; but despair is overcome, even though Satan depart only for a season and must be continually confronted.

V. DOUBT AS THE ABSENCE OF RATIONAL CERTAINTY

While Protestant theology finds that which is most *certain* to be the Word of God which comes down like seed to the ground and is received there (Mark 4_{20}), Catholic theology, being built upward from a foundation of rational certainty, takes rational demonstration as the type of knowledge to which theology aspires. In the sphere of revelation, reason by itself is indeed considered to be inadequate, but, because of the authoritative doctrines derived from revelation by the Church, theological knowledge is set forth in propositional form and, for the believer, is as objectively certain as are the proven truths of natural theology. Doubt has, ultimately, no place in Catholic theology.

The radical doubt that is despair is banished once and for all when the authority of the Church has been accepted. This 'objectivity' is very attractive, especially to those whose psychological certitude has been undermined and who have experienced the fear of falling into meaninglessness. Catholicism encourages the same whole-hearted devotion as is found among the devotees of ideological systems, appearing as unquestioning submission on the part of the unthinking and as confident exposition of orthodox teaching on the part of the intellectuals. For example, the Marxist who declares, 'History is on our side', believes equally that logic and nature are entirely amenable to explanation in terms of dialectical materialism, while the whole duty of the ordinary Communist is to see that he does not deviate, however unwittingly, from the party line.

The doubt that probes has, on the other hand, an important function to perform for Catholicism, although remaining itself outside. It witnesses to true doctrine by falling before it. It must exist in order that the latter may stand in all the glory of certainty. Thus, in the expository method of Aquinas, the objections to a proposition precede the positive statement. (It is noteworthy that Aquinas has been pictured with his foot on the neck of Averroes, whose teaching he opposed.) Then doubt, having made its entry and proved to be false, can be forgotten. When doubt appears incarnate in the heretic, and questions the certainty of the articles of belief by maintaining other beliefs, it is silenced whenever possible. Doubt is required simply to provide an object-lesson in the evils of doubt.

There is, however, a form of doubt which has a real place in Catholic theology, though it hardly deserves to be called *doubt* since it is rather *nescience*. Revelation, by decisively transcending the findings of reason, although remaining capable of being stated in an authorative form not contrary to reason, leaves an area which Catholic theology finds closed to it. The certainties of faith retain all the authority which belongs to speculative truth, but what can be said about them falls short of rational certainty, because reason cannot explain them. Thus, in the gap between man's understanding of the world by reason and his acceptance of the supernatural propositions of theology, 'doubt' is given scope. Before the mystery of divine things human reason acknowledges its inadequacy; it believes where it cannot follow, and, being unable to explain, 'doubts', i.e. does not know what to think.

One of the main themes of Geddes MacGregor's *Christian Doubt*
is that Christianity is a religion which reveals to us the depth of
mystery in all things: 'It is the revelation to us of God and it is the
revelation to us of mystery.'[26] He quotes in this connexion a statement by Gerard Manley Hopkins made in a letter to Robert Bridges:

You do not mean by a mystery what a Catholic does. You mean an interesting uncertainty. . . . But a Catholic means by mystery an incomprehensible certainty . . . the clearer the formulation the greater the interest. . . .
There are three persons, each God and each the same, the one, the only
God: to some people this is a 'dogma', a word they almost chew, that is an
equation in theology, the dull algebra of schoolmen; to others it is news of
their dearest friend or friends, leaving them all their lives balancing
whether they have three heavenly friends or one—not that they have any
doubt on the subject, but that their knowledge leaves their minds swing-
ing; poised, but on the quiver. And this might be the ecstasy of interest,
one would think.[27]

Such a confession seems to indicate an æsthetic appreciation of a
theological system rather than the wonder which says, 'I will lay
mine hand upon my mouth. . . . I will proceed no further' (Job 40_{4-5}).
The point of view which operates otherwise within certainties which
do not admit of doubt, and sees in one limited area alone an intellectual puzzle without a key, leaves behind *doubt* and concerns itself with
interest. (The uninstructed visitor who visits a laboratory or a factory
where he sees processes going on which he can follow only in a general
way is apt to murmur, 'All very interesting'; and will, as Hopkins
indicates, find that the more he actually understands clearly, the
greater his interest will really be.) It is no disparagement of Catholic
faith to suggest that its conceptual setting tells against an effective
sense of wonder. Quite clearly, doubt is incompatible with certainty,
and when a formulation of doctrine is taken to be indubitable, wonder is inevitably restricted.

Wonder, the recognition of finitude and humility before that
which passes our comprehension are essential to the growth of all
faith. Protestants and Catholics agree that the ways of God are past
the understanding of men. What Protestants query is whether the
range of uncertainty is so narrow that it embraces nothing more than
the lack of rational certainty. Catholic theology tends to mean by
'mystery' a dogmatic proposition which has no rational solution. In
its biblical sense *mystery* has a much wider significance. It stands
chiefly for some divine secret which cannot be fathomed except by
revelation, but which lies open to the believer's understanding

[26] p. 136.   [27] p. 141, n. 1.

(Mark 4_{11}, Rom. 11_{25}, I Cor. 15_{51}), and in particular it refers to the Gospel of the Incarnation (Eph. 6_{19}, Col. 1_{26}). The whole of God's dealing with men, and not just certain aspects of this, is to be received in humility without any assurance that our thought will be able to compass it.

Yet, while Protestantism can justly tax Catholic theology with an inadequate view of the mystery at the heart of faith, Catholic practice is in many ways more faithful to the New Testament sense of wonder and gratitude in the face of God's gracious acts than the Protestant tradition has been.[28] Catholic exaltation of the contemplative life has led to a richness of devotional experience which Protestantism can match far too seldom. Modern Protestantism has frequently been misled by an unduly pragmatic spirit which has led to a loss of humility, and in reaction against a Catholic sacramentalism seemingly sub-Christian and unethical, it has become over-intellectualized and over-moralizing. In reaction, Protestant piety has tended to assume the form of pietism and rely upon emotion separated from the discipline of theological thinking. We have already touched on this failure of Protestantism to remain true to its fundamental principles, and we shall have to return to other evidence of the same weakness again.[29] Yet, in spite of the need to face up to its shortcomings, Protestantism can still claim that its protest presents the interplay of faith and doubt more adequately than Catholic theology permits.

The mysteries of the faith in the Catholic tradition provide the basis for a mystical theology the subject-matter of which lies quite apart from the experience of the ordinary believer.[30] Protestantism has consistently refused to admit that there is any by-road on the path of faith requiring any special direction for those who would travel there over and above the revelation available to all. Mystery does not belong to one particular stratum of God's dealings with mankind, but characterizes the whole of His revelation of Himself. The grace freely given to the believer in faith does not remove the necessity for doubt as part of the spiritual equipment of every pilgrim to the Heavenly City, and there is no special exemption for an aristocracy which can leave faith behind and mount by mystical knowledge above the doubts and uncertainties of the pilgrim way.

---

[28] Although Geddes MacGregor says he has no sectarian axe to grind, his examples of denominational vainglory seem to be always drawn from Protestantism. Yet, if he appears to have 'imperfect sympathy' with the Protestant view-point, he certainly has no lack of material for his strictures.

[29] See Chapter 3, Section 2, *supra*; and Chapter 10, Section 4, *infra*.

[30] See Section 8, *infra*.

VI. DOUBT AS DISBELIEF

The dictionary meaning of *doubt* includes the elements of hesitation and uncertainty, and these may be said to be present in the purely intellectual inability to grasp 'mystery'. Geddes MacGregor also uses the word *doubt* in another sense still, however, where the 'doubter' does not waver in the slightest; he only 'doubts' what others believe.[31] In this further sense, which is secondary to intellectual nescience, 'doubt' stands for the state of positive disbelief set up by the assumption of certainty. If we believe that a fungus is poisonous, we will most assuredly 'doubt' the wisdom of cooking it for supper. The Bible also speaks of a doubt in which disbelief takes precedence over uncertainty, as when the disciples met the Risen Lord, and some *doubted* (Matt. 28$_{17}$). But here the element of hesitation is still present. In general, it is those of 'little faith' who doubt, and not the scoffers (Matt. 14$_{31}$). The *unbelief* giving rise to doubt has little to do with the positive assertion of an opposite belief, for it is essentially a negative condition which fails to attain to the conviction of a living faith; it stands back in fear instead of taking the plunge of confidence and trust.[32]

Doubt as disbelief is really doubt as the absence of rational certainty seen from another angle. The viewpoint is now the subjective one of the believer instead of the objective one of the situation. The objective view finds doubt existing whenever reason cannot furnish a complete explanation. The subjective view finds doubt existing whenever the believer cannot produce evidence to prove his case. For the first, the subject-matter of belief is doubtful; for the second, the ground of belief is doubtful—not being able to show that your own belief is *indubitable*, you beg leave all the same to doubt that any other belief is as likely.

Geddes MacGregor quotes the Athanasian Creed as an example (admittedly an extreme one) of how faith implies doubt and thus exhibits a moderate and humble spirit. When the Creed anathematizes those who deny that the Persons of the Trinity are equal and eternal it is doubting that a subordinationist view of the Trinity is adequate.[33] This is surely to strain intolerably the plain sense of the Creed. It is true that, as a matter of history, the great dogmatic state-

---

[31] op. cit., p. 7.
[32] The New Testament words for doubt, διακρίνομαι and διστάζω, imply a divided judgement, whilst the slightly different ἀπορέομαι and διαπορέω suggest resourcelessness.
[33] op. cit., p. 91.

ments of Christendom have been formulated mostly to prevent inadequate statements of belief being accepted. The creeds were often created rather to protest *against* what appeared to be error than to protest the faith in a final form. But, once made, the creeds say what they say and nothing less. And when they are held to be fully authoritative they allow of no doubt. If they define what is orthodoxy and what is heresy, and if we accept their definitions, we are bound to believe what they affirm and to disbelieve what they repudiate.

Protestants would emphasize another feature of the creeds which points in the direction of doubt, though in a different way. Doctrine is nearly always made up of paradoxes. The definition of the two natures of Christ given at Chalcedon is a supreme example of the method of paradox to express the data of revelation, but all explanations of Creation, Providence, and Redemption are paradoxical in the same way.[34] The Gospel as revealed has always been a stumbling-block to legalism and foolishness to rationalism (1 Cor. 1$_{23}$). Yet, though the *form* of dogmatic statements is a clue to their proper use (i.e. to elicit faith by reminding us that our certitude can never be rational certainty), if we accept that form as a final statement of what we must believe, faith and doubt alike give way to a certainty accepted on authority: we believe the statements themselves to be truths beyond, but not against, reason and the sting of their paradoxical nature is removed leaving simply an intellectual puzzle. If, however, we hold that doctrinal statements point to truths beyond themselves rather than representing intellectually valid objects of belief in themselves, a place for active doubt remains. We *do not know* that the most 'orthodox' doctrinal statement represents a fully adequate statement of revealed truth.

One place where Catholicism seems to hold a place for doubt more conspicuously than Protestantism is in its view of salvation. While maintaining that no one can presume to be saved apart from partaking of grace mediated by the Church, Catholicism teaches that God alone knows who is saved. This looks like genuine doubt, but it reveals itself as a special case of absence of rational certainty. For Catholicism does claim to know when men can be saved outside the Church in general, although not in particular cases. Man can be saved by the light of natural virtue alone, if he follows the light as he sees it and lives according to the law of reason. Even if he refuses the

---

[34] In D. M. Baillie's *God was in Christ* (1948), Chapter 5, the place of paradox in doctrine is well presented. The way of paradox is, of course, central in Barth's 'dialectical theology', as in Kierkegaard's teaching which influenced it so strongly. Both Barth and Kierkegaard look back to the paradoxical theology of Luther.

fellowship of the Church and submission to its teaching, he will not be condemned so long as his fault is one of 'invincible' ignorance. So if this is to be regarded as an example of Catholic doubt, it must be the doubt of disbelief: Catholics disbelieve in a man's attitude to Christ's revelation of God being the essential element in salvation, because they believe in the effect of his good works counting for righteousness in the sight of God. Protestants, on the other hand must protest that the Gospel requires faith from all; in this they are 'dogmatic'. Yet, since they believe that God saves whom He will, they cannot dogmatize about who will be saved. Even Calvin does not attempt to do so.

Catholics and Protestants who cannot agree upon a doctrinal basis for coming together in the interests of Christian unity might agree, Geddes MacGregor thinks, on the basis of their common doubts. He suggests that Rome would consent to join in such an approach.[35] Any way of meeting for a frank exchange of views would be much to be desired, but it is likely that the same difficulties would make themselves felt on this road also. For Catholic theology insists upon the strict limitation of doubt within dogmatic assumptions which do not seem justifiable by Protestant standards. Agreement on what both traditions do *not* believe (e.g. materialism) would mean little, unless both parties could advance to positive principles underlying the rejection. Christians and Marxists, likewise, agree in rejecting numberless beliefs, ranging from voodooism to Hegelian idealism, but reject them for very different reasons. An impasse would quickly be reached when Catholics insisted on including as an integral part of the faith what Protestants considered they must be free to doubt. In fact, there would be more dissension in all probability over doubt than over belief.[36]

VII. RELIGIOUS EXPERIENCE

We have called the attitude of mind which realizes that certain facts are in principle verifiable but which is content to take them on trust 'psychological certitude'. This is the way most of us believe that the earth is round or that the plays of Shakespeare were not written by Bacon. Flat-earthists or Baconians may have studied the evidence

[35] op. cit., Chapter 12: 'Doubt as a Basis for Christian Reconciliation.'
[36] C. S. Lewis sent the script of his *Broadcast Talks* (1942) on the Christian faith to four clergymen: an Anglican, a Roman Catholic, a Presbyterian, and a Methodist. None found fault, Mr Lewis said, except that the Methodist wanted more said about faith and, 'The Roman Catholic thought I went too far about the comparative unimportance of *theories* of the "Atonement" ' (Preface, p. 5). Thus the one positive disagreement was over the place of doubt in faith!

more closely than we have ourselves, but we are inclined to judge that their certitude comes more from some psychological unbalance than from the weight of the evidence. Yet we do not trouble ourselves unduly about the possible psychological cause of *our* subjective beliefs in these fields—we simply accept one set of authorities and reject the other as we think reasonable. It is this acceptance of authority which characterizes the person who rests content in a state of psychological certitude.

Apart from an infallible authority, or going on from certitude to certainty by way of rational proof, psychological certainty is a precarious basis for belief, and in particular for belief about religion. We have seen that neither Protestant nor Catholic rests content with psychological certitude. Catholicism allows that the truths of reason *may* be accepted in 'faith', as the truths of revelation *must be* accepted on authority, and so in fact leaves the believer in the state of relying, to a greater or lesser degree, upon this kind of certitude. Protestantism builds upon a certitude it claims is not psychological, but it cannot objectively prove that the certitude it proposes is of a different kind. Before we leave the subject of certainty and doubt, we must look at a third attempt at a solution which attempts to construct a basis for religion upon psychological certainty itself.

A partial answer along these lines was suggested by the celebrated 'wager' argument of Pascal.[37] We cannot be sure, says Pascal, that God exists and so that religion is true. But if it is true and God exists the consequences are so far-reaching that we cannot afford to risk being mistaken. We must 'bet' upon the uncertainty of faith. Bishop Butler, in his *Analogy* took a slightly different line, arguing from the widespread belief in a 'natural religion'. Christianity was as reasonable as the religion suggested by reason. Since we make probability and not certainty the rule of life in practical affairs, we ought not to boggle at a little uncertainty about religion. Pascal believed the issues at stake between belief and unbelief so urgent that the odds on his spiritual wager were irrelevant; the choice lay between the infinite and nothing. Butler considered the bet so safe that there was no need to trouble oneself over much about what was involved in accepting it; Christianity was not so very different, after all, from what every reasonable man must believe.

Psychological certitude is usually maintained by an implicit faith in authority, and doubt destroys it. Pascal and Butler tried to show how certitude can survive doubt. They said, in effect: There is no

[37] *Pensées*, 233.

objective authority to prove your certitude to be justifiable, but the need to choose some belief—or the universality of judgements based on probability—provide adequate enough substitutes for authority; believe on; you can count on a fair degree of certainty.[38] In contrast to these attempts to show that psychological certitude has a rational basis, a more recent effort has been made to show that psychological certitude is self-authenticating and provides its own internal authority. This approach (which had its genesis in the Romantic Movement, and was fully developed in William James's *Varieties of Religious Experience*) assumes that the dogmatic claims of the various faiths are unproven and unprovable. What cannot be doubted is that the religious convictions have objective consequences. Religion cannot therefore be wholly a subjective illusion: it is about *something*. The reality of religion is to be sought in the experience of religion. *That* experience is valid, even if its interpretation in terms of specific beliefs is not.

Unfortunately, the argument from experience claims both too much and not enough. It claims to have established the facts of religion as a certainty. A modern psychologist such as Jung is perfectly willing to follow James in admitting the phenomena of religion to be authentic matter for investigation, but he will then go on to show that religion itself is nothing but a symbolical mode of expressing the human *psyche*.[39] So religion's objective existence is established only by making its reality wholly subjective. All religions are equally true because none of them is true except as a means to provide symbols.

Protestantism cannot accept religious experience as a way to transcend psychological certitude, any more than it can accept infallible authority as a way to objectify certitude. Yet, more than anyone else, it was the Protestant Schleiermacher who opened the road for the Romantic 'religion of feeling' that was to bulk so large in such typical nineteenth-century thinkers as Carlyle and Emerson. Schleiermacher himself did not follow this road though he made it possible for others to do so.[40] Psychological certitude for the Protestant cannot be made into certainty by any device, because no cer-

---

[38] Of these two views, Pascal's is incomparably the more serious. At bottom, it rests not on probability but upon the existential situation of mankind and is a challenge calling for that 'protest' which none can avoid.

[39] *Psychology and Alchemy* (1953)—even more, perhaps, than his *Psychology and Religion* (1938)—gives a clear account of Jung's views of religion. Romantic poets, such as Blake and Holderlin, anticipated psychology here.

[40] H. R. Mackintosh (*Types of Modern Theology* (1937), Chapters 2 and 3) holds that Schleiermacher exploited an ambiguity of statement which allowed him to assert the objectivity of faith and yet led his readers to concentrate on the subjective content of the soul.

tainty is deemed absolute.[41] Religious experience cannot be allowed to possess greater authority than believing faith.

Yet, since Protestantism recognizes certitude to be the necessary form of human knowledge, religious experience is by no means without value for it. Experience can be regarded as God's gift and a sign of His presence, so long as it is not made into a condition of it, so that the believer imagines he can know it by consulting his spiritual condition. Protestantism is often thought to be based on religious experience. Luther's doctrine of faith has been described as 'an indubitable subjective experience of one's own salvation'.[42] Yet Luther was particularly insistent that experience must not be made the ground of belief:

And this is the reason that our doctrine is most sure and certain, because it carrieth us out of ourselves, that we should not lean upon our own strength, our own feeling, our own person, and our own works: but upon God, and upon His precious promise and truth, which cannot deceive us.[43]

But once the source of our confidence is understood, then experience can be corrected until it becomes a reliable witness to the truth:

Let every man, then, so practise with himself, that his conscience may be fully assured that he is under grace, and that his person and his works do please God. . . . These things do plainly witness that the Holy Ghost is present with us and in us. . . . Also He giveth us a true judgement, whereby we prove and try those things which before we knew not, or else altogether despised.[44]

Luther's understanding of how the certainty of God's Word lends its authority to our certitude in faith is echoed in P. T. Forsyth's words:

Faith is a mode of our experience, but the Word we trust at its core is not: it is *to* our experience.[45]

The sole authority which can make certitude into certainty is God's Word, and that we do not possess certainly, but accept in faith.

VIII. MYSTICISM

A special form of religious experience is that reported by the mystics. By definition incommunicable, the witness of mysticism purports

[41] Catholic theology is prepared to admit that religious experience gives a kind of certainty in so far as it is an internalizing of the rational proofs of God's existence (see Mascal, *He Who Is*, p. 92, quoting D'Arcy). Religious experience is thus identified with rational certainty.

[42] Erich Fromm, *Escape from Freedom*, p. 77. Compare Maritain (*Three Reformers*, p. 36): 'Christianity [according to Luther] is nothing but a continual exercise in *feeling that you have no sin although you sin*' (italics in the text).

[43] *Commentary on Galatians*, pp. 248-9.

[44] ibid., p. 243.

[45] *The Principle of Authority* (1913, edition of 1952), p. 80.

to describe a unique approach of the Divine to the human, culminating in 'union' between the two—'One and one at one'. Mysticism furnishes the extreme example of psychological certitude claiming to represent absolute certainty. It does not do so lightly, but on the basis of a severe discipline of contemplation that falls into various distinct stages on an upward journeying into the ineffable. And mysticism does not make its claim on the subjective level of individual experience, but maintains that it achieves *experience as such*, the very stuff out of which reality is made.

Mysticism has a recognized place in Catholic theology, where its claim to be certain is granted on the ground that the mystic is given a special revelation by God. What Geddes MacGregor calls 'a very neatly walled garden'[46] shuts out of the Catholic tradition of mysticism a great deal of what goes by the name of mystical experience. But it is by no means universally agreed that the mystical experience as such is necessarily a specifically Christian experience. Miss Evelyn Underhill has written:

We cannot honestly say that there is any wide difference between the Brahman, Sufi, or Christian Mystic at their best.[47]

Protestantism has had its mystics—Boehme, in Germany, Thomas Traherne and William Law, in England. Naturally, Protestantism has no 'walled garden' to delimit and guarantee the mystical theology its place within Protestant theology. Mysticism has been vehemently attacked by some Protestant theologians, including Ritschl and Barth. On the other hand, some Protestant thinkers, such as Dean Inge and Rufus Jones, have found a valued place for mystical experience within the Protestant protest.

The reason for Protestant suspicion of mysticism is plain. The mystical experience is direct and, in the last resort, finds no place for the revelation of the Incarnation and the Cross. It was on account of the mystic's tendency to by-pass revelation that Wesley parted company with William Law, whose friendship he had esteemed highly.[48] What it is imperative for Protestant theology to protest *against*, however, is not mysticism itself, but the status given to mysticism by Catholic theology. While holding that Catholic (though not non-Catholic) mystics preserve the centrality of Christ in a knowledge by faith and not by sight, E. L. Mascall can still write:

---

[46] *Aesthetic Experience in Religion* (1947), p. 128.
[47] *Essentials of Mysticism*, p. 4, quoted H. R. Mackintosh, op. cit., p. 145.
[48] See *John Wesley and William Law* (1945) by J. Brazier Green.

And as revelation surpasses reason, so does the experimental knowledge of God that is granted to the mystics surpass revelation.[49]

It is this confident setting up of mysticism as demonstrably superior to revelation that cannot but be contrary to loyalty to the confessional faith. As Nygren, following a metaphor used by Luther, has said, the ἀναγωγή ('inner ascent') of mysticism in Catholicism is made into one of the 'Heavenly Ladders' which, with the way of Merit in practical piety and the Way of Speculative Thought in rational theology, is used so that man may mount up to God in his own right and in virtual independence of the Way of the Cross.[50]

It may be, as Paul Tillich believes, that mysticism is a necessary companion to the faith, reminding us that, while faith must be understood in personal terms, God is more than personal and transcends all our categories.[51] Perhaps the attitude of Paul in treasuring mystical experience but refusing to allow this to modify his proclamation of the Gospel as from the experience of a sinner who has known God's forgiving grace in Jesus Christ (2 Cor. 12$_5$, 1 Cor. 2$_2$) is our best guide in this connexion. At any rate, Protestantism can find no certainty to proclaim *about* the mystical experience, whether the experience itself be indubitable or not to those who experience it. Doubt has its work to do here also.

[49] op. cit., pp. 82, 149.
[50] *Agape and Eros*, p. 633.
[51] *The Courage to Be*, pp. 177-8; *Systematic Theology*, I, 140.

CHAPTER SIX

THE FREEDOM TO BE WRONG

I. DOUBT, LAW, AND TOLERATION

THE BASIS for toleration lies in doubt. What is certain does not allow of difference in interpretation, and so there is no scope for recognizing the right of another point of view to exist. But, when doubt enters, diversity of opinion must be reckoned with, and the situation where toleration can be exercised comes into being.

Doubt by itself, however, does not create toleration. If we find ourselves in doubt, we usually try to find the 'right' course of action which will end our doubts. A scientist faced with two alternative hypotheses will not be inclined to tolerate both, but will by experiment determine the one which covers the facts most fully, and then reject the other.[1] Or, to take a more commonplace example, a motorist coming to a fork in the road chooses one way, and if he is wrong must come back to where he started and take the other way. Toleration only comes into the picture when human relationships are involved. The scientist may suspend judgement for a time between the rival hypotheses; this 'toleration' will be an internal affair between himself and his scientific integrity. But if the motorist has a friend with him who wants him to take the other way in the road, he will have a chance to exhibit toleration in a more exact sense.

Yet even the existence of personal relationships does not give the full setting for the exercise of toleration. In the above instance, the motorist would not be very pleased if his friend said that, while doubting his being right about the road to take, he would tolerate his opinion. He would object, very rightly, to the other adopting an air of moral superiority. For we *tolerate* always in the context of moral conviction. The sole justification of intolerance is the fact of moral conscience. Whenever men interfere with the freedom of someone else to do as he pleases, they do so by saying that they have a *right* to do so.

[1] An apparent exception to this rule serves to illustrate it very graphically. When Sir Arthur Eddington wrote of contemporary physicists, 'Sir William Bragg was not overstating the case when he said that we use the classical theory on Mondays, Wednesdays, and Fridays, and the quantum theory on Tuesdays, Thursdays, and Saturdays', he also stated that there was something radically wrong with theoretical physics, which would have to 'look forward to an ultimate reconstruction'. *The Nature of the Physical World* (1935 edn., pp. 192–3).

Now when we feel we are 'right' doubt vanishes. And when we feel justified in overriding other people's opinions it is because we claim to have a *moral right* to do so; we are 'morally certain'.

Moral certainty is, of course, not certainty at all, but certitude. That is why, between friends, any suggestion of *tolerating* one another's beliefs or behaviour is felt to be *intolerable*. It means that one party is claiming to have access to moral truth in a way the other has not, so setting himself up on a subjective pedestal. The other party, in turn, cannot prove his friend's claim to be incorrect, and can only oppose his own claim to have access to moral truth, and judge his friend to be in the wrong by this standard. Since friendship presupposes equality in social relations (an ethical quality), the appeal to moral truth to judge whether friendship has been broken is, in principle, correct. If his friend says, 'Your pretence to moral superiority is intolerable', the offending party may admit the truth of the charge. Yet, because friendship is primarily a relation of dialogue where an 'I' meets a 'Thou', any appeal to an external standard is a sign of a weakness in the relationship, just as referring the decision in a dispute to a third party would be. All the same, while the moral standard is recognized as being external only to the relationship of dialogue, but still internal because held in certitude, friendship can still remain unbroken. Tom can, without offence, say to Dick, 'I believe you have acted wrongly, but you must judge for yourself whether I am mistaken in thinking this'. Only when he says or suggests, 'You are wrong, and, if you cannot see you are wrong, I must just overlook your blindness', is friendship in serious danger of failing. For, in this case, Tom's certitude looks to an authority totally outside the relation of friendship.

The whole issue just discussed may be summed up by observing that friendship is made by love and not by law. Law is the inevitable form in which we come to know morality. We can know what is 'right' in the sphere of human conduct and ideas concerning conduct only by assuming the existence of *moral law*. 'Sin is not imputed when there is no law', said Paul (Rom. 5_{13}), and the law's very existence is bound up with the function of bringing home to men the wickedness of lawbreaking. The law of the land is the epitome of intolerance when it applies the sanctions vested in it, although it may be most restrained in the employment of its powers, and most lenient in its application of them to those who fall under its condemnation. And the laws of society under which we live are, in the last resort, nothing but the reflection of the moral law.

Jurisprudence has not always recognized the necessary foundation of human laws in the moral law. Jurists who emphasize the 'positive' function of the law point out that laws are obeyed, not because they are just according to some absolute notion of justice, but because they are laws. Certainly legal systems are made possible by being workable systems, actually enforced. Might rather than right ensures obedience to law, and particular laws may be extremely immoral. But laws do not create themselves. They are made by men who may be selfish, stupid, and power-loving, but who are also capable of understanding moral values and of cherishing moral ideals. As R. B. Perry has observed:

The ulterior moral purpose of the law is revealed at the point where law is created: when a decision is made as to what law shall be created, or why one law should be created rather than another, or, fundamentally, why there should be any law at all. . . . Law is traditionally associated with moral ideas such as justice, rights, and equity.[2]

It is by virtue of its function in mediating moral values to a community that law is intolerant and not merely self-assertive. St Augustine's famous saying, 'Set justice aside then, and what are kingdoms but fair thievish purchases?'[3] recognizes that the power of the State to enforce the law is founded on moral values or else is completely arbitrary. We do not speak of law being *intolerant*, however, because intolerance is law's positive function: it is organized intolerance. We speak of *intolerant people* because human relationships are never, even in the service of law, purely concerned with imputing sin. Law deals with personal relationships on the social and moral plane. It deals with persons and not just with actions, although its primary concern is with actions which prove that certain individuals have infringed the law. But law also has to take into account intentions as well as actual deeds, and decides on issues of personal responsibility; judges judge men, not wrong acts, though they judge men by what they have done. Human beings, on the other hand (who are always more than moral beings), are not limited to a legal relationship with other human beings. We therefore think it to be a defect in them if their moral perception is limited to legalistic attitudes. We do not expect others as fallible as ourselves to set their moral standards up as moral certainties; though we recognize that jural law, if it is to be effective in society at large, must claim to be final. At the same time, we do not admit laws of any country or time to be absolutely final.

[2] *Realms of Value*, p. 234.
[3] *City of God*, Bk. IV, Chapter 4.

Any relative law is judged by men's beliefs about the absolute moral law—hence agitation for the repeal or amendment of 'unjust laws'.

The difference between the necessary intolerance of law and the unwelcome intolerance of our fellows is seen very clearly when we contrast the abstract ideal of Law with the human lawgiver. A title said to be given to William Temple while he was headmaster of Repton School, 'A beast, but a just beast', represents the schoolboy's view of an unwelcome authority which is felt as less oppressive in so far as it is impersonal, but even then is described in personal terms. Justice may be discovered and honoured in the person of the administrator of justice, but those who suffer the penalties of the law —however justly—experience the 'beastliness' of it. Similarly, the administrator himself, if he is at all sensitive to his position, is conscious of the contrast between the servant of justice who convicts others of sin in the name of society and the fallible human being who is himself a sinner against absolute justice. The Lord Chancellor in *Iolanthe* who introduces himself proudly, saying,

> *The Law is the true embodiment*
> *Of everything that's excellent,*
> *It has no kind of fault or flaw,*
> *And I, my lords, embody the Law—*

quickly reveals himself to be 'a highly susceptible Chancellor' whose human lapses from perfection lead to some quite irregular goings-on. In a very different mood, the same contrast provides the setting for R. L. Stevenson's unfinished novel, *Weir of Hermiston*, which begins with the clash between an old judge and his son. The son is revolted by his father's callous behaviour in court and denounces the inhumanity of it. Old Hermiston sees only his son's defiance of lawful order, while Young Hermiston sees only his father's horrifying personal delight in the power his office brings him.

Human agents mediate human laws to their fellows. Human agents also seek to make laws effective and to grasp the meaning of moral law in its ideality. Yet human beings cannot even be trusted to act single-mindedly in regard to those moral principles that come within the range of their perception. Toleration therefore has its beginnings in doubt of a special kind: a doubt which centres round moral truths and the fallible human understanding of them. Such doubt is a suspension of the ethical. As we come to recognize the existence of consciences that differ from ours, so we come to apply doubt to our own consciences; we find that they are not universally binding, but binding upon us only as they represent the present range of our certitude. What is absolutely authoritative for us (and so uniquely valuable) may appear irrational and absurd, or immoral and a nuisance, to our neighbour. Yet this does not mean that conscience is treated as merely relative. The suspension of the ethical in toleration is for the sake of better ethics. The moral law is not ignored when we find we do not know it certainly but possess only our certitudes about it.

II. MORAL LAW AND SOCIETY

That toleration is fundamentally a moral question is not obvious, because it seems to be first of all a social one. Sociologists can examine the attitudes of different societies, or of different groups within the same society, towards those who do not share accepted ideologies and note the connexion between these attitudes and social structure, education, language, and similar sociological facts. Crass forms of intolerance seem to show a type of behaviour almost biologically motivated, like that of animals who turn against a sickly member of the herd when it fails to behave like the rest. Commonly in primitive societies deviations from social norms are not permitted, and individual rights depend upon participation in all the activities, beliefs, and practices of the community. The authority of custom and community is indeed very tenacious, so that even when the *barbarian* and the *gentile* cannot be kept outside the pale in practice they are still ignored in theory. When one community learns through the pressure of necessity to live beside another and co-operate with it, then toleration is, in fact, effective, even if both do not abandon exclusive claims and attitudes. At first sight, then, it would look as though intolerance were simply a social phenomenon, and toleration a stage of social development forced upon society by external conditions of social change.

Even at a primitive level, however, intolerance is linked to some stirring of the sense of moral law. It is the group *mores* which is offended by unconventional acts and beliefs. In sophisticated societies a lack of 'breeding', 'good form', or compliance with 'the done thing' is often regarded as a more serious fault than actual moral deficiencies—showing the persisting force of social aspects of behaviour. Yet here too social convention is far from indifferent to moral considerations. With the growth of self-consciousness in moral matters comes moral criticism of the traditional patterns of behaviour. The moralist who condemns as immoral what has hitherto been accepted as part of the common code of behaviour nevertheless owes his developed conscience to the moral conscience of the society which nurtured him. Human action is always moral (or immoral) action, since no one can free himself from the conception of the 'ought', sensing the necessity for universally binding moral law, however inadequately he may grasp it.[4]

To the extent that any one is conscious of the absolute claims of the moral law, and conceives it to be embodied in a 'good' that commands his assent, he is bound to be intolerant of those who do not give their assent also. This intolerance will of course be strengthened by the 'good' being, more likely than not, something approved by his social group and the non-conformists being usually *foreign devils* and *infidels*. Yet the *we* contrasted with the *they* may well be recognized to be a result of affinity in conceptual thinking as much as the product of the natural ties of community. Ideological strife divides families, and civil wars are notoriously the most bitter. The intolerant moralist is the more intolerant when obedience to the moral law is codified in terms of propositions to be assented to. Heresy-hunting is the prime activity of intolerance, for it recognizes that belief is the inspiration of action, and tries to quell revolt against authority by invading the conscience.

On account of the tendency of intolerance to push back its inquisition from behaviour to belief, it may seem that toleration is not concerned with the moral law but with religious and metaphysical beliefs. This is true to the extent that whether men are intolerant or tolerant depends upon an *attitude* springing directly from their total view of the universe. Toleration, we have seen, is impossible without doubt, and doubt is admitted or excluded by ultimate convictions. Yet tolerance, being essentially an ethical matter, does not ever lose its social reference. The attitude of tolerance, or its opposite, is always the result of beliefs applied to interpret the working of the moral law. Inquiring into a man's beliefs may be sufficient by itself to show that he is a heretic at enmity with 'true' belief. Nothing but the

[4] R. B. Perry thinks it advisable to separate *morality* and the *theory of morals* (the science which deals with what things are good and right) from *conscience* and *ethics* (the scientific description of men's approbations and disapprobations). He recognizes that to limit *conscience* to *custom* is not usual, but feels that its social reference is primary (op. cit., pp. 135, 160).

The separation takes account of a real difference. The moral law is never the same as the attempt to embody it under historical conditions. But it may be doubted whether the separation is a workable one. In particular, *conscience* can hardly be ignored by any *theory of morals*, since it represents individual insight into the moral law as well as a social attitude reflected by the individual (see p. 116 *infra*).

application of belief to the moral field, however, will produce the conclusion that the heretic is an enemy to the community of believers who must on that account be restrained, or eliminated. Our understanding of the moral law as it applies to social questions results in the formation of *conscience*.

Conscience is a hybrid, and that is one of the reasons why it causes us so much trouble, giving us 'pangs' and making us 'cowards'. It also explains why conscience has been so variously estimated, being thought, by Hobbes—who has a host of present-day followers here— to be private opinion largely detrimental to public good, and, by Bishop Butler, to be the power which alone has right to rule the world. Conscience is in part the sum-total of social attitudes, the approvals and disapprovals current at one place and one time. It is also the personal discovery of the absolute claims of the moral law and its relevance to a personal situation. Thus someone who has always accepted the 'rightness' of a specific act because the action has the approval of society may suddenly be faced with a prohibition from his conscience, telling him that the act is morally wrong. Here conscience has responded to the demand of moral law. There is nothing in the response, of course, which can prove conclusively that the response is correct, or that moral law actually forbids such an action. Social custom may well be wiser than individual conscience. From the other side, the attempt to objectify conscience by putting it under the rule of a theory of morals makes its own difficulties. A man may act in certain knowledge that his action is sanctioned by moral law interpreted in such a way as to set his intellect at rest over its 'rightness', and yet in the actual execution of the deed he may find his conscience in revolt against his intellect. Again, there is no final authority in conscience to decide whether the moral law was better served by theory or by individual intuition.

When we understand that conscience, the individual appropriation of the moral law, is inevitably involved in our application of the moral law to the context of social affairs, we are still left with the moral basis of toleration unaffected. But we are provided with some valuable help toward the solution of the problem of how toleration can be reconciled with the moral law, and the suspension of the ethical be justified.

III. MORAL SUBJECTIVITY

Toleration begins with the doubt that sees how men fail to mediate the moral law authoritatively to society. But the proposed 'suspension of the ethical' seems to deny the moral law's own authority; for there is no question here of an appeal to a higher source, as when, in his study of Abraham's sacrifice of Isaac in *Fear and Trembling*, Kierkegaard makes the 'teleological suspension of the ethical' transcend moral categories to discover religious values. Toleration of one's neighbour's conscience cannot be based on the brute fact of a divergence of opinion and the decision not to apply moral standards in our mutual relations. If there is such a thing as moral law, objectively we cannot both be in the right. Subjectively, it is strictly impossible for us to understand how anyone can differ from us in holding to be good what we believe not to be good, for even a strenuous effort of imaginative sympathy will scarcely give us true insight into another person's beliefs. When we try to explain other people's beliefs, what we usually achieve is a more or less plausible account of the psychological factors which we think led them to think as they do. It is the easiest thing in the world to unmask beliefs and prove them to be rationalizations. Unfortunately, the process does not help us to enter into an understanding of the beliefs or to test their validity.

Short of complete moral scepticism, toleration would thus seem impossible; and if that were so, then what goes under the name of toleration would be the sacrifice of moral truth to serve pragmatic interests. Some who defend intolerance have been accustomed to brand the ideal of toleration with the stigma of 'indifferentism'. But if we are forced to remain within the circle of our present beliefs in order to experience their full cogency, we know very well what it is to have changed our beliefs in the past. We are also familiar—or can make ourselves familiar—with the implications of both our beliefs and other people's. This brings home to us that subjectivity does not annul the moral law. Just as positive law must be interpreted by human beings, and involves human relationships which may frustrate its free course and inevitably modify its application to concrete situations, so the moral law is interpreted through conscience; and with conscience the personal element is essential instead of being incidental.

So the practical social demand to co-operate with those who disagree with us is supported by an understanding of the moral situation. While we pursue our moral ideals we do not wish to make it impossible for others to pursue theirs, because we recognize that we do not possess final insight into the moral law. Opinions may be incompatible, but it is men and not opinions that have to learn tolerance; and they learn it, without abandoning a passion for righteousness, by a restraint in self-righteousness. The process is not painless and may break down when conscience confronts conscience at a level where neither can admit itself mistaken, insisting that its ethical writ must run through society and no exception be allowed. The success of the tolerant attitude depends upon making sure that these head-on clashes of conscience do not occur unnecessarily. And again this is less a matter of practical machinery in the social scene (though it is that, too) than of an adequate moral insight into the foundation of toleration.

Healthy doubt about the objectivity of conscience provides the negative condition for toleration. The positive condition is a willingness to take as one of the supreme moral principles the need to respect the conscience of our neighbour. In the name of this principle we can agree to the suspension of the ethical, i.e. of the *ethos* of a particular tradition of moral judgements we have made our own. The tensions of particular beliefs are set within the framework of this larger belief, and can then be fruitfully employed to bring about a greater understanding of moral truths. It is sometimes objected that toleration in society does not mean very much, because few men are really able to enter sympathetically into another person's point of view. That true moral sensitivity based on personal insight is a rare spiritual gift can readily be granted. But it makes the social recognition of tolerance all the more valuable, because here custom and positive law hold in check our personal dogmatism and encourage an atmosphere where moral sensitivity thrives. Without this tutoring from the law, the grace of inward tolerance would be much rarer than it is.

Subjectivity with regard to the moral law has obvious similarity to the Protestant protest of subjectivity as truth in regard to the Gospel. Indeed it is a corollary of it. If it is asked where the moral law, so confidently appealed to in the demand for toleration, fits into the scheme of the sufficiency of faith, the answer is not far to seek. Law is a datum of revelation and the necessary presupposition of grace. We can no more know law than we can know grace without experiencing it. But we do indubitably experience the 'ought' whenever we experience practical activity in society. This was Kant's fundamental insight when he based his whole system of ethics upon the laws of the practical reason. What we do not know is whether our understanding of the moral law, as elaborated theoretically in our ethical systems and grasped concretely in conscience, is an adequate statement of the moral law. Kant believed that he could deduce the *form* of the moral law decisively through the practical reason, though the *content* was not so given. Perhaps he was over-optimistic, even in making this claim of a limited certainty. But he also saw that in the act of admitting the practical reason to be authoritative he had presupposed belief in certain unprovable realities which he called God, freedom, and immortality. There can be no moral law without belief in absolute values beyond the limits of the things which our reason can establish objectively. On the basis of belief in these transcendent values we can learn how to obey the moral law while respecting the consciences of those who differ from us.[5] The certitude of faith embraces doubt in the self-sufficiency of any individual conscience to grasp the moral law in its wholeness.

Put in the language of faith, the principle of toleration is a consequence of believing that our first duty is to love God. Loving our neighbour in God means seeking dialogue with him. We cannot achieve dialogue by asserting our own opinions over our neighbour's or even by accepting his for the sake of concord. We must learn from him in freedom and permit him freely to learn from us. It cannot be taken for granted that our first and essential basis for dialogue is in thinking alike, or in sharing similar emotions. Rather it is found in standing as children of God who are conscious of sin and of the power of grace, and who inhabit the same world of mystery and challenge, and live under the same providential order. Thus the law we recognize as binding for ourselves in society, and wish to see universally acknowledged, is suspended in our relationship with others until we reach the point where loyalty to God's Word forbids us to agree with our neighbour even at the expense of a breach in dialogue. But when we reach the limit of compromise and must say, 'Here stand I', we do not claim more than the certitude of faith for ourselves. Love to neighbour, as love to God, stands under no higher principle of authority by which it can be judged, and is known through subjectivity alone.

Common belief in the worth of dialogue is the very corner-stone of the toleration within a community, and implied in this belief is the recognition that individual or party moral theories and consciences are held in subjectivity. Ronald Knox, commenting on criticism of

---

[5] 'The free society . . . can be defended only by expressly recognizing the characteristic beliefs which are held in common by such a society and professing that these beliefs are true. The principal belief—or I should rather say the main truth—underlying a free society, is that man is amenable to reason and susceptible to the claims of his conscience'—Michael Polanyi (*The Logic of Liberty*, p. 29). Polanyi adds: 'The ideal of a free society is in the first place to be a *good* society; a body of men who respect truth, desire justice and love their fellows' (pp. 29–30). *Good* here has an absolute and not merely a social reference.

Rome for demanding for itself in democratic countries a freedom which it is not willing to grant to others, says: 'The contention is ill-conceived. For, when we demand liberty in the modern State, we are appealing to its own principles, not to ours.'[6] It would seem that the answer to the objection is itself ill-conceived, because the principle involves acceptance of common belief. Where the belief in dialogue is not accepted, but used to secure tactical advantage in a struggle for power, both the principle of toleration and the freedom that comes with toleration are destroyed.[7] Dialogue could be defined, in moral terms, as the belief that demanding privileges under the argument 'your principle, not ours' is immoral.

The emergence of 'fifth-column' methods, used by Fascists and Communists alike, has presented a severe challenge to the societies who believe in toleration. The challenge is first of all in the threat of a seizure of power by the intolerant through the abuse of freedom which toleration makes possible. It is also a challenge to preserve trust in the face of the fear which follows the abuse of freedom and which sees in every non-conformist an enemy. The foundation of belief on which toleration is built can be undermined from within as fatally as it can be shattered from without. There is a healthy tendency, where the tradition of toleration is strong, not to refuse to extend its privileges even to those who will abuse it, unless the security of the community is very plainly in danger. The ground for taking this risk is that every opportunity for dialogue must be kept open; once closed in one direction, toleration may easily be suppressed altogether.

IV. THE GROWTH OF TOLERATION

The combination of doubt and belief held in the certitude of trust is so closely allied to the similar combination in the Protestant conception of faith that the intimate connexion between the two cannot be doubted. Nevertheless, the growth of toleration within the Protestant Churches was a gradual affair, and the conscious acceptance of toleration as an ideal was a complex development. The ultimate triumph of the ideal was due in part to those who took their stand outside the Churches altogether. Locke's *Epistola de Tolerantia*, the first full

---

[6] *The Belief of Catholics* (1940 ed.), p. 242.

[7] 'The free society would cease to exist if its members ever admitted that some major conflict will have to be settled by sheer force within the society. Such an admission would therefore be subversive of the free society and constitute an act of disloyalty to it'—Michael Polanyi, op. cit., p. 31. If belief in dialogue is rejected, the only method of settling conflict must be by *sheer force*, though this will probably go under the less alarming name of *authority*.

statement of the modern view, though the work of a Churchman and a Protestant, uses the categories of secularist thought rather than those of Protestant theology. Though it was in Protestant countries where toleration was first established, the lesson was not easily learnt in a Europe so long dominated by Catholic ways of thought. Only gradually did Protestants discover the full implications of Protestantism.

Luther, like Calvin, was temperamentally autocratic and found it easy to fit into the authoritarian pattern of his age, as his refusal to treat with Zwingli demonstrates. In a controversial situation he could answer dogmatism with dogmatism and accusation with accusation. In face of these facts, the anti-authoritarian elements in Luther are remarkable. Discovering the whole Gospel in the twin truths of *grace* and *faith*, he insisted that everything else could have only relative authority. And in so doing he opened the door to differences of opinion within theology itself. Religious freedom is the precondition of every other freedom. Luther's understanding of faith as something apart from intellectual formulations of belief provided the necessary conditions for toleration to grow into a conscious ideal. In spite of his bitter controversy with Rome, he could grant what his opponents would not: that saving faith might be possessed by those who denied it in name. The mark of the true Church, as opposed to the 'synagogue' which was a Church only in its own sight, was faithfulness to the Gospel. Luther was prepared to draw the line between those who were outside the Church and those who were within on the basis of confessional statements, but the possibility of deciding certainly by external signs where the truth of the Gospel lay had been overthrown. Melanchthon expanded on Luther's conviction when he said: 'The gift of interpretation is with the true Church, but not bound to certain persons or places; it is sometimes with the many, sometimes with the few, sometimes more, sometimes less lucid and pure.' [8]

Calvin's attempt to set up at Geneva a perfect 'school of Christ' and his inflexible determination to stamp out heresy has to be judged in the light of his separation of the visible Church, containing hypocrites, and the invisible Church, whose membership is known only to God. Calvin's autocratic methods of deciding where 'truth' and 'error' lay had plenty of critics even in his own age, an age nurtured in authoritarian theory and practice. Protestant theology from the first pointed away from old dogmatisms to a better understanding of faith held in objective uncertainty.

[8] Quoted by Franz Hildebrandt, *Melanchthon: Alien or Ally?* (1946), p. 91.

The reading of history which sees toleration as the emergence of a 'modern temper', born of the struggle of minorities (each fiercely intolerant but demanding freedom for themselves) and of the bankruptcy of a policy of uniformity on the part of State Christianity, leaves out of the picture as much as it includes. The ideal of an enforced external unity was long-lived among Protestant Churches, and a persecuted minority could turn into a persecuting majority, as in the case of the New England Puritans. But the coming of toleration was much more than a matter of expediency and a weariness with ecclesiastical disputes, important though these factors were. Toleration was first advocated among the sects as a direct consequence of their religious beliefs. Humanitarian and latitudinarian sentiments grew in the soil of religious beliefs. When, with the advent of the eighteenth century, morality was separated from its dependence upon theology, and a dislike for all brands of 'enthusiasm' supplanted sectarian zeal, the Churches appeared to be the last strongholds of bigotry. But Protestant faith still continued to provide the ferment that worked in society towards social freedom and justice.

The Protestant urge toward toleration is typified in the seventeenth century in Oliver Cromwell. That Cromwell is popularly known as a dictator (with the modern associations of the word fully operative) who destroyed the liberty of the people, is a measure of the way we fail to understand the complexities of the history of ideas. Cromwell's letters and speeches, though less well-known than the magnificent literary pamphleteering on behalf of freedom by the Latin Secretary to the Commonwealth, John Milton, are unique documents in the story of the birth of toleration.[9] Under Cromwell torture was outlawed as an instrument of law. A religious settlement was made which gave complete autonomy to no one Church and which, though very imperfect, was capable of further extension. Cromwell himself attempted to reconcile denominational animosities, being on good terms with the uncompromising George Fox, and intervening personally on behalf of the unfortunate James Naylor. A man of action and a man of piety, but no theorist, Cromwell hammered out his convictions upon his conscience, sure that God's will was revealed to those who trusted and waited for Him to reveal His will in history. The aftermath of a Civil War, with the execution of the King and the suppression of the National Church conceived (wisely or un-

[9] So too are the early discussions in political theory of the time. See *Puritanism and Liberty. Being the Army Debates (1647–9) from the Clarke Manuscripts:* Selected and edited by A. S. P. Woodhouse (1938).

wisely) as political necessities, was hardly a favourable time for the advancement of liberal ideas; but the bloodless Revolution of 1688 and the subsequent establishment of liberty of conscience and the coming of modern democracy would hardly have been possible without the Commonwealth period of experimentation in freedom. What some romantic historians call an 'unfortunate interval' made the renewal of religious intolerance at the Restoration itself intolerable, a reactionary step which prompted a decisive counter-action.

With John Locke we step into another world, less the stage of a divine drama to contemporary consciousness than the testing-ground for rational speculation. Locke's liberty of conscience was grounded in assuming the rights of the individual to pursue his separate way to happiness—though, for Locke, this way was considered to be a Christian and a social way. From now on, toleration was to be argued mainly as an obvious good *opposed to* specific party beliefs. What was good seemed self-evident at the bar of reason and 'natural religion'. Locke's pupil, the third Earl of Shaftesbury (who was one of the first to treat ethics apart from revealed religion) urged ridicule as the best weapon against enthusiastic intolerance.[10] The American Declaration of Independence declared the individual's right to life, liberty, and the pursuit of happpiness to be the unalienable gift of the Creator. Toleration emerged as an undeniable 'good', and it was supernaturally grounded faith which had to justify itself, by proving itself to be a benefactor of mankind instead of an enslaving 'superstition'.

That the secularist creed sprang from high moral principles is clear from such instances as the passionate defence of the Protestant Calas family by Voltaire and of the Jewish Dreyfus by Zola. But the belief in individual rights here swallows up all thought of how that belief can itself be proved valid and how humanitarian ethics is to be defended. Having become a dogma, its dogmatic foundation is ignored. In the present age, the rise of collectivist and irrationalist philosophies has subjected the toleration of the Enlightenment to merciless criticism, while scientific dismissal of subjectivity has left it defenceless.

V. TRUE AND FALSE INDIVIDUALISM

By the nineteenth century there were many brands of humanitarianism: religious, anti-religious, non-religious, and ethical-with-a-

[10] It is noteworthy that Shaftesbury had nothing but scorn for the Jews, whose particularistic understanding of God was at the opposite pole from Shaftesbury's deification of Universal Harmony.

religious-flavour—all concerned to advocate toleration, conceived as 'the liberty of the individual'. In different ways, most of these actually advocated a 'religion of humanity' which, without destroying the essential Protestant approach, weakened it. The secularist-individualistic movements could display themselves as the true crusade against obscurantism, fighting for justice on earth while any fully religious programme (so the argument would run) meant escape into a pietistic concern for the next world to the detriment of this one. However, Protestant theology's category of the *individual before God* had sufficient resemblance to the atomistic individual of Locke and his successors to serve the same purpose: providing a unit capable of possessing unalienable rights.

Protestant individualism has been the target of much Catholic criticism. Catholic apologists are quick to point out the very real evils of unbridled individualism and to lay them at Protestantism's door. But individualism pure and simple has never been part of the Protestant protest, and this development must be traced from the Renaissance through the Enlightenment to its apotheosis in Romanticism[11]—which also produced individualism's antithesis, collectivism. We can see the turning-point in Rousseau, where the Romantic cult of personality gives birth to the impersonal 'general will'. And Hegel's conception of the Idea working in history grows into Marx's historical necessity which ushers in the reign of that concrete universal, the proletariat.

The fact of individuality is something which appears important only when history is taken seriously, for history is where the unique and unrepeatable appears. This category of history is extraordinarily difficult for thought to grasp, since conceptual reasoning proceeds by universalizing the individual existent in order to recognize it. The whole of the Aristotelian philosophy, which defines by means of genus and specific difference and finds matter to be unknowable to the extent that it is unformed, bears witness to the inability of thought to grasp the historical. So does language, in which each name for the category of history—singularity, individuality, the One, and so on—indicates first of all a single member of a class, so that the category is as hard to explain as it is readily understood. Christianity cannot escape a prime concern with the historical category because this is the central lesson of Scripture, and it is widely recognized that the

[11] Paul Roubiczek's *The Misinterpretation of Man: Studies in European Thought of the Nineteenth Century* (1949) shows the decay of the ideal of the individual in the contrast between the lives of Goethe and Napoleon. These two figures respectively illustrate the ideals of Enlightenment and of Romanticism.

problem of individuality is the specifically Christian addition to philosophy.[12] Aquinas, says Maritain, distinguishes between the *individual* who is part of nature and subordinated to the earthly City and the *person* who is created for an eternal destiny. But the post-Reformation State, which gives universal suffrage, equal rights, and liberty of opinion to the *individual*, blunders; for 'the modern world confounds two things which ancient wisdom had distinguished. It confounds *individuality* and *personality*'.[13]

Protestant theology finds the Catholic separation of nature and grace as unsatisfactory in the effort to understand individuality as in the effort to understand faith. Since it knows nothing of nature apart from grace, so it knows nothing of the individual who is a mere unit apart from the personality who stands before God. Persons on earth are always individuals, and individuals persons. To separate the two is to de-personalize the individual and thereby to degrade him spiritually, while it is also to de-individualize the person and in consequence not to take his historical existence seriously enough. Kierkegaard's *individual*,[14] who meets God in subjectivity, is also one particular man, a member of the human species linked to one particular time and place. This is the basic assumption of Protestant 'individualism', an individalism which makes Luther able to subject himself to God's will, and at the same moment assert his own independent individuality, saying: 'Here stand I.'

If personal existence is constituted by being an 'I' instead of a unit, the 'I' is a unit too. Every 'I' which is capable of meeting a 'Thou' can be made into the 'it' which is simply known *about*. A

[12] See, for instance, Langmead Casserley's *The Christian in Philosophy*, pp. 31 ff. Casserley prefers the word 'singular' to the word 'particular' because he says it represents the individual seen from the point of view of the man who is out to capture and enjoy the full flavour of its individuality. But the singular is also a unit opposed to the plural! A proper name, which has a minimum of descriptive meaning (see above, Chapter 1, Section 1), is the only satisfactory word in which to catch the historical individual. 'There is only one George' says George's mother or wife—and she is right, although there are thousands of Georges. In much the same way, traditional logic tries to make a link with historical fact by using proper names—'Socrates is a man', 'Socrates is mortal', etc.—or group names—'a fox is an animal'—and without these remains purely formal. The God of the Bible is a proper name before His nature is apprehended conceptually.

[13] *Three Reformers*, pp. 19 ff.—Maritain's italics. The correctness of Maritain's interpretation of St Thomas, here, has been challenged by other Roman Catholic scholars. Yet, whether or not his exposition interprets his source accurately, it certainly reflects very well one aspect of the Catholic *ethos*. See p. 143, n. 12, *infra*.

[14] R. Gregor Smith, translator of Buber's *Between Man and Man*, thinks that the phrase 'the Single One' translates Kierkegaard's *hiin Enkelte* better than 'the Individual' does (p. 207, n. 9). But this also is ambiguous, suggesting a Robinson Crusoe accidentally parted from his fellows. Every expression is inadequate to capture the thought which eludes definition, though grasped through the experience of what it means to find truth in subjectivity.

proper name, which is the label to distinguish an individual from all the rest, could be for identification purposes just as well a number, as it is in the armed forces. But a name is also capable of drawing into itself the personal attributes of a 'Thou'—as every lover knows. In the Old Testament, God is known by His personal name (Gen. 4$_{26}$, Ex. 6$_3$), and His people regarded Him as one god among others before they learnt to think of Him as the one true God. God's only Son appeared among men as another man, Jesus of Nazareth, before He was confessed the Christ of God. God, in His dealings with men, is known as the personal 'Thou', but when He is thought about He is perhaps less misrepresented as an individual God among gods than as the non-personal One of Neo-Platonism or the Absolute of modern idealism. We do not know God except through His Word which was made flesh and dwelt among us (John 1$_{14}$), very God but also an individual, a man among men. It is from this Biblical knowledge of God coming through history (the realm of the individual) and apprehended by faith (the realm of the personal) that Protestantism finds it necessary to preserve the notion of individualism.

It was the Hebrew prophets—whom Dean Inge has called the Protestants of the Hebrew religion[15]—who first clearly asserted the principle of men having individual responsibility before God (Jer. 31$_{29-30}$, Ezk. 18$_{2-5}$). They did so when showing how God made moral demands upon His people's lives, where common belief thought ritual worship and blood-membership of the theocratic community sufficient. Later the same message was given by John the Baptist; the individual could not shelter behind a supernatural status as a son of Abraham to avoid his particular obligations (Matt. 3$_{9-10}$). In the teaching of Jesus, forgiving grace goes out to that individual object which is lost (Luke 19$_{10}$). What the divine Love seeks, though uniquely valued, is yet *one among others*—as is a sheep, a coin, or a son (Luke 15$_{4, 8, 11}$). The prophetic demand upon the individual and the Good News of deliverance for the individual were both preserved in Protestant confessional theology.

The bearing of Protestant concern that the individual and the person shall not be sharply distinguished upon the question of toleration is easy to see. Catholicism may proclaim the right of every *person* to follow his conscience, and yet deny to *individuals* within any community the right to propagate, or even to hold, 'error'. The fact that the individual has rights as a member of society will not help the individual if the Church by its superior authority tells the State that

[15] *Protestantism*, p. 5.

its duty is to stamp out heresy. Protestants learn that, without the possibility of the individual being able to choose for himself what he believes to be true and to exercise freedom to teach to others what he has learnt, truth cannot reach any man as a personal possession. One cannot compel men to enter the Kingdom of God in the way Augustine interpreted the 'compel them to come in' of the parable of the Wedding Feast (Luke 14$_{23}$), thus opening the way for persecution in the name of Catholic truth. Persons are not free where individuals are restricted, even though the inward freedom of grace is not the same as the outward freedom of the citizen. Individuals must have freedom to be wrong if they are ever to be persons finding God's truth through faith. Though the Word of God is not bound even if His followers are in chains (2 Tim. 2$_9$), we cannot think we do God service by silencing those whom we believe to be speaking against God, but who may be conveying the Word of God to us.

VI. THE USE AND ABUSE OF FREEDOM

The freedom to be wrong is the most precious of all freedoms, as well as the most costly. Protestantism desires all individuals to be free to believe what they will in the knowledge that this freedom is a dangerous thing. Far from thinking that belief is a matter that concerns only the individual, Protestants value freedom for the individual so that he may obey the Word of God to him. But it is impossible to grant freedom and still control the use that is to be made of it. The parable of the Prodigal Son tells how the younger son was able to journey into the far country because his father was prepared to give him the means to go where he wanted to (Luke 15$_{12}$). Protestant individualism desires men to be free *under* the Gospel, but the same individualism may be welcomed by those who only wish is to be free *from* the Gospel.

One consequence of Protestant individualism is Protestant lack of unity. There is, humanly speaking, no way of ensuring that the freedom which enables men to hear the Word of God will not degenerate into a self-sufficiency which arrogates to itself the sole right to pronounce what hearing the Gospel means. Yet Protestants consider this to be preferable to the collective self-sufficiency which is the alternative. Denominational pride and sectarian bitterness show that even this latter evil is not wholly avoided within Protestantism. False individualism quickly turns into its opposite. The most eccentric sects are usually the most bigoted, and those who set themselves up as champions of Protestantism often claim to 'have the truth' as their exclusive possession.

Yet in weakness is strength. The individual can repent of his self-centred individualism to become again a true individual before God. Protestants can discover in their corporate life within the Church their individual sins 'writ large' and correct them under the guidance of the Spirit. Catholics, though knowing that the Church is composed of fallible men, are not free to admit that the Church itself is fallible, and so find it hard to question any practice of the Church as a historical institution. When faced with any manifest evil brought about by Catholicism, they are led to defend it, if that course is possible, or to excuse and deny any responsibility for it, if it cannot be defended. Hence there is a great contrast in the way reformations are brought about in Protestantism and in Catholicism. When witch-trials were ended in Spain, the ecclesiastical authorities simply recommended their discontinuance. In America the congregation at Salem joined in an expression of contrition for evil done and a repudiation of the methods used. In Geneva, Calvinists raised a monument to Servetus, recognizing the wrong committed by their spiritual leader and re-affirming the Protestant belief in toleration. Rome has dropped the clauses from the Canon Law giving the right to persecute, yet still claims that within Catholic nations permission to allow 'error' any voice is a concession dependent upon the call of a 'greater good'.

The same principle can be seen at work in the Protestant attitude to Biblical scholarship as compared with the Catholic. The early hostility to the historical study of the Biblical records (which still survives in many 'conservative' Protestant denominations) is a thing of the past in all the major Protestant communions. Since the condemnation of the Catholic 'modernists', Roman scholars have not openly acknowledged any contact with the results of modern Biblical scholarship.

But perhaps the greatest sign of the fruitfulness of the principle of the freedom to be wrong, is the Ecumenical Movement. In this century the tendency of post-Reformation Christendom to divide and re-divide Churches along confessional and national lines is being reversed. A will to the healing of the sickness of divided Christendom is again being created, and created in freedom, with the knowledge of what has been gained as well as lost by 'our unhappy divisions'. Willingness of ecclesiastical parties to tolerate the existence of other bodies calling themselves *Christian*, when the former think the latter to have no right to that name, is the first step to ecumenicity.

But the worth of that toleration which is willing to say, grudgingly, 'I have to live beside you, so I shall let you explain your impossible views, although they contradict my deepest convictions', depends on taking the further step from conversation to joining in dialogue. We stand now at the point where this further step is being taken. The declaration of the World Council of Churches at Amsterdam that 'we intend to stay together' is evidence of that step, which Evanston has confirmed.

Dialogue can never be sustained on a level of compromise, and it is nourished by complete sincerity of protest, even when individual protests conflict. Thus, at the risk of being misunderstood, Protestants are bound to say, to those Catholics who are willing to listen, that ecumenicity can grow only upon a basis of Protestant freedom to hear the Word—though not necessarily, of course, upon any particular Protestant denominational beliefs as at present formulated. Those who belittle the worth of the ecumenical movement are, in fact, those who take a Catholic view of the nature of the Church, even if they call their exclusivistic attitude loyalty to the Protestant cause. For it is Catholicism which states that dogmatic agreement is the presupposition of unity. Geddes MacGregor, for instance, who insists upon the place for doubt in faith, does not seem to give any real place for the doubt which underlies toleration when the realm of propositional belief is reached. He acknowledges that there is an approach to 'genuine understanding and fellowship between two very profound believers of widely disparate traditions (say, an Anglo-Catholic and a Congregationalist, or a Quaker and a Roman Catholic)',[16] but he argues that Rome's negative attitude to conferences to unite Christendom is the only truly realistic and honest one, and that 'she has at any rate grasped incomparably better than most other Communions the nature of the situation'.[17] Saying that no committee for the control of atomic energy could possibly exist if it did not agree on what atomic energy was, MacGregor asks: 'How can one promote Christian unity if even the word "Christian" has no uniform meaning?'[18] From the Protestant point of view, this way of posing the question refutes itself. If we knew what *Christian* was, there would be no need for dialogue, but only for political machinery such as is required by a committee on atomic energy. Do we indeed have no need of doubt on the question of what a Christian Church is? Is the Holy Spirit's operation established by a science possessing the same kind of certainty as nuclear physics?

[16] *Christian Doubt*, p. 120.   [17] ibid., p. 111.   [18] ibid., p. 108.

When MacGregor says that the union of Christendom cannot be attained 'without a radical change in the whole structure of Christian thought',[19] perhaps he feels that there can be no doubt about what *Christian* here means. The Protestant answer must be, in all humility, that Protestant thought does not require any such radical change (though Protestant practice needs it desperately), but that Catholic thought cannot surmount the barriers of its own construction unless it faces the possibility of this change. Referring to those who would welcome union at the cost of 'further alienation' from Rome or some other large communion, MacGregor writes,

They speak as though patching together half or a quarter of a broken vessel would be a notable achievement even if it involved making the remaining larger pieces more difficult to put together than were even the original fragments. Nor is there any wide agreement about how the vessel is broken; whether indeed it is broken at all.[20]

There are some obscurities in this metaphor. When you are putting something together it *is* usually an achievement to get part of the job done. But the question is really whether the metaphor illuminates the situation; whether the 'pieces' of Christendom are all needed, whether they must be fitted together just as they are, and whether there is one—and only one—right order of their fitting. When one comes to ask if the prior question to settle is where the pieces belong or how they will react to being put in place, the whole thing becomes absurd. Surely the issue is precisely *what we mean by the broken vessel of Christendom*, and true realism is to face this issue together, instead of assuming that some 'they' we dislike entertains such fantastic notions that it is a waste of time to reason with them. The doubt which MacGregor puts forward as a basis for Christian reunion is undoubtedly a prime condition of progress in dialogue; only it must be doubt which questions the presuppositions of our dogmatisms, and not simply discussion about issues which the dogmas we assent to leave open, or the disbelief those dogmas give rise to. The freedom to be wrong can breed an indifference which takes little heed of the obligation to care for the truth above our own opinions; but without it, and without the dialogue made possible by respecting it as a means of mediating between parties making contradictory protests, the reconciling Word will not be heard at all.

Freedom can be and will be abused, so long as men deny their service to the Gospel where alone perfect freedom is to be found.

[19] *Christian Doubt*, p. 112.   [20] ibid., p. 104.

But the burden of freedom which, as in Dostoevsky's parable of the Grand Inquisitor, authoritarian religion would take away from mankind can only be removed, as the Grand Inquisitor himself declared, by putting away the Christ who offers the dangerous freedom that is His gift.

CHAPTER SEVEN

THE SACRED AND THE SECULAR

I. THE ETHICAL DEMAND FOR SECULARISM

ALTHOUGH THE divorce between morality and religion in the humanist tradition which triumphed in the Enlightenment was ultimately disastrous, yet on a historical view it represented a great gain for morality. Without it, toleration would have made little headway against entrenched dogmatisms claiming to possess the final word about all things in heaven and earth. By Catholic standards the good life was neatly parcelled out between the natural and the supernatural virtues, so that there was no real place either for difference of opinion about moral values or for the education of the conscience. We have seen how the Catholic view of nature and grace was effective in forbidding criticism of Catholic findings concerning reason and revelation alike; and this applied equally in the sphere of moral values. The use of casuistry to draw particular conclusions from general moral laws—in practice a moral scandal, Pascal asserted in his *Lettres Provinciales*—made the exercise of moral insight unnecessary. Protestant ethics was hardly more satisfactory. The Protestant left-wing that stressed the 'inner light' of the Spirit was prepared to admit the need for an enlightened conscience to interpret the mind of Christ. But more influential was Calvin's attempt to establish a rule for all life drawn mechanically from Biblical texts, encouraging a legalism as destructive of finer values as the legalistic system set up by Catholicism. In the English-speaking world Protestant morality was most typically exhibited in its Puritan form. At its best, Puritanism through its piety, high standards of personal integrity, and emphasis on family life exerted a kindly and civilizing influence which modern Western society (in large part created by it) has largely failed to appreciate. But, at its worst, it stood for all that is implied in the unpleasant word *puritanical*. In addition, both Catholicism and Protestantism, where under the protection of the State, became subservient to it and largely acquiesced in the prevailing social values. In 1827 a *New Translation of the Lord's Prayer* by Dr Thornton caused William Blake to write a parody of it which he called 'Dr Thornton's Tory Translation'. The parody begins, 'Our Father Augustus Cæsar' and ends, 'for God is only an Allegory of Kings & nothing Else. Amen'; it is only too accurate a comment on much of official Christianity before and after that date.

Thus it can be seen why there was a pressing need to rescue morality from a religious authoritarianism in order to allow individual moral insight to develop. Humanitarianism and sensitivity to social wrongs grew with the spirit of toleration. Zeal for the reformation of society took the place of zeal for the reformation of Church doctrine. Where the State-protected and State-established Churches had always recognized a place for charitable works directed toward the needy in society, a new moral sensitivity felt the obligation to extend these remedial activities on a vastly greater scale. The eighteenth century showed the effective birth of private philanthropy, and prepared the way for the radical social reforms of the nineteenth century. A revolution in political and social thinking was brought about by the secularizing of moral theory, and the ideas, once launched, were soon put into practice.

As we have already noticed, secular thought found it hard to find a theoretical justification for valuing of toleration. To provide a reason why, if all beliefs are equally doubtful, the belief in the sanctity of individual conscience should be specifically exempt from doubt, it was necessary to bring in some quasi-theological principle, such as *natural right*. That this natural right was not a fact of nature, and entirely depended upon the extent to which moral values were recognized to be important, was never more than dimly perceived in secular thought. The famous opening of Rousseau's *Du Contrat Social*, 'Man is born free and is everywhere in chains', is an example of the slurring of the difference between the *is* and the *ought*. Man *is* never free in this world (at least, never as free as he would like to be), but freedom may be realized in part if man is convinced that he *ought not* to wear some of the chains which irk him most sorely. What is seen first to be a rightful ideal may then be transformed into a demand to be granted one's 'rights'. But the *right* of the individual to freedom can be nothing more than an assurance that society at large accepts the second part of the Great Commandment, and that love to our neighbour grounded in love to God is held to be the key to all other ethical precepts.

Secularist thought in the seventeenth and eighteenth centuries drew much of its inspiration from Classical philosophy, particularly from Stoicism with its conception of the basis of morality in universal law,[1] although there were also links which joined the new secular rationalism with medieval rationalism, which had been influenced by the same Stoic sources.[2] Almost alone among the ethical theories of its day, Kantian ethics showed some awareness of the religious dimension of moral truths. Kant's moral law, though stated to be autonomous, is always given as an imperative. It is a command directed to the conscience, not an idea perceived by the mind. Kant's various formulations of the moral law attempt to show that morality combines rational universality, recognition of the unique value of individuals, and the subordination of individual wills to a 'kingdom of ends' transcending their separate existences. Such a combination is clearly impossible to deduce from the bare idea of obligation, and looks toward the dialectical interplay of incompatibles found in the paradoxes of theology. When Kant makes the free will to consist essentially in the complete determination of the will by the moral law, he is simply putting into general terms the moral implications of the Christian belief that we are free from sin only when Christ lives in us. Kant's moral theory is based on the claims of faith over man, instead of on man's rational constitution, although rationalistic elements were very prominent in his thought and he had no wish to subject reason to revelation. Indeed, one of his battles was to uphold the supremacy of intellectual coherence over the empirical standards which more and more were gaining over the rationalistic ones.

Failing to push their conclusions as far as Kant did, most thinkers of the Enlightenment were content to consider ethical judgements doubtful and yet all-important. Ethical judgements were doubtful, because (once rationalism gave way to empiricism) they had no other authority except man's admittedly imperfect conscience. They were all-important because the ethical sphere was the real stage on which life's drama was played. Man in society was a moral being, and so ethics were a public concern. Religion, by contrast, was a private affair. It concerned individuals, or groups of individuals, instead of society itself. Locke defined a Church as a private association, although he was unwilling to believe that atheism could be tolerated. So secularist thought was chiefly directed toward the consequences

[1] The moral theory of Bishop Butler, for instance, is almost entirely Stoic. Butler bases the authority of conscience on the nature of man as man, and brings in Christianity solely to confirm his psychological analysis of human nature.

[2] Richard Hooker is an important figure in this continuity with the medieval world. Hooker looks back to Aquinas, and Locke drew much from Hooker. See Peter Munz's The Place of Hooker in the History of Thought. The Cambridge Platonists furnished another link, though not in the same direct Medieval-Stoic line.

of belief rather than toward the grounds of belief, and argued on the basis of social attitudes rather than of personal convictions. Utilitarianism, rallying round Bentham's formula of 'the greatest happiness of the greatest number', was the most typical expression of this intellectual approach, which was most confident when least self-critical. Bentham and the elder Mill, secure in their scorn of religion, had no doubts about social happiness as an end in itself, but the inconsistencies patent in John Stuart Mill's *Utilitarianism* reveal a hesitant spirit in search for something to make morality certain[3]— a quest which continued through the nineteenth century and ended by giving up hope of intellectual consistency in the interests of getting on with the practical business of living in society, as advocated by William James. Since Jamesian pragmatism could find no surer basis even for a 'concrete' ethics than a subjective *mood*,[4] Positivism in our own day has declared the problem of ethics to be meaningless, so that moral theory gives way entirely to sociological research.

The direct result of the secularist idea of toleration was to set up the secular State as an ideal. In the secular State, religion was separated from the jurisdiction of the government and equally from most aspects of community life: the ethical had displaced theology and metaphysics. Unconventional beliefs were not favoured, in case they led to anti-social actions. Yet Thomas Jefferson made it a point of principle not to reveal his religious opinions, although his silence made him falsely suspected of undue heterodoxy, simply to uphold the right of the citizen to enjoy his inner convictions unmolested. The United States was the first country to be able to build a secular State according to rule. In countries where a traditional link between Church and State continued, some means of countering ecclesiastical

[3] Mill's later willingness to consider Theism as a basis for morality is an interesting reversal of the outlook of Christian rationalists of an earlier age, who wished to prove the truth of Theism through the certainty of morality. He wrote in 1860: 'It would be a great moral improvement to most persons, be they Christians, Deists or Atheists, if they firmly believed the world to be under the government of a Being, who, willing only good, leaves evil in the world solely in order to stimulate human faculties by an unremitting struggle against every form of it' (quoted in R. H. Murray's *Studies in the English Social and Political Thinkers of the Nineteenth Century* (1929, I, 421).

[4] 'The deepest difference, practically, in the moral life of man is the difference between the easy-going and the strenuous mood. . . . The capacity of the strenuous mood lies so deep down among our natural human possibilities that even if there were no metaphysical or traditional grounds for believing in a God, men would postulate one simply as a pretext for living hard, and getting out of the game of existence its keenest possibilities of zest' ('The Moral Philosopher and the Moral Life', *The Will to Believe*, 1903 edn., pp. 211, 213). Even in expressing his anti-rationalistic creed, James's exposition contains traces of the rationalist's appeal to an 'essential' human nature.

power within the realm had to be devised if toleration was to become effective. In Britain one of the chief influences upon the pattern of parliamentary democracy was the existence of a strong body of non-conformist opinion. Where, as in France and Italy, the main counter-force to ecclesiastical power was anti-clericalism, the course of toleration was less certain. On the other side, the secularism of the State had to be held in check by moral forces effective in public opinion if toleration was to continue. The Secular State was able to make use of the political and social activities of individual Church adherents, whose religiously inspired moral convictions exerted a profound influence upon the whole of society. Where secularism became an end in itself, chiefly by the appeal of a quasi-religious nationalism as in Napoleonic France and the Germany of Bismarck and Wilhelm II, it shook the foundations of liberty. But only with the coming of modern totalitarianism has secularism been converted into its opposite and emerged as religious faith claiming entire juris-diction over public and private morality. The essence of totalitarian-ism being that the State's control over individuals is not limited by any law, moral or jural, except at the will of the Party which claims absolute right to rule by Party dictatorship, it makes little difference whether the Party derives its authority from the Party philosophy alone, or whether it gains support from an authoritarian church also. In either case the suspension of the ethical concept by which toleration lives is prohibited, and a militant Party ethic is universally binding. In the absence of a common belief in the moral worth of toleration, the secular State develops through crisis, brought about by clash of beliefs, into the theocratic State.

II. THE SCIENTIFIC DEMAND FOR SECULARISM

The ideal of the secular State was already a good deal of a reality when the idea of toleration arose and supported it on moral grounds. Renaissance preoccupation with the temporal values of this world had long been working to that end. The rise of nationalism and capitalism indicated that other powerful forces were disputing with religion for man's allegiance. Theology was finding its traditional categories inadequate to deal with the new fields of human activity and the advances of man's knowledge. Explorers were bringing to light a different earth, and astronomers a different heaven. Machia-velli was planning a political theory which should reflect the realities of the contemporary political and social situation, and classical scholars were discovering the past as the past, for the first time becoming conscious of *a sense of history*. A particularly potent element in the general ferment was the coming to birth of experimental science. If Marlowe's Faustus is the typical symbol of the Renaissance, science was the Mephistopheles bringing him his magic power. The universal genius of Leonardo da Vinci brooded over the machine as the instrument of power—in flight, locomotion, and warfare. Because it brought together theory and practice to such effect—(scientific method accomplishing tremendous advances both in 'pure' knowledge of nature and in technological control over it)—science raised searching questions on the theoretical and practical plane alike.

For the medieval world, *science* was the name for indubitable metaphysical knowledge. The transformation of the word into a title for the mathematical schematizing of the material universe, in order to permit the development of techniques to manipulate it, is a highly interesting phenomenon. Such a change indicates a revolution in the centre of human interest from thought to action. Karl Marx's celebrated saying about philosophers having hitherto explained the world in various ways and the task being now to change it was, after all, nothing more than a belated recognition of the aims of modern science. (Marxism itself, very revealingly, is in its own regard the embodiment of scientific truth, although so clearly an ideological structure). When today science is called '*natural science*' the phrase seems pedantic, so little sense remains of *supernatural science* being a kind of knowledge that can be called 'scientific'. Through the prestige it has achieved by its practical conquests, science has discounted the whole world that lies outside its particular territory. It is interested in those aspects of nature outside man and inside him, and those only, which extend our knowledge of nature in order to bring it under the control of human purposes. Although the 'pure' scientist is said to be concerned with knowledge 'for its own sake', this is true in no more than a certain sense. Such a scientist does not concern himself with the techniques which his theoretical formulations will require in order to produce results in the practical field, nor with the social consequences of the possible results which may follow technological exploitation of his discoveries. That is simply a consequence of the division of labour which science requires. Scientific knowledge, being progressive, creates an ever-expanding body of specialists to cover its ever-enlarging territory. But the 'pure' scientist is first of all a servant of science before he is allocated his corner in the workshop of scientific knowledge. Whatever cannot in principle be exploited by the technicians is not knowledge for him.

The basic pre-suppositions of science have been described as stemming directly from the Judeo-Christian view of nature, and it is probable that the Biblical valuation of history, with its stress upon the unique event within a Providential order, was the true inspiration of the scientific attitude,[5] just as Greek confidence in the world being made intelligible through mathematical abstraction provided science's intellectual foundation. But science is not concerned with the origins of its assumptions, but with the usefulness of its conclusions. It is not interested in ideas, except for those ideas essential to its formulation of hypotheses and their verification. Not merely theology but philosophy as well is unnecessary to it, and in our own day we have seen the emergence of the belief that the only useful activity of the intellect, apart from scientific research, is in elucidating the meanings of the propositions of science.[6] Positivism, which accepts this subjugation of philosophy by science in the interests of obtaining a unitary view of the universe, is forced to call all statements that fall outside the province of science *pseudo-statements*, knowledge being by definition nothing else than description of what is 'real' in space and time by means of 'laws'.[7]

By restricting its interests to what could be verified by experiment in the world of sense, science exerted its great and increasing influence on the side of secularism. In order to pursue its quest for knowledge it could tolerate no dogmatism about the objects of its investigations on theological or metaphysical grounds. So Galileo clashed with the upholders of scholastic-Aristotelian cosmology, and Huxley and the Darwinians with Biblical literalists. On its own territory science could admit no rivals or superiors, and the increase of knowledge about the world it brought (proved by increase of control over the world) was its charter of rights. Opposition to it had to retire from the encounter weakened as well as worsted. The scientific Moses had shown that the traditional Court Magicians possessed inferior magical powers. The fact that knowledge brought by science was progressive and accumulative, each discovery leading to new

[5] See p. 81, n. 41, *supra*.
[6] See Maurice Schlick, *Philosophy of Nature* (trans. 1949), p. 3.
[7] ibid., p. 21. Whitehead has written: 'If science is not to degenerate into a medley of *ad hoc* hypotheses, it must become philosophical and must enter upon a thorough criticism of its own foundations' (*Science and the Modern World*, p. 21). Whitehead speaks for the philosopher who wants to philosophize *about* science. But, if we accept science's own standpoint, we must accept the 'medley of *ad hoc* hypotheses' as the norm of all knowledge and attempt to form these into a coherent whole. To criticize science's foundation is exactly what cannot be done without abandoning the scientific approach to knowledge. From this angle Positivism is consistent in its single-minded and uncritical faith in science as the final authority.

control over nature, lent support to the supposition that scientific knowledge was 'true', whereas religion and philosophy were pretenders to knowledge with no way of substantiating their claims objectively. To make the world safe for science was one of the leading motives of the Enlightenment, and this could not be done without the freedom secularism gave. Then, from calling for secularism in the name of intellectual freedom, the this-worldly and anti-religious sections of the Enlightenment went on to prescribe secularism as a positive ideal. Under the unitary view demanded by Positivism, religion and metaphysics are outlawed. And with the banishment of theological dogmas and speculative systems, religious and metaphysical doubt goes too. Where the orthodoxy of scientific truth reigns supreme there is no need for toleration. The issue is presented as a simple one between 'true' knowledge and obscurantism.

The connexion between science and freedom is, in spite of widespread assumptions to the contrary, a very restricted one. Science is seriously compromised by the irruption of any extra-scientific conclusions into its special field, and needs complete freedom within its own borders. The cases of Galileo *versus* Aristotelianism and of Lysenko *pro* Marxism show how science cannot continue to function when a ruling orthodoxy insists that the scientist accept any criterion of truth other than the one demanded by scientific method. That these two cases of a head-on collision between science and an extra-scientific ideology are so exceptional points to the fact that freedom for the scientist is a very different thing from freedom for an individual. Because of its dependence upon the correlated findings of many different branches of scientific investigation, science favours the free exchange of information among scientists without discrimination, and so it is most secure and likely to preserve its own integrity in the 'free society' which extends toleration of belief among its members. But, although it is sometimes argued that science cannot survive in the atmosphere of a totalitarian society, this view is hardly borne out by the evidence and probably underestimates man's capacity for constructing water-tight compartments in the mind. The scientist may well hold an open mind in regard to the evidence presented to him in his scientific studies and yet, as an individual, submit to the mental blinkers of an unscientific ideology. A branch of scientific research, such as nuclear physics at the present time, may become partly subordinated to State control, so that the scientist loses his professional 'freedom', without scientific discovery being made impossible.

It is important to notice that the need for water-tight compartments only arises when a man's beliefs claim to present some infallible 'truth' of the same order as scientific truth. Aristotle's *physics* could not be harmonized with Galileo's astronomy, nor could the *Book of Genesis* as a historical record be reconciled with the Darwinian account of the *origin of the species*. Similarity of subject-matter does not of itself, however, imply a conflict between the scientific conscience of the scientist and his—or other people's—beliefs. A religious view of cosmology and history may very well co-exist with a scientific view of these spheres of knowledge, because the knowledge sought by the scientist and the religious thinker is different. In the same way, psychology and the social sciences seek to describe man's internal nature and his relation to his neighbours, which are also the concern of theology and philosophy; but, because different questions are asked in each case, so theology and philosophy, far from repudiating the answers these sciences supply will find them useful for the prosecution of their own tasks.[8] Conflict arises when a further question is asked, namely: which type of knowledge is most important for man to seek, and what corpus of knowledge is most comprehensive and 'essential' in the information it gives about the universe at large? This question is philosophical and theological. And whether the answer is given in terms of certainty, probability, or faith, it must be given as a belief.

From the scientific view, when scientific knowledge is taken to be final, all beliefs are simply ideologies. In this, scientific claim to represent 'truth' is on a level with any other dogma. Ethics, because it belongs to the same level of experience beyond scientific verification as religion, metaphysics, and art, is quite indifferent to it. But a scientific society cannot avoid asking ethical questions and seeking the ethical implications of scientific investigation and of the use of the power which science makes available. We are acutely aware of this in our post-atomic age. The specifically scientific urge to establish the secular society is thus a matter principally of historical interest, though it is one which has left a legacy of misunderstanding. The demand for freedom to pursue scientific truth, leading to a denial of the need for other types of truth, has obscured the importance of the ethical problem for man as such. Where science has created real confusion is in lending its prestige to further the dogma that moral

---

[8] This theme is admirably developed by Langmead Casserley in *Morals and Man in the Social Sciences*, with particular reference to the social sciences. The general theme has been treated in many studies, notably in Streeter's *Reality* (1926).

problems are 'pseudo-problems' and thus minimizing the need for existential choice of moral values; and, of course, behind ethical valuation lie theological and metaphysical beliefs. Science has no direct contribution to make here, although the information it gives about the kind of world we live in must be taken into account by all other kinds of knowledge, and has made certain dogmas untenable. Its chief influence has been a practical one. By putting enormous powers for good or evil at the disposal of society, it has made the solution of ethical problems more urgent.

III. THE MORAL BASIS OF SECULARISM

Since the growth of secularist society (linked to the technological advance of science) has thrown into relief the question of ethical standards, and since secularism finds it hard to give morality any meaning, it would seem that secularism cannot provide any moral justification for its own existence. To some this has implied that all secularism stands for is discredited and deserves to be swept away. According to this view, the revolt of authoritarian forces, Communist and Fascist, against all that nineteenth-century liberal democracy stood for reveals the hollowness of the ideal of the secular State. In *The End of Our Age* (written after the Russian Revolution but before the coming of Fascism), Nicolas Berdyaev looked forward to the establishment of a New Middle Ages that should end secularism and establish a theocracy. True, he admitted that it was not possible merely to put the clock back, and believed that religion would guide society in freedom instead of by external authority. But he gave no recognition to the worth of social freedom and ignored its roots in the Reformation—which, incidentally, he regarded as no more than one aspect of the Renaissance. And he could see in the Enlightenment and all that stemmed from it only the decay of Renaissance 'humanistic self-affirmation'.

Berdyaev's failure to see a theological element in modern individualism and secularism led to a one-sided reading of history, and on that account to a false estimate of the institutions which are a product of history. In particular, his understanding of democracy was strangely astray. He wrote:

Democracy is indifferent to truth because it has left its discovery to the votes of a majority, for it is only on the condition of ignoring or not believing in Truth that one can accept quantitative power and revere the opinion of a crowd.[9]

* 1935 edn., p. 175.

A democracy that indeed revered the opinion of a crowd would soon cease to be democratic. For democracy is not just the rule of the majority, but most essentially the agreement of a whole society to conduct its political activities within the framework of parliamentary procedure—a very different state of affairs.[10] According to Berdyaev there is in democracy no 'people', in the sense of 'a great historical whole' possessing 'a common organic will'; democracy knows 'only the wishes of an insignificant handful of contemporary individuals'.[11] This is an almost exact reversal of the truth. The most potent force in democracy is the accumulated wisdom of the past, which has shaped the national institutions and created the political temper. The ballot box may be the symbol of democracy, but it is not its god. The present opinions of its population, even at a time of national elections, have only a limited effect upon national destiny—unless one generation decides to throw away the heritage of the past and determine issues by overthrowing democracy. In a 'new' democracy the people does not change its will, but simply agrees to express its will in new ways, argument taking the place of force: the test here is whether a genuine tradition has been started, or whether it will fail for lack of 'a common organic will'. Democracy also implies a democratic *structure*, government at a local level and national government following the same principles, so that continuity is found in space as well as time. Montesquieu taught that the Separation of Powers (the executive and legislature set over against one another) was the secret of English liberty. If he was not entirely correct in his historical judgement, he estimated rightly how important structure is to a democratic State. Unless there are adequate checks upon sectional misuse of power in the interests of the 'people' against the 'crowd', responsible government breaks down.

A totalitarian State may well carry out the wishes of the majority of its citizens more thoroughly than a democracy can do but, in the latter, minority opinion also carries weight and the Opposition as well as the Government is elected and contributes to the process of governing. Willingness to allow the majority to shape and direct policy is a decision of the whole people, based neither on indifference to truth nor on a theory of *vox populi, vox Dei*, but on the recognition that society can only be just when there is a freedom for the individ-

[10] This thesis has been attractively presented by Ralph Barton Perry, arguing from the premise that democracy 'is in fact a social system, of which government in the strict sense is only a part' (*Realms of Value*, Chapter 16); it is also the starting-point of John Stuart Mill's *Representative Government* and *On Liberty*.

[11] op. cit., p. 180.

ual. The much criticized *individualism* of democracy takes into account that every attempt to ignore the individual in the interests of 'truth' assumes that some citizens (and not others) possess truth and that every attempt to subordinate the individual to 'the people', by taking away from the individual the right to speak as one of the people, assumes that some citizens (and not others) represent the people. The heretic in the theocratic State and the bourgeois in the Marxist State exist as individuals, but they do not exist as members of the corporate body of society: they are expendable. The words of Caiaphas, 'It is expedient for us, that one man should die for the people, and that the whole nation perish not' (John 11_{50}), ring down the centuries, the perennial authoritarian excuse for discriminating intolerance.[12]

According to the common faith that maintains a democracy in being, all individuals have the same rights within the community— all are 'persons'.[13] As a consequence, all individuals must agree to accept majority decisions for society, subject to the right of individual protest, and to propagate minority faiths within the bounds of dialogue. But so unwilling must a democracy be to interfere with the inner freedom of individuals that the 'conscientious objector' receives special consideration. Even the minimum faith needed to preserve toleration is not usually required to be assented to, *as a faith*. Within a democracy individuals and groups may hold this faith prudentially as 'your principle, not mine' so long as they do not attempt to put their contrary faith too obviously into action. Hence the democratic dislike of 'loyalty tests' and similar State insistence upon democratic orthodoxy. Even though democracy must be destroyed if the faith is extinguished, democrats know that it is a faith which can only survive through dialogue. Therefore the preservation of dialogue is more precious than formal willingness to declare agreement with the faith.

Thus the paradox arises: Protestant religious faith encourages secularism in the State, for secular society embodies the Protestant conception of faith as a theocratic society can never do. Faith must be what we *believe*, not what we assent to. It is most revealing that Catholic theologians are turning to this basic principle of Protestant thought when they come to accept the desirability of toleration, even

---

[12] Thus the Inquisition has been praised in this style: 'O blessed flames of the stake by which, with the sacrifice of a few crafty wretches, hundreds and hundreds of regiments of souls were saved. . . !'—*Analecta Ecclesiastica*, III, 29 ff. (1895), quoted by J. S. Whale, *The Protestant Tradition*, p. 242, n, 2.

[13] Ralph Barton Perry justifies the rule of the people in democracy by the existence of 'a finality in a human person' (op. cit., p. 276)—a moral claim which goes beyond Perry's professed empirical and pragmatic philosophy.

though this means admitting that it is the post-Reformation developments which have pointed the right relation between the sacred and the secular. Supporting 'Pluralist' society as against 'sacral', Father Victor White has written:

The transformation of Christianity itself into the established religion of a 'sacral' society for a millennium after the conversion of Constantine was an anomaly which produced many anomalies, as well as all that we call Christian civilisation. Not least of these anomalies was the Inquisition and the *De haeretico comburendo*. . . . Yet the 'sacral' idea has its attractions and the medieval ideal of the synthesis of Church and State is so impressive that we have been slow to see that it was an anomaly rather than a norm. But its departure should be a matter of rejoicing rather than for the nostalgic regrets of the apologists of the 'Europe is the Faith' school.[14]

For Father White, religion is 'an affair wholly of gracious election and individual decision', which is a view quite in harmony with the Protestant conception of faith, as well as with the Lockean belief that Churches are voluntary societies with which the State has no immediate concern.

The term *pluralist* describes the character of the 'open' society perhaps less ambiguously than the term *secular*, because it distinguishes the tolerant State from the State which is dogmatically anti-religious. The pluralist State may extend certain privileges to some religious groups and may actually recognize a State Church 'by Law established'. In spite of making religion a private affair, Locke thought that tolerance should not be extended to the atheist. Nevertheless, the use of the word *secular* reminds us that every pluralist State, though it may recognize and encourage the work of the Churches, must remain separated from them. Even an established Church within such a State finds its first task, as William Temple has pointed out, to be the preservation of its right as 'an association within the Community to live its own life'.[15]

The State's jurisdiction must stop short with the ethical. It may forbid religious practices which outrage the moral conscience, as the British government had to do in India, but it has no jurisdiction over beliefs which prompt social behaviour, only over social behaviour as such. The Christian Scientist may believe that matter does not exist and that disease will vanish with 'right thinking', but he will be forced to keep the drains of his house in accordance with regulations governing sanitation. State pluralism depends upon State secularism.

[14] 'Religious Toleration' in the *Listener*, July 30th, 1953.
[15] *Christianity and the State* (1928), Appendix II: 'On the Relations between Church and State.'

If once a concern for public morals passes into an insistence that morality must have a specific basis, then toleration is destroyed in principle. The theocratic State is necessarily a persecuting State, its mandate being derived from party principles conceived as being beyond criticism.

The notion that a society can have a 'common organic will', not alone to respect certain values, but also to accept some definite formulation of belief defining and delimiting those values, is a mistaken one. It is not mistaken about such a will being possible, for there are many instances of such a will being most undeniably present. It is mistaken in thinking that this will is moral or has spiritual value. The common organic will is found in primitive communities and under present-day dictatorships. It is the ideal of every type of authoritarian State. And it is perhaps most evident, in a local and transient form, in an act of mob violence.[16] A will of this kind is brought into being by an absence of critical thought and by an unchecked indulgence in emotional states of mind. The conditions favourable to its formation do not arise spontaneously, for tribal ritual (often of an ecstatic character) is a prominent feature of primitive communities. For the more sophisticated, the way of attaining to a common organic will is through the necessary psychological conditions being artificially created by their leaders. The demagogue makes an amorphous collection of individuals into a collective body moved by the will he instils into it. Modern totalitarianism uses all the resources of psychology to perfect its techniques of propaganda. 'Brain-washing' is a logical development of the desire to eradicate individuality in the interests of social unity, for it is individuality which destroys the common will and makes the heretic, the non-conformist, and the conscientious-objector. Commercial advertising is a mild type of brain-washing in its desire to *break down sales-resistance*; what is resistant is the individual mind rejecting the suggestion put before it. Worship itself can be corrupted and, from being a means to build up the common will to faith, can become a psychological incitement to carry out whatever policy strengthens the sense of corporate unity (generally a crusade where *we* are united against *they*). Religious fanaticism is the most extreme form of the common organic will which, in all its forms, is the expression of contempt for the individual conscience and uncritical acceptance of a social morality conceived as infallible.

---

[16] William Faulkner, in *Intruder in the Dust*, describes a lynching mob as 'not faces but a face, not a mass nor even a mosaic of them but a Face'. The face is the concrete manifestation of the will.

Berdyaev thought that democracy grew out of the break-up of the common will when the Middle Ages came to an end, and that it was a vain attempt to restore a common will on a basis of counting heads.[17] A more accurate diagnosis would be that democracy has tried, with some success, to substitute a common will to co-operation toward moral ends for an externally controlled will imposing uniformity of belief. Democracy assumes that there can be a common will, directed to establish certain values by particular methods found suitable for attaining the ends proposed. But this common will is a limited, conscious choice of individuals, which refuses to make an absolute standard out of its corporate decisions and which feels itself free both to draw from and to criticize the traditions inherited from its past.

This limited, secularizing will has been called by Paul Tillich *autonomy*. According to Tillich autonomy is opposed to *heteronomy*, which is the dominance of a dogmatic authority over society. The secular and the theocratic State thus exemplify autonomy and heteronomy respectively. Both of these, Tillich holds, are derived from another form of social existence—*theonomy*. Theonomy has its being when a religious meaning permeates all aspects of social life and is not imposed upon society in terms of an ideology (as in heteronomy), or neglected in the interests of self-development and national freedom (as in autonomy).[18] Tillich is conscious that theonomy is essentially an ideal. He writes: 'There is no complete theonomy under the conditions of existence.'[19] Yet, on the other hand, he identifies theonomy with the primitive life before rational thinking becomes self-conscious, and he speaks of definite historical periods as belonging to one or other of the three—the early Middle Ages are theonomous, the later Middle Ages heteronomous, the Enlightenment autonomous, and so on.

These three terms provide a useful tool for making a theological analysis of cultural history. But really only *autonomy* and *heteronomy* are put before men as practical alternatives, because society must be organized in terms of positive law ruling over it from without, how-

[17] op. cit., p. 178. Brushing aside the suggestion that the Reformation was the source of democracy, Berdyaev calls Rousseau the 'father' of modern democracy. In Rousseau we find the theory of the 'general will' used to the same effect as Berdyaev's 'common organic will' which, he says, cannot exist under democracy; both are incompatible with toleration as it exists under parliamentary democracy. Maurice Cranston has argued cogently that the liberal ideal of freedom must choose Locke's individualism and reject Rousseau's *étatiste* thinking. (*Freedom: A New Analysis* (1953). Part II: 'The Ambiguity of Liberalism'.)
[18] These terms are frequently discussed by Tillich. See, in particular, *The Protestant Era*, pp. 44 ff., 56 ff. and *Systematic Theology*, I, 83 ff.
[19] *Systematic Theology*, I, 85.

ever much cultural, religious, and personal achievements in any society may transcend the law and free themselves from legalism. The theonomous ideal may be the motive which inspires men to choose one or the other. A Catholic may believe that a theocratic State is a guarantee that the truths of religion shall not be allowed to be given over to Cæsar, or destroyed by the godless, as the first Protestants believed also. Even the Marxist has his own special vision of theonomy, for he looks for the withering away of the State and the reconciling of man with history as the result of the heteronomy organized by the Communist Party, which merely is the precondition of the Classless Society. If today Protestants are committed to choose a secular organization of the State, it is because they believe that men can best find their faith when they are given liberty to find it. While those who value religion also value moral integrity, secularism will remain an indispensable basis of society, not for itself but for its gift of individual liberty.

IV. THE ETHICAL LIMITATIONS OF SECULARISM

That the secular State must be accepted as the price to be paid for liberty of conscience brings about one of those tensions which are unavoidable in the Protestant way of thinking. If we possessed the truth in its entirety, then the State might be fashioned to truth's measure. Our concern would be the same as Plato's in the *Republic*— to prevent any change in the structure of a just order of society. Lacking any such objective certainty, we must expect change in social and political patterns. Yet we are also bound to strive to see the truth which we confess embodied to some degree in the State, and bound also to strive to prevent that truth from being lost from the community to which we belong. Confessional loyalty to the truth we protest may find its expression largely in free associations within the Community. (Freedom to form and join such associations is one of the outstanding gifts of the secular State.) But in the larger whole our full loyalties are not given full scope. Personal conviction may sometimes have to give way in order to preserve dialogue. Practical decisions for the whole of any society must be ethical in scope, thus ignoring the higher personal relationship of the love beyond the law; and they must be legal in form, thus ignoring the more perfect expression of personal relationships which appeal instead of command. These legal, ethical, and impersonal decisions of a people, embodied in their written legal codes and unwritten rules of conduct and procedure, are divorced from the ultimate reasons which make them binding, for they are not concerned with ultimate values. A legal definition of an 'act of God' is not a theological explanation of special Providence, and the State does not recruit men for its armed forces only after establishing that non-resistance is not a divine command. Yet no one who has definite beliefs can agree that all the demands made upon him by the State are morally justifiable. If he allows his beliefs to be overruled, it is for the sake of avoiding the greater harm of breaking dialogue. Until he can convince them of the rightness of his view, he will abide by the decision of his fellows; or, while asking for conscientious exemption for himself, will nevertheless respect the prevailing policy as one based on conscience.

Yet what is allowed at all seems for that reason good in itself; and so the secularist State, with its ethical relativism, is made into an end instead of a means. The practical divorce between ethical norms and the theological and metaphysical principles which alone can justify morality becomes considered quite natural—even necessary.[20] That absolute values are put into the background solely for the sake of tolerable social relations is forgotten, and society and what is good for society become the whole of the picture. It is not realized that this means a lamentable impoverishment of social relations, because the social is only one dimension of life. The social dimension is the sphere of the ethical, and social relations are made rich when dialogue takes place through the right use of this sphere. Human beings, if they are to meet at all, must meet in community. If personal relations are to develop, they must develop through the ethical sphere, by means of the security provided by law. Without some equality before the law and freedom from the conditions of social anarchy, dialogue cannot begin. Once made possible, dialogue can result in men sharing the most fundamental experiences: love, contemplation, and worship. But if *all* that men can share is in the social sphere, then personal relations remain superficial and dialogue is stifled at its birth. Instead of personal understanding there can be only exchange of individual views, expression of individual tastes, and co-operation in making possible individual amusements; or else individuality may be submerged in the sub-personal experience of being 'one of the crowd'. Such impoverishment of personal life follows where secular-

[20] This divorce between ethics and its objective foundation must not, of course, be confused with the specific divorce, which some insist upon, between ethics and theology. There are moral theorists who regard ethics as an autonomous science and protest against the subordination of ethics to theology (see, for instance, H. D. Lewis, *Morals and the New Theology* (1947)). This is simply a dispute between two parties who both believe that moral theory is objective, but differ about the *mode* of its foundation. Both are equally opposed to ethical relativism.

ism is accepted as a creed. Value, having been made relative to society, has been taken away from personal existence.

Secularism moves entirely within the dimension of the ethical and yet it has destroyed the necessary foundation for morality. It is not surprising, consequently, that its attitude to ethical questions is strangely unstable and contradictory. To begin with, moral judgements are its characteristic products. The typical secularist attack on religion is that it leads men astray and multiplies evil. Yet, since secularism's estimate of moral good is made in terms of social well-being, it judges according to utilitarian standards of *results achieved* instead of by intrinsically moral standards of *intentions in the agent*, and so tends constantly to belittle the need for moral consciousness and to exalt the mechanism of actually bringing about social progress as the essential factor. The advance of scientific method into the field of human conduct in psychology and the social sciences has led to the naïve belief that science can provide a way of salvation for humanity by its own power and without the prior existence of moral understanding;[21] and the prestige of the scientist as the person who gets things done is contrasted with the indecisive results achieved by other means. Secularism is apt to forget that moral progress does not depend upon techniques alone, but upon insight into moral values.

Again, secularism often assumes that moral values are self-evident because they are traditional, taking for granted a justification of morality which is explicitly denied. This is true of Bentham's crude utilitarianism which John Stuart Mill found it possible to support only by bringing in distinctions of moral worth entirely disruptive of the system. It is true also of much more carefully guarded forms of the same view, such as Ralph Barton Perry's ideal of *harmonious happiness*.[22] In this latter theory, what people like must be *good* and what they like best and longest because of the harmony of interests it brings makes mere *goodness* into *moral goodness*. *Harmonious happiness* seems the most reasonable of moral goals—so long as it is interpreted with the force of 'Thou shalt love thy neighbour as thyself'. But Perry's principle, 'When the good is greater the right is superior, and is entitled to moral precedence in case of conflict'[23] is simply

---

[21] 'The social sciences alone can teach the humanist man's most important dimension, the social one'—Georges-Henri Lévesque, quoted by John A. Irving, *Science and Values* (1952), p. 141. Irving himself writes: 'Amid the philosophical uncertainties of the mid-century there is ... one challenging certainty. The advance of psychology and the social sciences has brought humanity to the threshold of a New Enlightenment' (ibid., Preface, p. viii).

[22] op. cit., Chapter 7.

[23] ibid., p. 107.

Bentham's *greatest happiness of the greatest number* all over again.
Just because we should all be happy if every one were good, it does
not follow that morality is advanced every time more people are
given more of what they want. The persistent attempt to get rid of
the idea of obligation, and to make moral conduct consist in bringing
about what is socially acceptable, rests on the quite arbitrary belief
that all that men need to know in this world is a technique of happiness. Perry believes that the imperative of moral obligation is simply
a psychological accident due to our being used to being ordered
about by various authorities.[24] The obvious retort to this contention
is that it must be a psychological dislike of being under authority
which seeks to remove the imperative form of the moral demand.
Perry goes on to state that the only obligation found in morality is
the necessity of logic, by which right means are chosen to carry out
an intended end. Hume's 'Reason is, and ought only to be, the slave
of the passions' is recalled, being, as it is, the best expression of the
perennial secularist wish to make ethics a matter of enlightened self-
interest. While it is taken for granted that passions will be kept in
bounds by common agreement to be civilized and accept traditional
moral values, things can go along quite smoothly. But, once tradition
is put aside, the morality of successful technique knowing no *ought*
except the means to a desired end shows itself in a very different
light. Marxists will gladly accept *harmonious happiness* as their ideal.
Yet, since for them the logical means to achieve that end is the
dictatorship of the Proletariat, they just as gladly accept the Police
State, confident that this serves the majority interest until the time
when the withering away of the State brings the interests of all into
perfect harmony. Were a liberal (such as Perry himself) to object to the
suffering thus brought upon the bourgeoisie and all dissenters from
the Party rule, the answer could be made, 'When the good is greater
the right is superior'. That Marxist and liberal would fail to agree
about the measure of good would not mend matters.

A denial of objective moral standards has another consequence
which secularism makes evident. Men cannot, in fact, live without
encountering the claim of the *ought*. If it denied in principle that
there is any such *ought* binding upon all, individuals will avoid complete anarchy by erecting their own moral standards and insisting
upon following these *as though* they were authoritatively binding
upon them, regardless of the consequences. The 'tough' heroes of
many modern novels of the Hemingway school show this situation

[24] *Realms of Value*, p. 109.

and its working-out; a purely individual *credo* is held with intolerant zeal, and any one unfortunate enough to come in between such dedicated individuals and their self-appointed duty is ruthlessly removed. When morality is reduced to purely subjective terms, all that remains of the ethical is its intolerance.[25]

V. THE FAITH BEHIND SECULARISM

Although, as we have seen, the secular State is supported by a belief in ultimate values, the State itself cannot establish the reality of the faith by which it lives. Thus it is always in danger of being destroyed by lack of faith and by the emergence of another faith from within its own institutions which is hostile to it. The ease with which democracy passes into its opposite—rule by a single tyrant—was described by Plato and has been proved again with tragic force in our own day. When existence is without faith to give it meaning it becomes intolerable; and democracy ceases to have meaning when it degenerates into a naked struggle for power between parties without a faith in what is above party. Rule by a crowd is tyranny, whether the crowd is a majority, a minority, or a single individual who represents in his person the will of a party within the nation. The dictator is the creation of a crusading faith. Both Napoleon and Hitler used enthusiasm (in the former sense of that word) centred in national destiny in order to climb to power, and then played upon the cult of the national leader as a 'man of destiny'. Whether a national leader shares the faith or not, he depends for his power upon his ability to kindle that faith in others.

The enormous importance of propaganda in totalitarian States today is evidence of the part played by faith in preserving a social order. It may easily be overlooked that the purpose of lying propaganda is only secondarily to keep the masses in a state of ignorance and is primarily to inspire them with common beliefs. The full extent of despotism's dependence upon eliciting a spontaneous faith has been portrayed very cogently in George Orwell's grim novel of life in a fully totalitarian world, *Nineteen Eighty-four*.

---

[25] It is interesting to observe that the form of the ethical judgement, according to the school which denies all objectivity to ethics, is what may be called the *dictatorial imperative*. C. L. Stevenson sets forth his 'first pattern' analysis thus: ' "This is good" means "I approve of this; do so as well" ' (*Ethics and Language* (1944), p. 22). The *do so as well* here represents a non-rational, emotional command. The representatives of 'justice' (as portrayed by Dashiel Hammet, Raymond Chandler, and Mickey Spillane), who fight and shoot themselves through to final triumph, are the individual exponents of the dictatorial imperative, just as totalitarian propaganda and commercial advertising are its collective exponents.

Orwell describes a régime where Party authority rules supreme. Technology has given it the means to make outward revolt impossible, so that its resources are devoted to forcing obedience at an inward, personal level. The hero-victim of the book, Winston Smith, has to learn to 'love' Big Brother (the leader-symbol of the régime), and Smith's story ends with his surrender of will to the official dogma his intellect knows to be a lie. The world of *Nineteen Eighty-four* is a consistently secularist world. Men's lives move solely on the social level, bounded by the single ethical norm of duty to the Party, a norm which supplants all personal desires and obligations. In this world, not only can there be no religion, there can be no friendship, no art, and no joy in the senses. Existence means now carrying out one's function in the State. The dimension of the spirit, where man is confronted by absolute value, is totally destroyed. At the same time, the secular power of the State is used to make a complete theocracy. The Party, omnipotent, omniscient, and omnipresent, stands in the place of God, and by its will supplies the absolutes which must be accepted in faith. Party members live in the faith that the power exercised by the régime is an ultimate good, and insist that this faith shall be shared by every citizen, who must 'love' the Party will represented by Big Brother. Yet, while every social institution, including language, is devised with the single aim of ensuring that this faith shall be universal, the Party needs to encourage individual rebels—Winston Smith and his kind—in order to exercise power through punishing the heretic.

Orwell's fictional parable shows that the need for faith and for recognizing absolute values cannot be banished by throwing out the notion of objective truth and by seeking to restrict human life to the dimension of the secular. Such a restriction merely results in bringing back dogmatic beliefs in a perverted and unendurable form, where faith is a manufactured myth at war with truth, and law exists in order to multiply the penalties for breaking it. Definite values, calling forth loyalty to the community and making possible a practical philosophy of life, cannot be established without the intrusion into the secular of explicit or implicit absolutes derived from personal faith, either conscious or unconscious. Without faith there can be no will to discover truth or bring good into existence; and a weak faith, however reasonable or well-intentioned, will always be driven out by a strong faith, however irrational and self-destructive.

VI. THE SACRED WITHIN THE SECULAR

The faith of a democracy is a faith in the creativity of dialogue. Of course, this faith does not stand alone, for it is the achievement of democracy to allow for a variety of faiths to flourish simultaneously within society. It is this freedom for a diversity of faiths which characterizes the 'open society' and makes it 'open'—a freedom which gives opportunity for beliefs to propagate themselves and not, as is often supposed, a freedom which frees men from the need to believe anything at all.[26]

If we look to history, we can see how the secular State was founded on passionate faith. The *philosophes* of the eighteenth century were motivated by a moral fervour inspiring their rationalism and anti-clericalism. Their faith in a moral order working through history is summed up in Voltaire's cry, *écrasez l'infâme*. Wordsworth's well-known line,

Bliss was it in that dawn to be alive,

is found under the disenchanted title, *French Revolution, as it appeared to enthusiasts at its commencement*; he had known what it was to have enthusiasm and to lose it. In the nineteenth century, freedom conceived as democratic liberalism was championed by men as temperamentally diverse as Abraham Lincoln, Mazzini, and John Stuart Mill, and appealed to national consciousness and to supra-national idealism in different proportions. Abraham Lincoln has actually become a symbol both for the American people and for the democratic principle.

Nineteenth-century liberal faith found itself confronted with increasing doubt as the century progressed; for nationalistic politics claimed that political individualism destroyed the basic historic unity of a people, and socialism preached that economic individualism destroyed the effective freedom of the majority of citizens in a democratic State. Nationalism and socialism, as faiths, seemed to deny the suspension of the ethical necessary for the secular State, and in their extreme forms coalesced in twentieth-century totalitarianism to challenge the liberal ideal of freedom for the individual. The survival of democracy today depends upon the ability of secular liberal-

---

[26] Cranston's *Liberty: a New Analysis* argues that freedom is always a negative 'freedom from'; yet in reviewing the various brands of liberalism Cranston supports a positive ideal of society found in the Locke-Mill tradition. K. R. Popper's *The Open Society and its Enemies* (1945) advocates a similar ideal without making it clear how an empirical philosophy can support it.

ism to incorporate what is just in the nationalist and socialist criticisms of the open society, while insisting that these must be subordinated to an over-all faith in dialogue.

Secularist democracy, which seems to leave room for no worship except the worship of Mammon, can conceal great reserves of common faith. Napoleon called the British a nation of shop-keepers, and Hitler poured invective upon the *plutodemocracies*; yet both lived to see their will to power founder against the united will to preserve a way of life they thought to be a hypocritical façade. The will to dialogue in a democratic State is a complex one. It is made up of reverence for tradition (uniting individuals into a people) and devotion to 'free associations' within the State—each valued for its own sake and yet recognized to be bound up in its interests with the welfare of the State as a whole. Nurse Edith Cavell's timeless declaration, 'Patriotism is not enough; I must have no hatred or bitterness for any one', illustrates the true depth of democratic patriotism: Edith Cavell died because of loyalty to country. The loyalty inspired by a democratic State is all the stronger because it is a conditional, and not an absolute, value. The individual stands by his own faith, which may not be that of the community as such, and yet finds the community an expression of that faith. Thus the secular State is justified in so far as it allows the growth of faith within itself; or, to use Tillich's terminology, when theonomy is achieved through autonomy.

The enemy of democracy is the theocratic State in any form. Religious faith recognizes this when theocracy is secularist-absolutist, or the theocracy of an alien religion. Protestantism has learnt that any ecclesiastically supported authoritarianism is intolerable. Such authoritarianism makes it impossible to implement the second part of the Great Commandment in social life by forcing men to obey the first part according to a prescribed form, or else to forfeit their standing as citizens. Using Tillich's terminology again, we could say that heteronomy is the enemy of theonomy.

Christianity faced the theocratic State in its early history over the issue of Emperor worship. This issue of conflicting loyalties was ended by the conversion of Constantine, resulting in official patronage of the Church in place of persecution. As we can now see, this changed the complexion of the problem without really resolving it. Not until the rise of the *dissenter* in post-Reformation times to take the place of the *heretic* did a solution force itself upon the Christian conscience. The State learnt respect for faith, as distinct from alliance with or opposition to faiths in their organized capacity, and at the same time organized faiths learnt to live beside one another. The sacred could only exist within the secular when it was willing to allow the secular State a limited separation from its religiously based ethical claims.

'The blood of the martyrs is the seed of the Church.' In the martyr's refusal to abandon faith at the behest of force is the test of faith's rule over the believer. It is not the test of faith's validity. The secular realm cannot be indifferent to faith, but it can refuse to allow any faith to destroy the appeal to dialogue. Modern totalitarianism excuses the existence of concentration and labour camps on the grounds that they are necessary to control 'criminal elements'. Roman Catholics brush aside the charge that Rome permits persecution of religious minorities by pointing out that anti-religious persecution is more widespread. In all such cases the secular right of freedom for the individual is the only effective preventative. The secular State has no vested interest in creating martyrs.

It seems clear that until religious unanimity reigns and man's social institutions can be brought within the range of the sacred without violence to any individual's faith, the secular framework must be accepted, along with the rubs and antagonisms and tensions which necessarily arise between diverse ethical outlooks. In the absence of any 'natural law' which can be confidently appealed to, certain wide areas of agreement must be found on which to carry on social life. Fortunately, good will and human sympathy can create much greater agreement among the followers of different faiths than discursive reasoning can establish in respect to ethical principles. Men can suspend the ethical whenever the urgency of dialogue is taken seriously enough.

CHAPTER EIGHT

PROTESTANT MORALITY:
I. GRACE BEYOND THE LAW

I. THE PLACE OF MORALS IN RELIGION

PROTESTANTISM AND morals go together. The close connexion between the two is not disputed, and most judgements about Protestantism are based on the attitude taken towards Protestant morality. Either Protestants are praised for their 'practical' Christianity, or they are censured for making conduct the whole of faith. It is said that a Catholic will keep his religion even when he loses his morals, while a Protestant will keep his morals after losing his religion. However superficial such generalizations may be, they agree about the prominence of the moral emphasis in Protestantism. There is also a widespread agreement that Protestant morality is of a recognizable type with certain definite features. Its friends say that it is a morality of firm principles which builds character. Those less sympathetic find it narrow, negative, and unlovely, breeding hypocrisy and censoriousness, and leaving in its train a multitude of 'repressions'. In the English-speaking countries this type of moralism is linked with *Puritanism* more particularly than with *Protestantism* as such—but, of course, this Puritanism is Protestant Puritanism. There are Puritan movements outside Protestantism, however, and the prominence of one kind of morality linked to a particular understanding of religion opens up the large question of the relation of religion as such to morality as such.

Although many religions concentrate on ritual acts and seem to have little concern for the ethical aspects of life, yet all influence deeply the day-to-day habits of their devotees and thus, in fact, establish moral values. The 'higher' religions are higher because, among other things, they are more fully self-conscious, and critical awareness inevitably concerns itself with shaping moral codes as well as with developing coherent systems of doctrine. This trend is to be seen in the Bible. Judaism looks back to Mount Sinai and the giving of the Law (which is so prominently ethical as well as ceremonial) as the central event in God's revelation of Himself to Israel. And historical criticism would place the true beginning of Hebrew religion, as a separate faith distinguished from the general pattern of Canaanite religion, with the moral teaching of the eighth-century prophets—the culminating phase of the attempt to free loyalty to Yahweh from the dominant cult of Baal. Christianity, through its conception of the Church as the Israel of the New Covenant, carries on the same ethical tradition. Though superseding the Law by bringing Grace, Jesus is a new Moses (John 1_{17}, Rev. 15_3), whose teaching resembles a new Mosaic Law as it is given upon the mountain (Matt. 5_1); and He carries on the ethical message of the prophets, insisting on the primacy of the ethical over the ceremonial (Matt. 9_{13}, 23_{23}).

Whenever the prophets, bringing a message of ethical reform, teach that God requires mercy and not sacrifice, a tension is at once set up between religion and morality: ethical requirements have been ranged over the ordinances of religion. It is true that this is done in the name of religion. Being *religious* reformers, these men do not propose to abolish the established cultus in the name of morality. Yet the fact remains that true religion is described in terms of enlightened ethical practices and not vice versa. The foundation of moral principles is laid down by the character ascribed to God, but this character is presented as being one which is morally admirable because it conforms to standards considered acceptable to the moral conscience. God is compared with a shepherd, a husband, a parent; and in each case we are asked to see divine goodness in terms of human behaviour. In the New Testament an equilibrium between the ethical and the religious demands is reached in the Great Commandment. This resolution of the tension, seemingly so simple, is a profound statement of the meaning of faith in the moral life, and of morals in the religious life. It underlies that other tension which is so prominent in the New Testament—the opposition between faith and works.

In the Great Commandment, love to God takes precedence over love to man: it is *first*. Similarly, in the Pauline exposition, as Luther saw so clearly, faith justifies apart from works (Rom. 3_{28}) although works follow, exemplified in the love of our fellows, 'for he that loveth another hath fulfilled the law' (Rom. 13_8). The ethical content of Christian faith is abundantly illustrated through the whole of the New Testament, where the practical demonstration of brotherhood is regarded as a test of a right relationship with God. For Jesus, the doing of the brotherly act determines the status of men at the Last Judgement (Matt. $25_{31\,ff.}$), and for the Church of the apostolic age it signifies true participation in the community of faith (James $2_{14\,ff.}$).

Love to man is *second* and derivative (so the Great Commandment states), but it is also inseparable from the love of God.

All social and inter-personal relationships fall under the sphere of morality, so that morality cannot but be a lively concern of religion, since religion claims every dimension of personal existence as its proper sphere. Hebrew religion had been at first, like all primitive religions, so closely bound up with the corporate life of the community that its later course was much taken up with establishing the inwardness of faith, showing that it was an affair of the heart and not of the lips alone, and holding up as an ideal the life of righteousness springing from delight in the Law as well as obedience to it. The emphasis in the teaching of Jesus was laid upon the inadequacy of moral endeavour *of itself* to win merit. He tried to upset the complacency of those who believed that they had fulfilled the Law's requirements, first of all showing that ethical norms must take precedence over ritual requirements, taking up the prophetic insistence upon inwardness. We are defiled from within (Mark $7_{18\,ff.}$ and parallels). From there Jesus went on to undermine belief in righteousness as a status guaranteed by moral achievements, preaching against those who considered themselves to be righteous (Luke 18_9) and teaching that even after doing our duty we are still 'unprofitable' (Luke 17_{10}). Those who would be commended at the Last Judgement for their brotherly love were, according to Jesus, those who had not thought of their actions as being in any way meritorious (Matt. $25_{31\,ff.}$). So the New Testament as a whole exalts the religious category of faith above that of the moral conscience. Even the inwardness which is the essence of the genuinely moral, as opposed to mere ethical conformity, is subordinated to a direct dependence upon a right relationship with God. At the same time, the higher call of faith does not release us from the obligation to obey the moral law.

In *Fear and Trembling* Kierkegaard found in the story of Abraham's call to sacrifice Isaac an example of the religious 'teleological suspension of ethics'. The absolute demands of faith, according to Kierkegaard, here cancelled the relative values of ethical conduct existing only on the social plane. Yet this reading of the Biblical story is only possible if we read as modern Europeans and without all historical understanding. Abraham's testing is in line with other accounts of the trial of men's faith involving sacrifice of what the individual holds dear. That Abraham found the command hard and felt the price of submission costly is certain; there is no indication that he found ethically repulsive the form of the sacrifice demanded.

Religion cannot demand the violation of clear ethical principles. This is not to say that it cannot *appear* to do so. Faith may well call an individual to act against the commonly accepted judgement of what is ethically fitting; yet this will only be to illuminate and develop further ethical insight.[1] Nevertheless, though we may dispute some of the steps by which Kierkegaard reached his conclusions, the case he argues is sound: namely, that the personal response of faith is far removed from the interpretation of life in terms of moral rights and duties, so that, inevitably, it must often appear to be absurd to the latter: Kierkegaard's contention that the dimension of faith establishes itself without necessarily conforming to morality must be granted true—for our consciousness. Faith must transcend the ethical if it is to be distinguished from it. We shall see that religion, when we try to state it in conceptual terms, conflicts with our moral vision.[2] But in so far as our own moral activity is concerned, religion cannot ask us to violate ethical principles without itself losing its authority. The faith which sharpens conscience and gives it authority, is itself judged by conscience wherever moral issues arise. In its social manifestations, religion is proved worthy or unworthy by the morality it teaches.

II. CONFESSIONAL THEOLOGY'S ATTITUDE TO MORALITY

On the face of it, Protestantism's reputation for a militant moralism seems odd. Stressing the all-sufficiency of faith and denying the merit of good works to the degree of being called antinomian, historic Protestantism has nevertheless been associated with an exacting and sometimes harsh discipline covering the whole range of personal and social life. A simple explanation, of course, lies conveniently to hand. Does not one extreme lead to its opposite, and one error produce its counter-error? So it is said that Justification by Faith, if it is not to encourage sinning that Grace may abound, must fall back upon an irrational authoritarianism in moral matters. Grace without law for the soul brings in law without love for the body, and the

---

[1] Oliver Quick has pointed out that the Atonement constitutes an apparent contradiction of the moral ideal of justice. It can only be understood as 'moral' by deepening the understanding of the concept of justice so that it includes more than a demand for 'fairness' (*The Christian Sacraments*, pp. 90–1). We may add that the whole conception of Atonement, as of self-sacrifice, involves more than moral issues and raises the question of the ultimate presuppositions of morality. When morality is taken seriously enough it tends to transcend itself because it seeks to appropriate for itself the ground of its own existence. See on this question Paul Tillich's 'The Transmoral Conscience' (Chapter 9 of *The Protestant Era*, especially pp. 145 ff.).

[2] See Section 3, *infra*.

devil takes over the management of the social realms from which a just God has been expelled.

A danger certainly exists in Protestant concentration upon revelation and rejection of natural law. It is the danger of creating a moral vacuum into which sub-Christian values can enter. Quite apart from the extreme sects, Protestantism has suffered from a tendency to replace a consistent moral philosophy by isolated Scriptural references brought together in a literal and legalistic way. And since Biblical precedence can never cover every aspect of contemporary life, large areas of conduct have been left outside moral direction. The history of political life in the Lutheran German States and of race relations in the Southern States of the U.S.A. and in South Africa show how far wanting Protestant ethics have been in certain important respects. A 'Sunday' religion, without relevance to the week-day world, is also a familiar enough phenomenon within Protestantism to point to a grave weakness in Protestant witness. The Evangelical movements which were so widespread in nineteenth-century Britain did little to mitigate the harshness of the Industrial Revolution.

Yet, however revealing these failures in the moral field may be, they witness to the distortion of Protestantism rather than to its essence. The simple view that would see only error and confusion leaves out of account the great positive achievements of post-Reformation society; and a more candid appeal to history and to the implications of confessional theology presents us with a very different picture. Some of the historical evidence will be reviewed in the next chapter. We must now consider the theological side of the evidence.

To begin with, confessional theology appeals to revelation as contained in Scripture for its point of departure. Although there is no systematic body of moral philosophy to be found there, the close connexion between the service of God and moral righteousness in the biblical record can hardly be overlooked. An objection may follow that, though it cannot be overlooked, yet it can be explained away by mistaken exegesis. The case against Justification is that it does just this. So Maritain pillories Luther:

Behind Luther's appeals to the redeeming Lamb, behind his outbursts of confidence and faith in the forgiveness of sins, there is a human creature which raises its crest and manages very well in the mud in which it is plunged by Adam's sin.[3]

3 Three Reformers, p. 37.

Such criticism turns a blind eye to the way Lutheran and other branches of orthodox Protestant theology emphasize sanctification equally with justification.[4] Confessional theology regards the two as different sides of a single process rather than as two stages in the spiritual life; and this has real force because sanctification has a moral reference, while justification regards the soul's standing with God where moral valuation is strictly out of place. No moral achievement can, by itself, win the free forgiveness of sins which is God's gracious gift. It would not be free if it were earned. No belief in being forgiven is more than self-deception if it does not issue in moral victory. It would not be the gift of God if it did not embody the fruits of the Spirit, which are ethical. The primacy of faith is given in the prevenient Grace which is 'first' because external good actions, to have moral worth, must have their origin in an inward movement of the Spirit.

The subordination of morality to faith no more makes morals superfluous than the subordination of religious authority to the personal reception of revelation makes authority in faith arbitrary. Both are fundamental elements in a theology which finds its centre in God's Self-revelation to His people. God is related to the whole personality, and morality takes its place within that whole without usurping the place of the inward subjectivity or 'singleness' where the individual stands before God. Just because people are more than bundles of impulses and interests, it is impossible to separate these elements from the individuals they belong to, and still find a moral agent or a believing soul. The unity of personal existence is seen from the fact (considered above) that a right relationship with God— the relationship of faith—cannot be proved apart from its effects in ethical action. 'By their fruits ye shall know them', said Jesus (Matt. 7_20). It is seen also by another fact closely related to the first one, namely, that the need for faith is proved by moral failure. The discovery that, though we intend to do good our will seems impotent to follow the promptings of conscience, is a moral experience of Christian and non-Christian alike. 'I see and approve better things, but follow worse', says Ovid in his *Metamorphoses*, and St Paul enlarges on the same theme (Rom. 7_15 ff.). The Christian, being obliged to refer his moral experience to his religious understanding, interprets moral inadequacy in terms of disobedience to God's will. 'For I delight in the law of God after the inward man', Paul comments,

---

[4] Watson notes how even Wesley misunderstood Luther's view of sanctification (*Let God be God*, p. 171).

'but I see another law in my members . . . the law of sin' (Rom. 7$_{22-3}$).

Sin—the anti-law to the law of God—is not properly a moral term. When we talk of a sin against society or a sin against truth we lend a metaphorical personality to truth and the social order, for no one sins in the exact sense of the word except against the divine law, and so against the divine Lawgiver. But the law of sin would remain unrecognized by the individual were he never conscious of particular moral lapses, of doing things which society and his social conscience condemn. The pattern of repeated lapses leads him to admit a defect permeating his whole personality, a defect more than moral in range because it reaches beyond what he ought to *do* to what he ought to *be*. Society can arraign him for being immoral, but only a holy God can communicate to him a conviction of sin. Sin differs from all other law-breaking by its absolute character.

This discovery that moral inadequacy is bound up with spiritual needs is the starting-point of confessional theology's understanding of morality. Confessional theology does not hope to solve its moral problems through any moral theory, because it does not find that moral conduct can be adequately approached through morality taken by itself. It does not even consider that the moral law is self-evident, or that conscience reflects the truths of natural law, and so what the individual needs is supernatural grace to enable him to carry out what the law demands. In rejecting the notion of natural law and natural virtues, Protestantism seeks for the clue to right conduct in a right relationship to God, believing that a right relationship to our neighbour will follow. The Protestant does not seek to live without law just because he believes that Christians can live by the grace which is beyond law. Positive law—the law of the land—is necessary for every human society, and the various institutions of society (including the Church) must have their own laws by means of which they can function as organizations. But none of these forms of law is complete or absolute in itself. As nature is not to be understood without revelation, so morality is not to be understood without the grace which constantly transforms the moral situation and shows to be inadequate every attempt to fix the moral law in order to give it finality of form. In place of rigid moral precepts, Protestant moral theology looks to the Spirit for moral understanding according to the mind of Christ. Since the Great Commandment of Christian morality is the commandment of love, legalism as such is transcended in the Christian life.

III. THE MORAL AND RELIGIOUS SPHERES OF INTEREST

There is an inevitable tension between the claims of morality and the claims of faith. The moralist, who wishes men to be virtuous, sees in religion a possible ally which also exhorts its followers to live the good life. But the moralist is also aware of a different emphasis in the exhortation, because religion wishes men to be sinless—which is not the same as being virtuous, even if it approximates to it. Morality takes its social reference as a final criterion, whereas religion looks beyond social ills and social health to the will of God in His creation. The theoretical discipline of ethics, equally with practical morality, is bound to morality's social reference, even though its first concern is to define and delimit moral conduct and not to inspire it. Ethics cannot concern itself wholly with moral *persons*, but must concern itself with moral *acts*. Religious consciousness may find that he who hates his brother is a murderer (1 John 3$_{15}$) and both the deed and the intention equally damning evidence of sin. But the moralist, while admitting the truth of the religious claim that inward attitudes cause external acts, is bound to rate very differently the man who only feels an urge to kill and the man with blood on his hands. In this respect, positive law is only a particular application of ethical thinking. The law recognizes acts alone as falling within its jurisdiction. It cannot call the hater to account, except for those deeds which have been prompted by his hatred and which are explicitly accounted criminal. Guilt before the law is acquired by 'sinning' against an external rule which carries its prescribed penalties. Yet even the law, in judging the act, recognizes that it is dealing with a moral agent; people, not acts, are sent to prison or fined. The law distinguishes various degrees of guilt in respect of the same act. A man may kill while insane, or to defend himself, or when grievously provoked, or in 'hot blood', or as a habitual killer. In each case, the law will take *circumstances* into account, i.e. it will examine the context of the act to decide the degree of responsibility in the agent.

Moralists are thus bound to find religion wanting in the distributive and quantitative aspects of conduct which bulk so largely in social morality. A moralist is compelled, either explicitly or implicitly, to judge individual morality in its social context. Religion is concerned first of all with human guilt in its universality, and only secondarily with specific wrongdoing. Indeed, both divine holiness and human sin, in primitive religions, are bound up with ritual acts which seem to bear little relation to moral conduct and may often be opposed to moral enlightenment and social well-being. But, even where religion becomes the inspiration of morality instead of an obstacle to the education of conscience, its call to men to be holy is never simply a demand that they shall behave morally. Hence the suspicion with which the moral philosopher regards the theologian; for what is all-important to the one is peripheral to the other. This is particularly the case in regard to Protestant theology, which has always been averse to the legalistic weighing of degrees of guilt by means of casuistry and has not attempted to make any definitive union between moral theology and one particular ethical system. 'Liberal' Protestantism at times has tended to join hands with the moral interest and speak as though the Kingdom of God were to be identified with the ideal society, but this tendency has usually been countered by a vigorous reaction. Neo-orthodox Protestantism, complains H. D. Lewis, depreciates individual responsibility and the moral predicament by insisting upon the universal condition of sin and guilt.[5] It is the old cry of 'Obscurantism!' raised whenever religion takes its own categories of thought seriously enough to disentangle them from the moralists' similar-seeming ones.

If ethics and theology clash when they view human behaviour, we ought perhaps to consider whether psychology can settle the issue, since psychology investigates the mechanisms of the mind which give rise to notions of right and wrong, guilt and sin. Like religion, psychology is concerned with the whole person and not with the status of separate acts or intentions. In this respect the psychologist is not interested in ethical questions, so that, more often than not, moralists and psychologists seem to be opposed to each other. The psychologist judges the quality of acts in the light of their reaction upon mental health, and he has no particular desire to have men conform willy-nilly to one particular code.[6] Being an inquirer into the subjective origins of beliefs about human conduct and the motivation of acts, he may well not accept as proven the fact of human responsibility and thus be sceptical of the whole dimension of moral action. When psychiatrists are called in to help with a criminal charge, judges and others involved are often reluctant to accept their findings on the question of whether the accused was responsible for his actions. Very understandably, the agents of law have reservations

---

[5] *Morals and the New Theology*, Chapter 5, 'Universal Sin', and Chapter 6, 'Collective Responsibility'.

[6] Because of this freedom from upholding the standards of morality obtaining in contemporary society, Tillich classes depth psychology with religion in its appreciation of the transmoral conscience (*The Protestant Era*, p. 149).

about the psychiatrists' conception of what is involved in being morally responsible, even though they may respect their professional
opinion about a condition of mind which their technical knowledge
alone can classify. The psychologist possesses special information
which is useful in forming correct moral judgements. Yet possession of
that knowledge does not in itself mean that correct judgements will in
fact be made. The psychologist does not supersede the moral thinker.

Psychologists are sometimes prone to over-simplify the relationship of their science to morality, claiming that they stand for
'scientific detachment' as opposed to the emotionally based preconceptions of the moralists. It is true that a scientific training
greatly helps to get rid of the stock responses and conventional ideas
which commonly cloud the moral vision. All the same, a psychologist, though he may perhaps personally accept a theory of the mind
which denies the objectivity of moral judgements, must always work
within the framework of some moral standard or other. If he holds
the view that a particular wrong-doer *ought* not to be punished, this
view cannot be derived from his belief that the man could not have
helped acting as he did, but only from adopting the moral principle
that society *ought* to re-educate its unruly members to observe the
laws instead of breaking them, or else that society *ought not* to make
such laws and expect its members without exception to obey them.
The moral judgement is simply transferred from the individual to
the collective group. Somewhere, the *ought* is imported and thus the
ethical is brought into the psychological picture. Similarly, when
psychology passes judgement upon the claims of religion to speak
about man being in a state of guilt due to sin, or being saved by
grace, its judgement cannot be a purely psychological one. Usually
it makes use of moral values in the process of its analysis. Thus it
may disapprove of religion for generating feelings of guilt among its
devotees, or it may support a religious faith which proves useful in
decreasing neurosis. It will then be building on the moral premise
that integrated personalities are socially desirable and that neurotic
persons are cases to be cured and made socially profitable. From the
vantage-point of a particular psychological theory psychology may
claim to be able to 'explain' and evaluate both religious systems and
moral convictions, but in practice it is forced to adopt a moral
standard as a norm of judgement. The psychological critique of
morality is always at bottom another moral theory, and the psychological critique of religion is always a valuation of religion in moral
terms.

The moralist, whether he wear the cloak of philosopher or of psychologist, is unable to cope with the categories of guilt and sin, although he is at home with the related concepts of personal responsibility for wrong-doing and moral failure. The moral and the religious spheres of interest lie near together, but there is a great gulf fixed between them. How much theology is a stumbling-block to the moralist is sometimes obvious, sometimes disguised. If liberal Protestantism has been willing to make a common cause with moral endeavour, evangelical-pietistic Protestantism has been willing to offend it. Protestantism here has only inherited a tension evident throughout the history of Christianity. Christianity is beyond all question a religion which takes morality seriously. But does it therefore put morality first? The issue was first unmistakably stated in Christian theology when Augustine opposed Pelagius.

Pelagius interpreted the Christian faith as a moral struggle in which God strengthened the moral will; Augustine interpreted faith as the demonstration of the ways of God with men in granting them the will they needed by His gift of irresistible grace. Pelagius, with all moralists, insisted on individual freedom and responsibility as the prerequisite of moral endeavour, and he was scandalized by Augustine's seeming denial of the very basis of morality. Augustine's insistence that it is precisely our will—the motive-power of the total personality—which is beyond our control, was an assertion of the supra-moral dimension of religion. When later Catholic theology tried to reconcile the moral interest with the religious, saying that both the primacy of grace in moving the will and the freedom of the will to turn to receive grace were equally real, the radical assertion of religion's claims against the supremacy of the moral interest passed to Protestantism. Luther wrote about the *Enslaved Will* against Erasmus's treatise on the freedom of the will. Calvinism has become popularly identified with the denial of free-will contained in the second edition of the *Institutes*, and still today members of the Reformed Churches are to be found complaining that Lutheranism concedes too much to human freedom.[7] Against the semi-Pelagianism of post-Tridentine Rome, Jansenism tried unsuccessfully to maintain an unadulterated Augustinianism within the orbit of Catholicism. Through the genius of Pascal, Jansenism had an influence upon later Protestant thought, which was wider than its distinctive tenets.

[7] As Barth does in *Credo* (1936), p. 196.

IV. THE MORAL SCANDAL OF PREDESTINATION

The conflict of the moral and the religious interests is shown so vividly in the question of predestination *versus* free-will that we may profitably digress to look at this issue. Religious belief in the providential rule of God as naturally expresses itself in the doctrine of predestination as moral belief in human responsibility expresses itself in the theory of free-will. And the two cannot be made to agree.

Since ethical ideas lie closer to a common-sense view of the world than theological ones—or, at least, seem to do so for most people who have learnt to think about things in general—the issue of predestination creates something of a scandal whenever it is raised. This is no modern prejudice. St Paul felt the force of the moral objection when he wrote of God's predestinating ordinances, and he was driven to resort to the (ethically) inadequate argument that God, like a potter with his clay, cannot be judged by human moral standards (Rom. $9_{18\,ff.}$). When Calvin adopted the theology of predestination and irresistible grace from Paul and Augustine, he recognized the need also to assert individual responsibility, and so he argued that the wickedness of those destined to perdition arose from the evil within those persons and was not caused by the divine Decrees.[8] Augustine before him had been content to use a similar argument.[9] The widespread belief that Calvin was being extravagantly and wilfully perverse over predestination[10] substitutes an assumption of moral superiority for a readiness to face the issues involved. Calvin was not prepared to assert, any more than other Christian theologians before or since, that God is the direct cause of evil, even though this seems to be implied in several passages of the Old Testament.[11] But he was at least consistent in preserving the primacy of the religious interest which makes God's will the source of all events, not least those where human wills are involved.

T. S. Eliot has asserted that the Calvinists, by emphasizing the degradation of man through original sin, 'thus fell into the doctrine of predestination'.[12] The condescending tone of the remark is un-

---

[8] *Institutes*, Bk. III, Chapter 23.8.

[9] *City of God*, Bk. XII, Chapters 1 and 6.

[10] Thus Maurice Cranston cites Calvin's reply to his critics, 'Who art thou that repliest against God?' as a proof of Calvin's personal arrogance (*Freedom: a New Analysis*, pp. 118–19), though Calvin was giving St Paul's own answer to objections raised against predestination and giving it in direct quotation from Romans 9_{20}.

[11] For example: 2 Sam. $24_{1,\,15}$, 1 Kings 22_{23}, Amos 3_6.

[12] Preface to Pascal's *Pensées* (Everyman's Library edn., 1931), p. xvi. The doctrine of total depravity has no necessary connexion with the doctrine of predestina-

fortunate, for *falling into the doctrine of predestination* must be taken as an equivalent phrase for *engaging in theology*, since it would be hard to imagine any serious theology from which the conception was absent. Predestination is an implicate of the doctrine of divine Providence, which itself arises whenever man is confronted with the living God. A God whose will is not effective both in space and time cannot be God except in name.

Not long ago several eminent thinkers favoured the idea of 'emergent deity'. From the theological point of view such a 'God' should rather be called a *daemon*, i.e. a mixture of human and divine, bearing a divine principle yet part of creation since it develops in time along with creation itself. Yet even so theologically inadmissible an idea as the *god-who-is-to-be* witnesses to the central place of predestination in all religious thinking. For the only reason for fixing upon some aspect of the universe and calling it *God* is to secure a conviction that somehow or other the process of creation is destined to display the victory of good over evil—and indeed exists for that very purpose. The Universe is ascending spiritually as it wastes physically, says Whitehead.[13] How does he know this? He will not admit an omnipotent God for fear of falling into the doctrine of predestination, for he sees that the two go together without fail. But, he says, though not omnipotent yet, God is growing more nearly omnipotent every day! History is on His side!

This transmutation of evil into good enters into the actual world by reason of the inclusion of the nature of God, which includes the ideal vision of each actual evil so met with a novel consequence as to issue in the restoration of goodness.[14]

Whitehead's abstract terminology here gives us nothing more than a paraphrase of Tennyson's optimistic belief in some 'scheme of things' as described in *Locksley Hall*:

tion, though, of course, the Calvinist *statement* of predestination is presented in terms of the former doctrine, and more 'optimistic' views of man's nature after the Fall are anxious to preserve human independence under God's providential rule. As Calvin pointed out, the desire to avoid predestination springs from the wish to harmonize the claims of religion with philosophical views of man's dignity as a free moral agent.

[13] *Religion in the Making* (1926), p. 144.

[14] ibid., p. 139. Whitehead deplored the habit of paying God 'metaphysical compliments' (*Science and the Modern World*, p. 222). Yet his God is no more than a metaphysical construction—its other name being the *Principle of Concretion*. It is strange that Whitehead should wish to pay the *Principle* a religious compliment, and most of all that of calling it *God*. But then, a principle only illustrates a law; while God, through His predestinating power, ensures that law brings about some specific result. And it is the result which Whitehead desires to have guaranteed above all.

Yet I doubt not thro' the ages one increasing purpose runs,
And the thoughts of men are widen'd with the process of the suns.

When belief in an almighty God decays, men still cling to the notion of an indubitable Providential order.

Thus the doctrine of predestination is so necessary a consequence of belief in God's rule over His creation that even a God who does not rule is still called upon to function as some sort of a predestinating power. Another side of the same picture can be seen in the persistent conviction which grips all kinds of people, making them think of themselves as being passive instruments to carry out the designs of a predestinating Will over-ruling all individual human wills. Irrespective of creed upheld or scepticism professed, this religious consciousness keeps on reappearing. And it is essentially religious whether the predestinating Will be named God, Fate, Necessity, the Will to Power, or the Life Force. It is seen in Thomas Hardy and Bernard Shaw as well as in the Greek dramatists. It expresses itself through Matthew Arnold's tentative appeal to 'the enduring power, not ourselves, which makes for righteousness' as well as through the Marxist's fighting faith in the dialectic of history. What will be, will be. But, more than that, what will be *must be right*, because the Will which foresees and ordains is itself the source and standard of all good.

At the same time, all forms of predestination present an offence to the moral understanding, finding (as we have seen) no room for that free-will which is the foundation of morality. Catholic theology has tried to reconcile moral and religious demands by holding that human acts can be initiated both by God and by free-will in the agent. Yet, in so far as predestination is asserted, free-will is inevitably made into a mere appearance; while in so far as the will is made self-determining the prior will of God is made ineffective.[15] For free-will is, by definition, that which is not bound by any other consideration, including the Providential order. Although here, as in other cases, the intellect is readily lulled into accepting a wedding of incompatibles because of the mental discomfort of admitting a plain paradox, for-

[15] Calvin was surely right in insisting that the issue cannot be side-tracked by reducing predestination to foreknowledge. God is not a spectator merely. Nor is it satisfactory simply to say that men live in time and God beyond time, as C. S. Lewis does in his *Miracles* (1947) in the Appendix 'On Special Providences' (pp. 208 ff.). This simply reduces time and free-will together to a mere appearance. Lewis also uses the analogy of an author writing a book, and making his characters behave according to their nature. But there is no place here for free-will. Who but the author is responsible for Mr X being saintly and Mr Y being weak and cowardly?

tunately the imagination is less easily deceived. In *A Defence of Poetry* Shelley pointed out how impossible it is to reconcile the God pictured in *Paradise Lost* with moral values:

Implacable hate, patient cunning, and a sleepless refinement of device to inflict the extremest anguish on an enemy, these things are evil . . . Milton's Devil as a moral being is as far superior to his God, as one who perseveres in some purpose which he has conceived to be excellent in spite of adversity and torture, is to one who in the cold security of undoubted triumph inflicts the most horrible revenge upon his enemy, not from any mistaken notion of inducing him to repent of a perseverence in enmity, but with the alleged design of exasperating him to deserve new torments.

Morality depends for its very existence upon the reality of the struggle of good against evil. Where, as in Milton's epic, what is styled *evil* fights against omnipotence, there can be no true struggle, and so omnipotence cannot be presented as *good*. War in heaven, like war on earth, can be conceived to be just only where there is a righteous cause in real danger of defeat. Morality demands an ultimate dualism of light against darkness. And religion cannot tolerate such dualism.

The opposition between predestinating omnipotent Will and moral freedom has appeared again in another form for the modern world. It is seen in the clash between ethical thinking and the scientific dogma of universal causality. Here the doctrine of predestination has been taken out of the sphere of theology and impersonalized as the rule of Law. But the result is the same, so far as morality is concerned. No moralist can afford to admit that the universe is an unbroken nexus of cause and effect where no new cause can arise spontaneously; just as no natural scientist can afford to admit that nature is essentially irrational and incapable of being reduced to orderly processes. Hence the eagerness with which some ethical thinkers and many religious ones have grasped at the scientists' admission of 'indeterminacy', however limited and problematical the evidence for this may be. Those who represent religious interests are the more anxious to do this because religion asserts the need for a Law-giver behind any 'law of nature', and equally must preserve the reality of moral action. Yet the theologian who is concerned to combat at once Deism and fatalism in the name of faith should beware of putting his trust in today's scientific hypotheses which will be modified or abandoned tomorrow. Scientific data alone cannot establish or refute these philosophies. It is naïve, also, to regard indeterminacy in physics as a victory for faith. An unpredict-

able universe may well be a self-sufficient universe, requiring no
Creator and governed by no Providence; while the outlook of the
scientist who believes in an inter-locking system of unalterable laws
governing the least part of the whole is by no means incompatible
with theological truth. For the scientist who assumes the rule of law
in nature also takes for granted that he can discover the truth about
these laws and make their manipulation for human betterment possible. In other words, he believes both in determinism and in freedom.
In the same way, the theologian believes in God's Providence and
also in the fact of human obedience and disobedience to His omnipotent will.

Moralists, confronted by scientific determinism, may take refuge
in the argument that determinism has not been proved to be complete and universal. This is the conclusion reached by Maurice
Cranston in *Freedom: a New Analysis*; and he admits it to be an unsatisfactory one. Or they may dogmatically state that moral experience is indubitable, and that therefore freedom must be granted to
the will before any human interpretation of experience can begin;
and that is perhaps the better way. Similarly, theologians who are
also moralists have a choice before them of simply asserting man's
responsibility for his actions as a given fact, or of saying that God's
Providential rule is not universal, but is restricted so as to allow scope
for human freedom. This latter view, however, tends to assume that
moral achievement is the really important thing, and that human
freedom is that which all creation has been groaning and travail-
ing to produce. Leonard Hodgson, for instance, has argued that
what we know of the evolution of life on this planet indicates that
God intends men to discover 'perfect finite freedom'.[16] God, it seems,
is like a stage manager who arranges the scene so that the actors in
the theatre of History can play their parts as they choose.

Any theory which conceives human freedom to be an absolute
value has surely fallen short of a truly religious vision of life. Leonard
Hodgson thinks that the doctrine of predestination is a deduction
from the bare idea of omnipotence.[17] But this ignores its very close
connexion with the doctrine of grace in Christian theology. In St
Paul and those who followed him, grace was the leading and con-
trolling concept, and predestination followed from it. The paradox

[16] *Towards a Christian Philosophy* (1942), Chapter 6, 'Freedom, Grace and Providence'. Hodgson's views are precisely those which Calvin opposed when he
argued that God does not simply prepare man's heart so that he can afterwards 'do
some good of himself'.

[17] ibid., p. 148 n.

of the will, free to disobey Omnipotence, yet enslaved to sin until freed by no power of its own, is rooted deeply in the heart of the Gospel, and no moral categories are adequate to resolve it.

V. MORAL FREEDOM AND MORAL EFFORT

Free will depends upon the ability to make real choices. A moral agent, to be moral, must stand between good and evil and be capable of choosing one and rejecting the other. This is the moral viewpoint; but religion takes another stand. To the religious sense 'true' freedom lies in being completely subject to the holy will of God and in being incapable of sinning. This religious sense of freedom has continually irrupted into philosophy. To any one with an ethical outlook the notion that freedom can be defined in terms of recognizing necessity, or even that it can be defined as a positive freedom *to*, instead of a negative freedom *from*, seems an inexcusable misuse of language and a wilful obscurantism.[18] Yet the persistence of such types of thinking point to the fact that if morality is to be justified it can only become so in terms of that which transcends its own categories. To say that we stand between good and evil had meaning only if good and evil themselves have a positive meaning. In order to discover such a meaning, ethics necessarily has to fall back upon some metaphysics of value, and so enters the same area as theology. Here the question as to whether man is free to choose between two alternative courses of action gives place to the question as to whether he can achieve what is good, and where good is to be found. Though it might be assumed (as some ethical thinkers take for granted) that what is good is a purely ethical concern, philosophers since the time of Socrates have been by no means willing to believe this to be so. And religion has always claimed that it alone holds the key to the problem of good and evil.

In this regard, Kant's analysis of moral freedom is extremely illuminating. Kant begins by assuming that there is no need to believe that freedom is part of the natural order of the universe as man observes it. Yet, since moral conduct is real, freedom of the will exists. This freedom is a freedom *from* causal necessity. Although Kant asserts that the two realms of necessity and freedom are compatible because they belong to different orders, he does not in fact demonstrate their compatibility. Though it is, of course, possible to

[18] Maurice Cranston, who investigates freedom as a moral ideal (op. cit., Chapter I), emphatically rejects what he calls *rational* and *rational-compulsive* definitions of freedom. See *supra*, p. 153, n. 26.

argue that every action may be wholly conditioned and predictable *phenomenally* and at the same time be *noumenally* free, the argument assumes that the two orders never meet. Clearly, no predictable action is free in the sense of being a choice between two possible courses of action. Kant's determination to uphold the course of law in the physical universe and of freedom in the moral universe is similar to that of the theologian who posits the simultaneous existence of Providence and of moral effort. But Kant does not only see freedom as freedom *from* determinism; he also sees it as freedom *to* obey the moral law. Freedom has its own causality, and here it is bound to obey its own nature. While Kant speaks of the law of freedom as being self-legislating, this freedom *to* is in no sense a matter of a choice between alternative courses; it is strictly an inability to legislate other than according to the rule of right. The good will which it is possible for man to exhibit stands under the holy will of God, although the latter is for ever inaccessible to frail humanity. In this second view of freedom according to its own essence, Kant shifts from the moral to the religious view of freedom and goodness. In the latter view the primacy of choice as the meaning of freedom drops out of the picture and is replaced by a conception of obedience to a call to holiness. This departure is all the more remarkable because Kant is wholly concerned to keep within the circle of moral ideas and has no place for religious faith as such.

Historically, belief in the religious call to obedience has been much more productive of moral effort than belief in freedom of choice has been. Mohammedanism, Calvinism, and Communism are known as highly militant faiths, while hinayana Buddhism, which (being atheistic) gives unqualified freedom to the will, has been remarkably quietistic and pacific. The Ethical Societies show no ambition to turn the world upside down. It is religion and the religious interest that, for good or evil, really display the will in action. After all, once the will has been directed to a particular course, there is no need for debate about its freedom of choice. Since they claim to know what is ultimately good, religions are all to some degree intolerant, even when they are world-denying and theologically accommodating, as Hinduism is. They exist to demonstrate the effectiveness of the moral will and not its uncertainty, while they direct moral valuation by an appeal going beyond morality itself.

The religious interest unchecked by ethical insight, however, brings only energy and single-mindedness to bear on matters of conduct. Religion's responsibility for encouraging moral blindness is all too evident. *Tantum religio potuit suadere malorum*. Achieving holiness may mean committing or condoning enormous crimes. Those who are united by a common faith also come to think of themselves as the children of Light and of all who differ from them as children of Darkness. The difference between belief and unbelief is so all-important to them that it tends to wipe out, as of no account, all other differences. And so what is done by the faithful 'for the faith' must be right, irrespective of its moral quality. In the *Inferno* Dante, after giving a solemn promise to Friar Alberigo to free his eyes from the icy tears which cover them, at once breaks his promise, making the casual comment, 'to be rude to him was courtesy'. Such complacency in sheer immorality is characteristic of that religious outlook which regards holiness alone as determining moral virtue. There is never a lack of those who think that killing their fellows is the best way of doing God service.

Religion may often make its followers morally unenlightened. But it must also be remembered that the goal of religion is not at all the same as the goal of morality. The gifts that piety seeks to obtain—peace, joy, victory, blessings, riches of the spirit, and the like—may look like the ends which a moral philosopher would deem desirable, but all of them are to be interpreted in a very different sense from the values 'of the world'. The very choice of words is founded in paradox. Religious blessedness has no more than a slender connexion with the ethical conception of happiness. Faith finds strength made perfect in weakness, and freedom in absolute obedience; it is rich when poor, and at peace in the midst of strife. The two cities which Augustine described, the earthly and the heavenly, go their predestined ways; the one miserable in its seeming prosperity, the other rejoicing in its seeming misery. So Augustine can write: 'That the saints in their loss of things temporal lose not anything at all.'[19] This transvaluation of values is integral to the spiritual vision and constitutes a true 'teleological suspension of ethics'.

Of course, no personal experience of the blessings of faith can justify an attempt to impose religious values upon any society by any process of law, either secular or ecclesiastical, when these values negate the values of morality. It is blatant hypocrisy to oppose social reform on the grounds that wealth makes sanctity difficult and that poverty is beneficial to the souls of the poor. Because religion urges men to live according to supra-moral standards, this too often becomes an excuse for those who profess a religious faith to avoid the

[19] *The City of God*, title of Bk. I, Chapter 9.

demands of morality altogether. This kind of unethical religiosity on the part of the Pharisees called forth from Jesus the rebuke: 'These ought ye to have done, and not to leave the other undone' (Matt. 23$_{23}$).

If the energy of religion is not divorced from moral effort, it is released for the better prosecution of moral ends. Those ends may be unenlightened, and then the result is the ugly phenomenon of religious fanaticism. Communism today has become an enemy to humanity, less because of being an inflexible dogmatic theory which closes men's minds than because of being a disciplined way of life which hardens men's hearts. The Class morality preached by Communism, and invested with infallibility as part of the Communist creed, is inhuman because it subordinates every moral standard to the good of the Party. Faith and morals—religion and ethics combined—cover so large a part of human life (indeed the greater part of all existence which is specifically human) that a faith with a moral mission is one of the most powerful agents of violent social change. The spreading force of Communism the Western world watches now has its parallel in the spread of Islam in the seventh and eighth centuries, and the Christian Church itself was by far the most important factor in bringing Western civilization into being.

Protestants inherited from Catholicism, with its ideal of Catholic Christendom, the belief that doctrinal unanimity within the believing community must embrace detailed codes both of faith and morals, and only gradually have they won through to a moral perspective free from legalism. For the most part, the Bible was used by them as the final objective test of the rightness of a moral judgement. Thus, in the issue of slavery, both the abolitionists and their opponents could appeal to the same authority to support their case. Yet legalism, the ethically limited vision of the spiritually hidebound, was not—in spite of all appearances—the most typical aspect of Protestantism. Reformation faith lapsed too often into theological scholasticism and religiously tinged moralism, but it had begun as a union of religious and ethical concern such as had informed the prophetic movement in Judaism. This dual drive is exemplified in Luther's attack upon Papal indulgences. And in spite of sad declensions, that faith never disappeared wholly. To have 'the mind of Christ' in order to follow the pattern of the Biblical ordinances was the aim of the Reformers, and not vice versa. Discipline, the training in good works which, though they could not save, were evidences of a state of salvation, was a consequence of this attitude. The Puritans, who gained their title as a result of their concern for pure doctrine, soon became recognized by their scruples concerning pure conduct.

Puritanism, as a branch of Protestantism and by no means an untypical one, has been held up as a horrid example of a narrow and negative morality stifling the natural instincts. Some of the strictures levelled against the Puritans are justifiable, although very many are based on historical misapprehension and blame Protestant theology or social habits and perspectives which were commonly accepted by every one at the time. But just as the theology of grace and faith expounded by the Reformers showed a way, from the very start, by which Protestantism could free itself from exclusive theological intolerance, so this same theology in its moral aspect pointed the way beyond fanaticism in ethical matters to the refinement of conduct which should renew Western society and lead to the advancement of humanitarianism and social progress. Protestantism, particularly in its Puritan form, has been the architect of much today that we take for granted as being 'civilized behaviour'. The moral effort put into effect by the Reformation has left its mark on the conscience of modern man. The Protestant takes for granted that religion entails a moral challenge. And that he should accept as self-evident what is by no means a universal assumption is a proof of an undeniable achievement of the religious consciousness.

VI. THE PROTESTANT VIEW OF THE RELATION OF FAITH TO MORALS

In the social realm Protestantism separates faith from ethical precepts in order to ensure individual freedom. But in the personal realm it makes plain that ethics stand under faith. It regards the Catholic approach to moral knowledge (which is to add the supernatural virtues to the natural and thus give a Christian overlay to pagan-classical moral theory) as an inadequate way to establish Christian standards of right and wrong. The Protestant theologian does not try to know nature apart from grace, but interprets nature in the light of grace. Similarly, the Protestant moral theologian does not try to interpret morality apart from revelation, but finds the meaning of human goodness in the Incarnate Christ.

In the New Testament practical ethical instruction is found side by side with the Gospel story: a *didaché* linked with the *kerygma*.[20] Since the Incarnation had initiated a new relationship between God

---

[20] See C. H. Dodd, *Gospel and Law. The Relation of Faith and Ethics in Early Christianity* (1951), Chapter 1.

and man, that relationship is crucial in all matters, and most certainly for every aspect of conduct. Granted that the Old Covenant stands behind the New and that the way for grace is prepared by the giving of the law, yet the Great Commandment makes clear that the New Commandment of love puts the whole subject of guilt and innocence before the law in another dimension. Living by grace, the Christian is no longer under the tutorship of the law, but has achieved a new standing with God and with his fellows (Gal. $3_{24-5, 28}$). Being one in Christ, Christians walk in a new and living way characterized by the works of love (Heb. 10_{20-4}).

One of the marks of this new relationship with God is that the external sanctions of the law, with the objective certainty of the law that knows no exceptions, is gone for ever. The near-certainty which casuistry tries to establish, seeking to find out how the law bears on each individual case with its complicating individual factors, is equally ruled out. The unique quality of the single individual and his personal destiny now stands for something that cannot be discounted by a legalism thinking of individuality only as something problematic and indeterminate to be set under a general rule. In the New Testament we can see how difficult and dangerous the early Church found this supra-legal freedom to be. All the internal problems of the young Christian community, as well as questions of its external relations with its parent Judaism and with an environing paganism, were pressing in upon it. Issues of economics and sexual ethics, of circumcision and food taboos, of Church order and doctrine, of standards of membership and of obedience to the civil authorities —all these had to be settled. How St Paul cherished a 'word of the Lord' which could serve as a new law to settle things once and for all! From the Gospels themselves it is evident that the teaching of Jesus was presented there in a form which would give assistance in the local congregation's practical difficulties.[21] Yet, though guiding rules were found, derived if need be from tradition ('We have no such custom, neither the churches of God') (1 Cor. 11_{16}), or from *ad hoc* common-sense stipulations ('This we commanded you, that if any would not work, neither should he eat') (2 Thess. 3_{10}), the liberty of the man in Christ was paramount. Personal and social ethics were regulated by the love which was an inward possession, given direction by imitation of the Lord's example (1 Cor. 11_1, Phil. 2_5, 1 Pet. 2_{21}, *passim*).

Protestantism, seeking to model its ethical existence upon the

---

[21] See, for instance, G. D. Kilpatrick, *The Origins of the Gospel according to St Matthew* (1946), Chapter 6.

New Testament model, has found all the difficulties experienced in New Testament times and made most of the mistakes recorded of the young churches in which Paul worked. Protestantism's ugliest feature has been its frequent relapse into literalism, usually caused by making a fetish of biblical authority and by the attempt to establish an objectively provable orthodoxy. Its finest achievement has been that of bringing the standard of inwardness to bear on the whole dimension of life, thus encouraging spiritual sensibility which could permeate the body of society at large.

Personal piety, devotion to ideals, heroic service and self-sacrifice do not admit of competition. No Protestant would wish for a moment to claim any superiority in these things over Catholics—or indeed over non-Christians. We can only be thankful for all that shines with splendour in a dark world, whatever its origin. Every tradition has its roll of saints which is its true glory and pride. Every tradition has also its record of evil and shame. If we like to think that our own cause compares in some respects favourably with others, the reason for rejoicing may be an accident of history rather than the result of any innate righteousness. 'We Baptists have never persecuted', Spurgeon, the great Baptist preacher, is reported to have said at a meeting; and, when the applause had died down, he added, 'We never had the chance'. But, without making any tendentious claims to having been right where others were wrong, Protestant morality, imperfect as history shows it to have been, has had some qualities which have contributed to ethical progress. It has shown these qualities when, under God, it has been true to the Protestant conception of grace beyond the law. Out of the theological principle that we do not possess the truth, and can only approximate to truth as we stand under the Gospel and can share the mind of Christ, comes the possibility of lessening the evil we perpetuate by our moral blindness. For this principle is very relevant to the moral life.

Just as Protestantism does not think of faith as accepting a number of dogmatic propositions, so it does not think of virtue as obeying a certain number of approved precepts. Taking seriously the unity of faith and works as two sides of a single process to which faith provides the key, it does not hope to achieve the good by first finding out what is good and then aiming at it (as almost every moral philosopher assumes to be the only possible method),[22] but instead seeks to

---

[22] Kant here again is an exception. He insists on the 'paradox' of the concept of the good and the evil not being definable prior to the moral law, and of the moral law being the means by which good and evil are themselves defined.

obey God as His will is revealed. Law always appears as a series of definite commands, objective and unambiguously defined. Grace is quite another matter and takes quite another form. The form of grace can only be that of a relationship in which dialogue takes place on the level of subjectivity. The objective command on this basis is transformed into a personal authority which is recognized and given rightful respect only to the degree to which dialogue is successfully maintained. There is always room for misunderstanding and always the opportunity for more perfect understanding. Following this way of dialogue, Protestantism can never lay down any moral prescriptions which must be followed implicitly by all people at all times, although this is the ideal which rational moralists and religious legalists aspire to. The Protestant will rather be compelled to say 'Yes' to one moral course of action which is proposed and 'No' to another, the basis of his action being loyalty to what he believes to be God's will for him at one particular time. If charged with lack of principle or the subjectivity of his choice, he can only answer that there is no other course open to him and no surer guide than the One who speaks with the command of love. Any other course must result in separating the life of faith and the life of good works and in making the latter control the former. The virtuous life is no independent pattern, operating by a law of its own, but is faith itself issuing in the fruits of faith.

VII. THE IMPLICATIONS OF MORAL SUBJECTIVITY

If the Protestant principle of discovering virtue through dialogue in subjectivity is carried through, there are obvious implications which become apparent. The first is the efficacy of doubt to give moral insight an opportunity to develop. What is good is revealed by personal appropriation of the gracious self-revelation of God rather than by a legal code of rules; it follows then that the one who receives may be receptive in a greater or a lesser degree, but he can never be confident that he is perfectly aware of what he ought to do or that he has not more to learn. 'The Catholic woman is never in Doubt', an advertisement issued by the Knights of Columbus proclaims. If the present views of the Roman Church upon marriage, divorce, contraception, and the education of children indeed perfectly reflect the will of God, then the Catholic woman is certainly relieved of all burden of doubt when she 'knows' that will by accepting the authority of the Church, and her conduct will infallibly follow the way of righteousness. If these views do not so perfectly comply with ultimate good, she may be doing wrong, though the wrong she does will be in ignorance and from the best of motives. In either case, the absence of doubt (however psychologically consoling) does not contribute to a developed conscience; for conscience must always be self-critical. As we have seen, there is no social conscience which can function without the willing suspension of the ethical, and therefore without doubt. Equally, there can be no advance in the individual moral sense without a continual readiness to test our preconceptions—and particularly those preconceptions which we label *principles*. If we receive our principles without examination on authority, believing ourselves secure in so doing, these principles are also removed from all possible criticism.

In addition, when doubt is thrown out of the arena of moral action and ethical principles are declared to be objectively valid, there is no room for further light on the subject, and no change in conduct can be tolerated. Since there is, fortunately, some gain in moral insight both in personal and social history—we no longer torture witnesses at law or burn heretics—the need for adjusting our ethical notions is constantly apparent. While we recognize that that most essential moral quality, conviction, is rooted in subjectivity, we will always be ready to accept the fact that we were wrong. And the price of being prepared to be ethically instructed is to bear the burden of doubt on our conscience. Doubt allows us to be tolerant of the views of other people who are as fallible as ourselves, without believing that all views are equally valid. It also allows us to welcome truth which comes through these fallible channels. But if we are wholly convinced that we cannot be mistaken in our beliefs, and claim their indubitable validity, then we shall be forced to resist all change, even though it be for the better, or else to change without admitting we have done so, and thus compromise our integrity seriously.

The second implication of the principle of the subjective appreciation of ethical truth is acceptance of individual responsibility. If the end of moral effort is a reward proportioned to that effort, most people will not exert themselves more than they consider absolutely necessary.[23] By contrast, a personal loyalty knows no limits. Loyalty means the dedication of the whole self: the end and aim of moral effort is to satisfy the claims of that to which loyalty is owed by every means in one's power. When the object of loyalty is objective and external, and is seen in a Fuhrer, a Cause, a Church, or a Party, then

---

[23] F. J. Sheed laments the fact that the average Catholic is content to go to heaven and does not aspire to the *best* heaven his merits could win for him (*Theology and Sanity*, p. 329).

the loyalist's moral sense will always be limited to the ethical level
of his ideal. And nothing so debases and perverts moral understanding as an inadequate ideal given absolute personal devotion; the
result is a destruction of personality such as that described in *Manon
Lescaut* where the chivalrous des Grieux is reduced to the meanest
crimes through his unworthy love. Only when the object of loyalty is
itself known by subjectivity is the conscience kept active. Loyalty
thus called forth will never be content to follow blindly, because the
possibility of following at all depends upon individual decision and
individual insight. This decision is not taken once and for all—as
when a loyalty oath is sworn—but continually; and only through this
insight can the ideal be known and kept in view. Without continual
renewal the object of loyalty disappears, becoming falsely objectified
in a static image which is nothing but a semblance of the original.
Thus true friendship can continue only when two people love and
respect each other as they are, without imagining that the other
possesses virtues he has not got or mistaking the existing person for
an idealized picture in the mind. In this situation, friendship can
prove to be the inspiration of more consistent moral action for each,
as each strives to be worthy of the best in the other, without any
limitation of the moral ideal to the actual achievement of one of the
two.

Every moral act is performed as the only one possible for a particular individual at one particular time. There may be general principles
which can help in a large number of cases, but in any one instance the
genuinely moral act must be performed out of responsibility freely
shouldered by the agent. 'Here stand I', is the criterion of action for
every one who stands within the dimension of dialogue. Yet the individual knows his stand *may* be mistaken. Atheistic existentialism
of the type popularized today by Sartre would agree so far with the
analysis of the moral situation, but would here add a gloss to the
effect that every stand, though necessary, *will* be useless, because
there is no meaning in the universe as such other than human moral
decision. But the one who believes that dialogue is possible with Him
who gives meaning to the universe—and indeed is His gracious
approach to us—will see in his moral decision not an expression of
his own moral freedom but an occasion of his being obedient to the
will of God for him, if God grants him that grace. He learns what
perfect obedience means by the freedom to be wrong and by insight
which enables him to discover and correct his error—again, given as
God illuminates him. Yet he can never shelter under the excuse that

in his moral mistakes he was only acting under authority and that he acted in good faith and failed only through ignorance; for the authority was one he himself has accepted and interpreted.[24] Thus his conscience becomes an instrument progressively capable of responding to Infinite Subjectivity. He finds that grace is always needed, a grace which transforms and supersedes the law.

A third implication of the principle of subjectivity in the ethical sphere is belief in the way of dialogue as the only possible means to achieve moral development in society at large. Not only is moral insight capable of growth and decay in the individual, but the whole moral climate of a culture can be radically altered for better or worse. Change in moral standards is largely brought about by social change, which itself is promoted by the technological advances achieved by a society. (This process was acutely analysed by Karl Marx, who, however, was over-influenced by the notion that technology *determines* the way of living and hence the ideas of those whose lives are affected, and neglected to take account of the fact that the same social conditions can give rise to different and contradictory 'ideological' systems). The enormous development of the humanitarian spirit through society during the past three centuries is directly linked with the advance of science and scientific technological discoveries. In our own age, large-scale scientifically organized countries have suddenly turned against the humanitarian ideal. This return to torture and terror as a declared instrument of policy in totalitarian countries has gained much of its horror by being set against the gradual—and largely successful—banishing of brutality from the general pattern of Western civilization. This up-surge of what we call *barbarism* (and which is really the reverse, being a deliberate rejection of humane and liberal values by those who enjoy full knowledge of the workings of civilization) is seen as well in the smaller but equally alarming growth of crimes of violence within those societies where humane standards of social conduct are the accepted rule. Dachau, Buchenwald, and the Soviet labour camps stand out starkly from the background of the Welfare State, and juvenile delinquency from universal education and rapid advance in the social sciences. The forces working in complete opposition to the

[24] Kant's formula of the moral will being self-legislating reflects this truth, although Kant, in correctly analysing the form of moral action, thought solely in terms of law. Because of this legalistic outlook, Kant imagined that reliable moral rules could be arrived at simply by summoning the idea of moral duty before the mind. Thus his practical ethical counsel is as unsatisfactory as his formal analysis of what moral action entails is illuminating.

direction of our scientifically directed culture show that social techniques in themselves are effective only where there is the moral will to make right use of the possibilities inherent in them. The same psychological knowledge which can be used to remove neuroses can also be used to achieve the result intended by 'brain-washing'.

Large-scale breakdowns in the morals of modern societies, it is often pointed out, furnish evidence of the urgent need for moral and spiritual values. Men, it is urged, cannot live without religion, and religion alone can restore health to the body politic. This is true, but it must be remembered that a religion may be successful in uniting a society in allegiance to a common creed and a common set of values, and yet these accepted beliefs may be morally debasing—as the religio-politico-dictatorships of our age have proved. If the house of civilization today is empty, swept and garnished, bereft of ideals and scornful of religion, ideals and religion are not in themselves the answer: these may prove to be devils worse than before. Only the will to extend dialogue can preserve moral order and prevent ideals from being corrupted by self-righteous ideologies, each claiming to be the 'true' faith. For it is a will which draws its strength from religious faith and expresses itself in a search for the moral ideal. It may often be mistaken, even tragically so, but it contains within itself the means for correcting its moral deficiencies, because it does not claim anything for itself, but waits in trust upon the Source of all goodness.

So it is that Protestants cannot identify the advance of religion, or the success of any particular Church, with the cause of righteousness. True religion goes hand in hand with true morality, and both are not in our possession, in spite of all our zeal for what we conceive to be true and right. In the last resort, we can only wait upon God to show us what we must do, as what we must believe, and do so in fellowship with our neighbour whose beliefs may not be ours.

CHAPTER NINE

PROTESTANT MORALITY
II. 'THE FRUITS OF THE SPIRIT'

I. BEYOND DUAL STANDARDS

THE UNITY of faith and morals in Protestantism is seen in its rejection of dual standards. Protestantism finds no place, among other things, for the Catholic separation of venial from mortal sins. While a scale of offences is a normal requirement of positive law, because law must judge the external act, the casuist's manual is not competent to measure sin, which is essentially internal—a wrong relationship of man's will to God's will. Christ taught the inward origin of evil: a casual word or a glance might incur God's condemnation as readily as the most deliberate crime (Matt. 12_{36}, $5_{21-2, 27-8}$). To try to weigh and measure sins is to split the unity of will and to import legalism into the sphere of Christian obedience.

An immediate objection likely to be made to this abolition of dual standards is that it will produce moral and spiritual anarchy. It being a matter of common experience that there are little sins as well as great ones, to treat them all alike would seem to drive people into absurd scrupulosity or to complete moral indifference. Yet this objection only confuses the moral and the religious interests to the benefit of neither. We do not free ourselves from sin by making separate moral efforts against particular sins, nor do we cause grace to abound by relaxing the moral struggle either wholesale or piecemeal. We do not presume to judge which sins are grave in God's sight and which appear to Him to be trivial. Rather, with St James, we are conscious that whoever offends the law of God at one point is guilty of all (James 2_{10}). We are thrown back, not upon our own ability to keep the commandments, but upon God's free forgiveness. And it is the assurance of being forgiven which gives us the confidence that God will enable us to show the good works of morality.

A dual standard in regard to sin must tend to obscure the religious interest, for an acceptance of forgiving grace made more grateful by the thought that the sin we have been forgiven is 'mortal' will be the less grateful when the sin is believed to be merely 'venial'. The relationship between God and man is thus conceived in legalistic terms of greater or less merit instead of in terms of personal confrontation with holiness, and of love and sorrow, repentance and forgiveness. And the moral interest is hurt by this approach, for men are not best taught to love the good by being told that some acts are permitted, some discouraged, and some absolutely forbidden. Genuine moral insight is most commonly prevented by an unquestioning habit to obedience to law, just because it is law. Responsibility is shifted away from the internal conscience when an external authority is relied upon for distinguishing between right and wrong.

At this point another Catholic dualism appears, in the dual standard of the religious and the secular calling. Catholic biblical exegesis finds in Martha and Mary distinct types of the active and the contemplative life. Protestantism sees these two women of the New Testament story rather as possibilities for every human existence than as distinct and exclusive callings. The separation of the religious from the secular, which may be needed on the social level where men deal with one another through the rule of law, does not apply on the personal level where man stands before God directly. In the Protestant view, it is probably essential to recognize one who follows a 'religious' vocation, while others have their various 'lay' occupations. This is a simple division of labour made necessary by diversities of gifts. But it does not follow that this distinction makes a radical difference in the status of individuals as Christian disciples. A dual standard here splits the unity of human personality.

The objection to this might be that to try to put all souls on one plane is to ignore spiritual realities, and that the religious and the secular vocations represent two levels of spiritual capacity. Behind this objection stands the belief that Dostoevsky portrayed in his fable of the Grand Inquisitor: that freedom is too heavy a burden for frail humanity to carry, so that, for their own good, men must be kept under the yoke of law, with the Church as lawgiver. Again, the answer from the Protestant side must be that such a view confuses the external with the internal and builds on a basis of legalism—a confusion which derives from the basic Catholic dualism of nature and grace. If the basic requirement laid upon God's creatures be that they obey the law of nature, while grace comes as an addition perfecting nature, then obedience to God's will is conceived in terms of an ascending scale of merit depending upon fulfilment of a higher or lower law. Some rise no higher than obedience to the commandments binding upon all men (because belonging to the natural order), while others follow of their own choice the 'counsels of perfection'—

which are still specific, legally defined rules of conduct. Grace comes through the hierarchy of merit, mediated through those who have earned the right to intercede for their less perfect brethren.

This notion of a grace which is limited and partly exclusive is foreign to Protestant thinking. Externally, it is true, men vary in native capacity, interests, occupation, and moral character. Internally, they all stand alike confronted by the Gospel and dependent upon grace. Therefore their calling by God differs not at all, and their progress in the life of faith does not depend upon their external condition. It is a continual scandal to the moralist that a man's standing before God is not determined by his moral record, that forgiveness does not depend upon proven evidence of reformation: and that there is more joy in heaven over one repentent sinner than over those of conspicuous virtue (Mark 2_5, Luke 15_7)—a scandal removed by the Catholic invention of Purgatory. In the Protestant view, the sacred and the secular are one and the same for every man's experience, because every man's experience of nature and grace is basically the same. We are all sinners, and all able to know full forgiveness through the Cross of Christ. Certainly, there are great differences in the way men seem to react to their experience and in their apparent awareness of it. Yet it is not for us to decide who has advanced farthest into 'spirituality'. It is Christ who knows His own and is known of them (John 10_{14}).

The legalism which would establish a defined division between the two realms of secular and sacred is one which perpetuates a social condition which has serious consequences. Instead of recognizing a difference between the religious and the non-religious interests of citizens which can be maintained with some degree of success in spite of inevitable friction, the society pledged to recognize the interests of 'religion' (identified with one social group) over against the interests of the laity, is tied to a policy where power and the maintenance of power is the chief concern. The Church becomes a political force which calls upon the State to perpetuate its position of privilege and to extend its authority over the whole range of social life.

Thus the need to transcend the dualism of the religious and the secular has both a religious and a moral basis. The interest of religion demands that the whole of life and every department of society shall be regarded as a sphere of religious endeavour. The Church of God is made up of the people of God and not of any one priestly caste. All of existence is capable of becoming the sphere of service to God, which is not particularly bound up with the practice of exclusively religious observances. And the interest of morality demands that no social programme shall be forced on society because of the claim by any religious organization that such a programme is required to safeguard the rights of religion within society, or because a religious party declared the programme to be morally obligatory.

II. THE ALTERNATIVE TO CLERICALISM

Every religious system leaves its imprint upon the culture within which it is found. The tree is known by its fruit. So, while the appeal to history is never beyond question—there is no infallible method of evaluating the past—the ethical legacy of any religion is an important factor in helping us to judge that religion's strength and weakness. The fruits of the spirit in the Protestant tradition are sufficiently distinctive to be recognized. Yet, because they are so much a part of the world we have grown up in, we do not always realize what they are nor value them until, after almost losing them by indifference and neglect, we come to ask ourselves urgently how we may again securely possess them. The precious gains to humanity of toleration and democracy have already been reviewed as the fruits of the Protestant attitude to ethical standards. The belief that individual convictions, conceived in subjectivity and shared in dialogue, should determine social action, rather than a battle for survival between ideologies in which the victor liquidated the vanquished, was basic to these achievements. Toleration and democracy also required some actual—if not always formal—separation between Church and State. But, in this process, what was perhaps most important was the Protestant principle of the equality of all before God and the rejection of the special status of the cleric.

When Protestants are blamed for breaking up the Medieval synthesis of Church and State, and so for introducing the consequent confusion of the modern world, it is often seen that the root of the matter lay precisely in this matter of ceasing to accept the validity of the distinction between religious and secular vocations. Protestantism, on this count, is accused of trying to achieve an unworkable perfectionism in the secular realm, and in this way of being responsible for a reaction leading to the complete secularization of society. Christopher Dawson argues along these lines:

The Puritans attempted to popularize asceticism by making it binding on every Christian, and the result was that they rendered it repulsive. The ordinary man was ready enough to recognize the self-devotion of the mediaeval ascetic, but he resented the claims of the Puritan saints as hypocrisy or spiritual snobbery. Consequently, every fresh assertion of the Puritan claim was followed by a reaction that tended to the secularization of culture. Where Puritanism was defeated, as in eighteenth-century England and Germany, the state-churches became more secularized than the medieval Church at its worst, and where it was victorious, as in Scotland and New England, it had a narrowing and cramping effect on life and culture.[1]

Now the Puritans fell short in many respects—enough, at least to lend plausibility to some of Dawson's strictures. But that Puritan 'asceticism' was merely repulsive is hard to believe. The Puritan ideal of personal discipline was adopted by many who did not share its religious basis (one need only think of Benjamin Franklin and Abraham Lincoln, or of Kant and Goethe) and shaped, more than any other factor, the pattern of domestic and civic life which today we call 'humane' and 'civilized'. Nor was eighteenth-century secularism a simple reaction to Puritanism as such. Where in Protestant Europe of the time could such a society have been found as the one described in Stendhal's *La Chartreuse de Parme*, with its priest-lover-careerist hero? It was the 'ordinary man' who kept alive the Puritan tradition of moral rectitude until middle-class supremacy in the nineteenth century brought a large measure of success to Protestant values. In England, for instance, the Wesleyan movement was a popular re-affirmation of Puritan morality, which took *Christian perfection* for a rallying-cry, and its effect was to stimulate the Evangelical movement within the Established Church and to re-vitalize the older nonconformist bodies. Puritan narrowness—itself a reaction from the laxity encouraged by a dual-standard culture—often wore a forbidding aspect, and yet it was attractive enough to win the allegiance of succeeding generations. Those who revolted against its negations usually continued to admire its virtues after they broke away from it. On the other hand, rebels against the Catholic way of life have most often conceived a profound hatred for the Church and all that they thought of as in any way connected with religion. This hatred has been usually a moral protest and expressed in anti-clericalism.

It is the monastic ideal—with its assumption that religious merit is to be sought by an exclusive path chosen by a spiritual élite—which has contributed so much to clericalism. Monasticism has been an enormously productive influence. There can be no overlooking the formative contribution it made to Western civilization during the

[1] *Enquiries*, p. 302.

Middle Ages. But it is not to belittle the achievement of the monastic orders to recognize that these, products of history as they necessarily were, have no eternal foundation in the Christian heritage. The Church of God is not bound for all time to retain a form of organization which proved beneficial over a certain period of time, even though the period be a very extended one. Early Protestantism's opposition to *monkery* had good historical justification in its day, and its objections still carry weight. From the first, the real cause of the opposition was far more than dissatisfaction with corruptions and abuses in the institution. Corruption can always be remedied from within. The criticism which went to the heart of the matter was a denial of the dualism on which the system rested, and an assertion of the freedom of all men to pursue the highest in the spiritual life without distinction of vocation.

Clericalism creates a vested interest opposing all that threatens its own security and privilege; but, in itself, it consists more essentially in a claim to authority than in a claim to power—although the one tries to express itself in the other. It identifies the right order of society with the willingness of the State to grant it 'freedom', i.e. priority to the secular power and immunity for its own members from the jurisdiction of secular law.[2] Clerical intolerance and exclusiveness within Catholicism is no by-product, but the direct result of a theological standpoint. And the foundation of clericalism's power is in maintaining intellectual submission to its authority. Since the strength of the rule of a religious caste must be in the weakness of any movement toward dissent, moral responsibility in the individual is its chief enemy. In the context of Spanish Catholicism, Miguel de Unamuno has written:

The real sin—perhaps it is the sin against the Holy Ghost for which there is no remission—is the sin of heresy, the sin of thinking for oneself. The saying has been heard before now, here in Spain, that to be a liberal—that is, a heretic—is worse than being an asasssin, a thief, or an adulterer. The gravest sin is not to obey the Church, whose infallibility protects us from reason.[3]

[2] Gerd Tellenbach's *Church, State and Christian Society at the time of the Investiture Contest* (1948), trans. by R. F. Bennett, gives an admirable analysis of the logic of Catholic thought on the rule of the Church, as well as providing a historical study of the medieval conception of churchly 'freedom'.

[3] *The Tragic Sense of Life*, trans. by J. E. Cornford Flitch (1921), p. 71–2. Compare the sentence from the Encyclical of Pope Pius X, *Vehementer*: 'As for the multitude, it has no other right than that of allowing itself to be led and, as a docile flock, to follow its shepherds' (Quoted by Jenkins in *The Nature of Catholicity*, p. 112).

Unamuno himself saw the appeal of the rule of clericalism, where simple faith is kept away from all that might disturb its peace of mind. But equally he saw that it prohibits adult rational responsibility. He agreed that when men break away from the unthinking 'faith of the coalheaver' they are likely to fall into complete scepticism. His own scepticism retained the will to believe along with the refusal to abandon responsibility, but the highly personal solution of affirmation within despair which he adopted did nothing to solve the moral and social aspect of the problem.

More than any other factor, the Protestant moral sense has been instrumental in combating the social evil of clericalism. This moral opposition has not been peculiarly Protestant, of course, in its quality of being a moral protest. In many battles for reform Protestants have found themselves partners with 'freethinkers' and other liberals, who took their stand on ethical principles alone. But it remains true that only where Protestantism is influential can it be assumed that the Church is not an enemy of civil freedom and social reform. In Europe, only the advent of modern totalitarianism convinced the anti-clericals that the Catholic Church was not the sole enemy, and might even be an ally in the struggle to preserve social freedom.[4] Happily, it is possible for a Catholic to be a liberal (in a deeper sense than that of belonging to a party bearing that label), and Protestants gladly acknowledge the Catholic contribution to the ranks of the martyrs of the cause of humanity. In Nazi Germany, Protestants and Catholics were brought together under persecution in a common struggle which in some instances built up an understanding between the two to a greater degree than possibly at any time since the Reformation. Yet, Protestants must also point out, at the risk of seeming self-righteous, that the Catholic liberal, to be consistent, must embrace an essentially Protestant principle in subordinating the claims of his religious party to the process of dialogue in a community. And Protestants cannot avoid moral opposition to Catholic illiberalism where it seeks to obtain special privileges for itself which it denies to others.

III. RESPONSIBILITY IN SOCIETY

The root-evil of clericalism being its stifling of individual responsibility, its disastrous effect spreads over the whole range of moral development; but it is most easily seen in the atrophy of the social conscience, for morality belongs essentially to the social dimension of

---

[4] See, for instance, Michael Polanyi, *The Logic of Liberty*, pp. 108–9.

existence. When religion is denied the right to speak to the total conscience, conscience will most certainly be silenced if it challenges any accepted social or political institution supporting the current religious régime. The consequences of this strangulation of the moral sense are writ large in the course of modern history, and are still working themselves out. There are those for whom the phrase *nine-teenth-century liberalism* is nothing more than a term of derision, and who believe that the whole development of toleration and democracy deriving from the Protestant tradition was a mistake. The world has had full opportunity to see what abandoning liberalism really means, however, and those voices pleading for a return to dogmatism and authority are not quite so many or quite so vehement as they were only a few years ago. Perhaps the most noticeable trend in Western society these days is a willingness to seek for reassurance in re-affirming the virtues of conservatism, i.e. a moderate liberalism dis-sociated from a crusading radicalism. But the very tradition on which this conservatism rests, and which gives it its appeal, is the Protest-ant-democratic tradition of political responsibility which emphasizes the moral duty of the citizen to create the good society by individual effort.

Liberal-conservatives and liberal-radicals differ in their view of the function of the State and how it can mediate justice in the social order. They are united in their belief that the just society can only be built upon the foundation of moral conscience brought to bear upon social problems by the whole community. There is within Protest-antism an element of pietism which is apt to think of politics as 'worldly' and to disassociate social questions from religion, sometimes acquiescing supinely in current national and social attitudes and standards. This element has never been allowed to go unchallenged. The concern of Protestants with social righteousness has been con-stant and persistent, even where it has gone astray in adopting an impossible Utopianism or sub-Christian 'realism'. Any serious *theological* contention that the believer ought not to trouble himself about social justice because of the prior and conflicting claims of religion would be hard to find in Protestantism. And Protestants cannot but be concerned with Catholic arguments which seek to justify authoritarian government and to discourage individuals from taking social responsibility seriously.

For example, Rosalind Murray, writing from a Catholic stand-point, quotes with approval the 'very definite opinion' of those who opposed parliamentary democracy in nineteenth-century Spain, that

the attraction of interest to party politics was 'in itself a deteriora-
tion'. She also brings as evidence for the blessings of having no
political rights the high level of culture attained by the average
Chinese and pre-1914 Austrian.[5] It is surely remarkable that Spain
and China, after a long period of political tribulation of a particularly intense nature, have achieved their present state of national
existence through bitter civil war and are both under totalitarian
government; while Austria, after not dissimilar upheavals, produced,
as its most influential citizen in the post-1918 period, Adolf Hitler.
The preoccupation with the political elevated into a religion, which
Miss Murray deplores and blames on Evangelical Protestantism,
does not in fact exist to any degree in Britain and North America,
where that influence was paramount. But it is rampant in all those
countries where effective participation in political responsibility was
withheld from the people at large. In all the European countries now
under dictatorships or menaced by large totalitarian movements,
Catholic teaching (Roman or Orthodox) was predominant until recent times.

The theory that social and political interest conflicts with 'higher'
interests flies in the face of all history. It is completely contrary to the
biblical prophetic teaching concerning the unity of social justice and
true worship. If kingdoms are, as St Augustine said, just great
robberies apart from justice, then to acquiesce in prevailing injustice
and immorality, caring nothing about how our neighbours are
robbed, must hurt the soul in its ability to distinguish right from
wrong. This moral truth is recognized far beyond the Christian
tradition. In the wisdom of Confucius, men would prefer to be
slaughtered one by one by wild beasts rather than dwell under a
tyrannical prince. The twelfth book of the *Analects* contains the
verdict that rule by consent of the people is the prime requisite of
government, to be preferred above military protection and food:
'From of old, death has been the lot of all men; but if the people
have no faith in their rulers, there is no standing for the State.' The
healthy organization of society is inevitably the first condition of the
right functioning of all other activities within it: and although religion is independent of the state of society it cannot be indifferent
to it.

Nor can we plausibly contend, with Miss Murray, that 'culture'
can be an adequate substitute for a just social order. If the best we
can do in an overwhelmingly wicked world is to cultivate our garden

[5] *Time and the Timeless* (1942), pp. 26–7.

(which is questionable), at least we are not justified in letting the weeds grow while we cultivate our good taste. Art pursued apart from its relevance for society produces the kind of culture that is with real reason called *decadent*. Certainly, art does not wait for ideal conditions in order to exist, or flourish only in one set of social circumstances. Art may be popular, traditional, revolutionary, peasant, aristocratic, bourgeois, indigenous, derivative, eclectic, learned, primitive, sophisticated, escapist, didactic, or 'pure'. But no art recognized as 'great' has ever been created in a moral or social vacuum. This is most plain in the great writers. Virgil, Dante, and Milton were active patriots, and Shakespeare's concern with the moral lesson of his country's history was elaborated in the great cycle of history plays. Rabelais, Cervantes, Molière, and Fielding, preaching a moral lesson to their countrymen through their humorous vision, also immortalized the spirit of their land and age. The visual arts point the same moral a little less obviously, and the musicians still less so. Yet neither Bach nor Beethoven—nor even Mozart, who might on a superficial view be thought an exception—can possibly be fitted into any art-for-art's-sake category. From the author of *Piers Plowman* to the author of *The Waste Land*, from Giotto to van Gogh, the artist has embodied, directly or indirectly, by acceptance or by revolt, the ideas and ideals of the society to which he belonged and has not been content to turn his back upon them in order to confine himself to 'his' art. A clue to the paradox of art, which is in itself quite unconcerned with moral and social questions and yet in its production most intimately dependent on these, is found in the unusual (and for that reason typical) case of the poet, painter, and system-maker William Blake. Blake combined with his faith that the content of art was pure imagination the most vehement concern with the evils of contemporary society and the most searching criticism of current morality, religion, and metaphysics. The artist expresses his moral and social message in ways not easy to understand. The Nazis condemned as *decadent* the art which embodied the real problems of the inter-war period and would not fall into step with the social programme of the Party. The artist is always, in his own right, a preacher with a message.

What is true of art is also true of other aspects of cultural life. Poets, painters, and music-makers are not so very different from philosophers, critics, educators, and propagandists. Not only is every metaphysical system linked to an accompanying ethic, but is inspired by the conception of the good life derived from the thinker's experience of society, and it reflects the insights and limitations of that view. Plato and Aristotle, Aquinas and Spinoza, or Kant and Hegel provide admirable examples of contrast in theory arising from different presuppositions concerning man's relation to his fellows and to the community at large. Those who are not so much interested in the analysis of experience so much as in pressing forward, by precept and example, what they take to be sound values to live by, are even more dependent upon the current stream of civilization than are the system-builders—very naturally so, since they are attracted to the near and concrete rather than to the remote and abstract. An Erasmus, a Samuel Johnson, an Emerson or an Irving Babbitt passes on to his contemporaries his personal convictions about the things which count for him, and in so doing assumes many of the current psychological, sociological, and ethical beliefs he has absorbed unconsciously, while he criticizes and develops others. What he can never do is to advocate 'culture' apart from moral and social values revealed to him through the society of which he is a part. An illuminating example of this is seen in the life of John Ruskin who, from a detached and dilettantish interest in the fine arts, was driven by the logic of his pursuit to a passionate concern for social righteousness.

It does not matter where we start. Any human activity, intellectual, artistic, cultural, educational, or religious, brings us up against the moral question; and morality is rooted in the social, and hence in the political and the economic. There is no escape from this circle except a dishonest one, that of deceiving ourselves that we are 'above' such matters. That does not mean, as the Marxist concludes, that politico-economic considerations determine all. It does not mean that every other human activity must be subordinated to serve these ends. It does mean that when they are artificially excluded that the whole of life is corrupted. Every total view of existence depends for its soundness upon the soundness of its moral insight. Moral development thus holds the key to every other personal achievement, and moral blindness destroys or impoverishes every other spiritual capacity.

IV. MORAL DEVELOPMENT

Moral development begins when conscience rebels against accepted beliefs to lay hold upon an internal standard of right and wrong. Albert Guérard describes the beginning of his spiritual development in these terms:

My teacher was the Dreyfus Affair. Circumstances compelled me, when I was still in my teens, to question the sacred character of the Flag, the Army, the Nation, the State, the Law, the Masses (*vox populi*), and even the Church. Their authorized representatives strove desperately to impede justice; and justice prevailed. We were then called in derision the *Intellectuals*; but we were first of all the *Believers*. We rationalized our passions—holy, I still claim—into a method.[6]

Guérard records that he afterwards progressed beyond Orthodox Dreyfusism, leaving behind its simple anti-clericalism and other dogmatic articles of faith, while retaining the lesson he had learnt from it. An affinity with Protestantism can readily be seen in this attitude of *Belief*, however much its content may have differed from that of Evangelical Christianity. It was a positive faith (a *protest*) accepted on the basis of direct insight. The *holy passion* produced the method, not vice versa, and had a validity beyond the terms in which it was expressed. Though positive, it realized itself in opposition to existing institutional beliefs; and its opposition took the form of a moral stand against a specific contemporary abuse.

In spite of the fact that Orthodox Dreyfusism was avowedly materialistic, its disciple could abandon materialism and still feel that his *Belief* had not been mistaken. Protestantism has often changed the formulation of its Gospel without departing from the Gospel under which it stands. The central events of the Gospel which are concerned with Incarnation and Redemption (the revelation of the Word) are many-sided, so that theology is ever-changing. Yet, whenever Protestants are tempted to lose sight of the events in the interpretation, they are called back to the 'faith which was once delivered unto the saints' (Jude 3). But in the ethical implications of the Gospel there is more room for further understanding. Protestants have undergone revolutions in ethical thinking: a fact they thankfully admit.

That is why, when ethical questions are at stake, Protestants can easily co-operate with those of other creeds. They recognize that in the matter of moral development we are all learners. What we need most is *belief* in that degree of moral insight which has been granted us and readiness to allow for further insight reached through dialogue. Present agreement is not nearly so important as a common will to be enlightened. The Catholic basis for agreement with other faiths is on the basis of natural law. This assumes that co-operation is possible only when we agree about the *answers* to moral questions;

6 *Bottle in the Sea*, p. 5.

so that our dialogue is formal only, limited to the occasions on which we happen to agree, and co-operation is carried on with no better foundation than that of power-politics, where the allies of yesterday may well become the enemies of tomorrow.

Moral development as an idea is not recent, deriving from eighteenth-century belief in the perfecting power of reason or from nineteenth-century evolutionary theory, as it is sometimes said to be. It is rooted in the record of the Old Testament, where the revelation of the living God is seen to bring about the transformation of a tribal cult into a highly ethical universal faith. It underlies the New Testament teaching of a New Law of Christ in the Christian community, a law characterized (as C. H. Dodd has put it)[7] by *direction and quality* instead of by specific ethical commandments. And it has been recognized, fitfully and often no more than half-consciously, in Protestant history. 'The Lord hath more light and truth yet, to break forth out of His holy Word', was a principle ethically as well as theologically valid. Although always threatened by the tendency to relapse into legalism, Protestant morality was never entirely subordinated to an external standard. It was too closely bound to the internal conscience to become altogether sterile and retrogressive. If Protestant communities have often fallen into the condition of those geese which Kierkegaard saw as the symbol of spiritual torpor—praising flight without trying to fly themselves and trampling those of independent mind under their foolish, clumsy feet—there has always been a Kierkegaard to remind them of their state and to lay down once more the challenge of living faith.

The right to private judgement (which we have seen to be better described as the recognition of subjectivity) has of course played a decisive part in Protestant moral development. The stress which has been laid on conscience as the prime arbiter in ethical judgement within the Protestant tradition has had very great consequences in making men aware of the place of morality both in personal and in social life. In this it has built upon the great achievements of the Middle Ages in educating men through a Christian conception of conscience. But, since in Catholicism conscience became identified with natural reason and was made subject to the rule of authority, Protestant reliance upon conscience was commonly condemned as sheer individualism, defying reason, lawful authority, and established custom. That scrupulosity which marked the Puritan caused scorn in the less particular: 'He that hath not for every word an oath . . . they

[7] *Gospel and Law*, Chapter 4.

say he is a puritan, a precise foole, not fitte to hold a gentleman company.' The Puritans, Hooker complained, 'simply oppose their *methinketh* unto the orders of the Church of England'.[8] Nevertheless, by the pertinacity of their witness to conscience, the Puritans finally won recognition for their views. It began to be recognized that a minority opinion, even if it seemed simple, cranky, or revolutionary, was not necessarily to be despised and suppressed. Eighteenth-century philanthropy, which prepared the way for later social action, was carried out by individuals more sensitive in conscience than their contemporaries and was largely inspired by Protestant piety. In nineteenth-century Britain the *Non-conformist conscience* was a widely recognized factor in social and political reform.

Today any direct attack upon morality usually takes the form of denying the worth of individual conscience. It is not difficult to show that conscience is largely a social phenomenon, varying enormously in different ages and among different races. Conscience is thus identified with social convention, and morality declared to be a figment. If it is objected that conscience often stands in opposition to socially accepted values—a *methinketh* against established order—then this difference is put down to a psychological quirk in the individual. Against the subjective view, others may appeal to 'objective' morality, urging that private decisions cannot, in themselves, be made into trustworthy standards. Thus, although Catholic theory admits that an individual must follow his conscience even if it leads him away from Catholic truth, it will not allow him the right to persuade others to think as he does; so conscience is permitted no greater freedom than that of a prisoner on parole. Only where the principle of subjectivity is granted can conscience come into its own. In that event, it is evident that the moral conscience is not justified unless enlightened, but that it cannot be by-passed, because there is no substitute for it which is itself moral. All satisfactory ethical progress waits upon individual moral development. But where conscience is valued, the conscience of the whole community is likely to be itself progressively enlightened.

When instances of intolerance in Roman Catholic countries arouse Protestant complaint, apologists of Rome usually fall back upon the defence that we must take into account differences of temperament and history: the Latin, for instance, does not behave with the restraint and lack of emotionalism found in the Anglo-Saxon. Yet it seems very likely that national character (that elusive entity!) is

[8] Quoted by Peter Munz, *The Place of Hooker in the History of Thought*, p. 31.

largely the product of those moral ideals which arise out of men's beliefs and determine their attitude to society. We know that the Englishman at the time of the Renaissance was thought on the Continent to be dirty and over-emotional, and that the pre-Reformation Scot was considered by his southern neighbours to be shiftless and lazy; so that nationality evidently confers no indelible stamp. Dr Thomas Arnold's experiment at Rugby School is credited with having produced an entirely new type of English aristocrat. What is most probably true of nations is certainly true of historical ages. Ronald Knox has written:

The employment of torture by the Inquisition was in accordance with the judicial practice of the time, as Protestant England can witness. It is utterly out of accord with the spirit of our own age, and a Catholic authority would be no more likely to inflict it now than a Protestant authority.[9]

Since the revival of judicial torture is one of the features of 'our own age', it should be abundantly clear that the spirit of the age which finds the use of torture immoral is the liberal spirit of post-Reformation times, that individualistic and secularistic spirit which (regretably, some think) took the place of the Medieval synthesis of Church and State. Where Protestantism has firm roots, liberalism has best triumphed over sectarian zeal. It is from the United States, where the separation of Church and State has been accepted from the founding of the nation, that the first Roman Catholic protest against the excesses of Spanish clericalism has come. Moral development does not arise of its own accord. The ground must be prepared for it.

V. EDUCATION AS A MORAL FORCE

Protestant moral development has been largely achieved through the institution of education. Though with its roots in classical antiquity, education in the Western world grew under the patronage of the Church of the Middle Ages, and the legacy of that great tradition has been rich indeed. As in the realm of faith, Protestantism had no wish to repudiate the tradition in its largest reach, although it was intent upon re-directing it. The chief alteration brought about by the Reformation was the abolition of the dualism which took for granted that education was primarily of, for, and by the clergy.

Protestantism was necessarily an educational force because of its belief that all, without exception, should be able to read the Bible—a conviction which has led to many races having their first scripts created under missionary initiative. *Reading* in this case meant very

The Belief of Catholics, p. 240.

much more than technical literacy, because interpretation was considered an integral part of the 'hearing of the Word'. (Besides the
preachers who proclaimed the Gospel to elicit saving faith, many of
the early Protestant churches had teachers, whose duty it was to give
detailed exposition of the scripture readings of divine service.) From
the basic assumption that no one was too ignorant to have personal
contact with the Gospel, and so must be content to believe on
authority, came the impulse that finally resulted in national schools.
Scotland provides a good example of the strong Protestant impulse
to democratic education. Here the poverty of the country did not
prevent either a national love of learning or its wide dissemination
through all classses of society. Scottish education was directly inspired by Knox's *Book of Discipline*, which laid down (in addition to
a plan for responsible local government) 'for the most culturally
backward nation in western Europe, the first programme of universal
compulsory education'.[10]

Reform in teaching methods also had strong links with Protestant
principles. When Erasmus condemned the brutal cruelty of contemporary schoolmasters, he was referring to the same conditions which
Augustine had deplored more than a thousand years before. In spite
of rapid strides made by humanitarian feeling, milder ways were slow
in penetrating the schools, as Charles Lamb's reminiscences of
schooldays at Christ's Hospital show. The Dissenting Academies of
eighteenth-century England were the first institutions to adopt new
standards of education, early experiments in 'free discipline' as well
as in a revised curriculum being especially evident in Quaker schools.
The hymn-writer, Isaac Watts, who was also a proficient author of
educational text-books, in his writings for young children proved
himself to be one of the founders of juvenile literature and a pioneer
in a completely revolutionary attitude to the child and his educational
needs.

The Protestant view of education was influenced most strongly
from the start by the fact that the Reformation followed close upon
that aspect of the Renaissance called the *Revival of Learning*. Many
of the Reformers were scholars, and vice versa. Thus the idea of
knowledge being valuable for its own sake grew up beside the idea of
knowledge being valuable for the sake of moral and spiritual development. Against Renaissance humanism, however, evangelical
pietism waged an anti-rationalistic campaign. The intellect could not
bring salvation, and hence all 'worldly' knowledge was at best super-

[10] Lord Eustace Percy, *John Knox*, p. 378.

fluous and at worst distracting, likely to lead the believer to forget his soul, and even to scorn the truths of faith. Pietism took the Protestant principle of the uselessness of reason in the sphere of religious conviction—Luther's great discovery that the intellect, most fitted for understanding things 'below it' is impotent to judge things 'above it' —and turned it into a proof that everything could be settled by trusting in warm feeling instead of in cold thinking. Where this outlook triumphed it led to crude theologizing and crass sectarianism; but, fortunately, the attitude is one which tends to destroy itself. On the one hand, as it becomes self-reflective and tries to justify itself it is forced to come to some sort of terms with reason. And on the other hand, the call to moral duty (which is never easily ignored in even the most heterodox Protestantism) is likely to exert its influence to force an appeal to the head as well as to the heart. A concern for moral development leads to a concern for education, even though the stress be laid upon *education of character* more than upon intellectual attainments. Thomas Arnold's revolution in the schooling of the English upper-classes was inspired by this motive. His 'muscular Christianity', borrowed from the Broad Church party in Anglicanism, was a very liberal version of pietism and far from Evangelical in dogmatic content, but genuinely Evangelical and Protestant in its moral tone. The success of his work shows how it has been possible for Protestant pietism to transform itself from a world-forsaking into a world-changing force through the strength of its moral interest.

The Protestant view of education as a means to character-building had a point of contact with other historic philosophies of life which were totally unlike it, yet also held an instrumental theory of education. The thinkers of the Enlightenment believed that, if only individuals were subjected to proper training in the use of reason, they would leave behind old habits of superstitition and tyranny, and create a new world. The Romantics also believed in changing society by putting away old errors, though instead of service to the rule of reason they desired for the individual complete freedom for self-expression. If the ends sought by the Protestant and the Rational-Romantic ideas were very different, yet they looked equally for social progress through education. And, since Protestants were averse to the dogmatic control of education, there could be no guarantee that one kind of progress would be constantly pursued. In the United States, Protestant theory established the public school system; but the acclaim given today to the educational philosophy of John Dewey is evidence of the triumph of a tradition going back to Locke, to the Encyclopedists, and to Rousseau. By banishing clericalism and opening the way for moral development, Protestantism could not be certain that the development actually achieved was of a kind that could be approved by the Christian conscience.

Yet, while the Protestant knows that when schools are not put under the control of a religious party they are always liable to be won by some crusading or fashionably dominant ideology, he will not wish for that reason to fall back upon a closed dogmatic system. Rather, since non-sectarian democratic public education allows for criticism of any dogma that emerges within it, he will consider it more effective in the long run to hold up all theories to free criticism, insisting that moral and intellectual training shall go hand in hand, governed by changing ideals of what constitutes good citizenship.

It follows also that, while Protestants find it eminently reasonable that every family shall have full opportunity to have their children trained in the specific dogmas of the faith they profess, they must deplore the Catholic demand that education entirely directed by dogmatic standards shall be provided for those who desire it. Such segregation, making in effect clerically controlled communities on a small scale, is a serious obstacle to dialogue. Minds trained at the most impressionable age to view all differences of belief and standards of morality in the inevitable context of *we* against *they* will find that habits of sympathetic understanding are inhibited, and also that an atmosphere of incipient hostility and misunderstanding prevails. If moral responsibility is to be an educational goal, doubt as well as faith is an educational asset and must be acquired in the willing confrontation of the 'I' with the 'Thou' in the relation of subjectivity.

VI. SOCIAL MORALITY

Protestant piety has always been centred in the personal life of the individual *in his relation to possibilities of dialogue*. It is this relationship which prevents Protestantism from lapsing into mere individualism. Equally with individual personal faith, the Protestant is confronted with the social demands of morality—the two halves of the Great Commandment. In the personal situation, men are bound to find that their moral duty comes most demandingly in the relationships nearest to them: the more intimate social groups present the clearer call for ethical decisions, the more remote having less force. Thus the family and the local church community have traditionally been the centres around which Protestants have focused the life of piety. But, if charity begins at home, it does not prosper if it stays there; and concern for the family passes naturally into concern for the wider community where the family is placed, while the local church, as an organization, is one among other organizations which are part of social existence.

So it has come about that Protestant piety, being judged by an inclusive standard demanding quality of life rather than ritual observances, has made for social righteousness. In the early days of French settlement in Canada, a petition was sent to France urging the recall of Huguenot colonists, on the grounds that their exemplary conduct was having too much influence upon their Catholic neighbours.[11] Such a representative example of the Protestant view of how men ought to fulfil their duty to God and their fellows as Richard Baxter's *Reformed Pastor* shows how far removed from the popular caricature of Puritanism this view was; while the same author's *A Christian Directory or Body of Practical Divinity* illustrates the seriousness with which social ethics were regarded. In the latter work, Baxter tried to draw out the implications of the Great Commandment to cover the economic and other practical problems confronting men of the seventeenth century, relating each case to the principle of *Justice* which he found in the command to love our neighbour as ourselves, and insisting that good habits must be continually tested by the light of an active conscience.

Protestant personal piety could shrink into pietism by being unduly restricted to 'spiritual' interests, and so ignoring the wider dimensions of life. But such a denial of social responsibility, with its implication of a radical separation of the spheres of nature and grace, had to meet the continual pressure of Protestant moral consciousness. With every development of pietism came a reaction from it. John Wesley, who began his evangelistic work under the inspiration of the Moravians, broke with them because they 'were not zealous of good works, or, at least only for their own people'. It is not often remembered that Wesley's message of individual salvation was accompanied by a strong social message. He made private philanthropy a strict obligation, and his converts were expected to prove their new condition by bettering themselves economically. In an age ignorant of hygiene, he wrote a popular guide to 'Physic', opened the first free

---

[11] This was in 1742; the petition was rejected by the King. I am indebted to a mimeographed treatise on French Protestants in Canada by J. E. Boucher for this reference.

dispensary, and brought into currency the phrase, 'cleanliness is next to godliness'. After Wesley, Evangelical religion became less socially conscious, partly because the rising middle-classes who formed so large a part of its supporters found the system then prevailing a comfortable one for themselves. But even then the Protestant urge towards social morality was not moribund. It had been continually evident in humanitarian crusades, such as those of John Howard and Elizabeth Fry over prison reform, and of Wilberforce and Henry Ward Beecher over the abolition of slavery. Beecher's successor, Lyman Abbott, created the development of American Protestantism which later became known as the Social Gospel. And while Abbott departed very far from orthodox Protestantism in his desire to reconcile Christianity with contemporary categories of thought, the moral drive behind his Social Gospel has been taken up by the neo-orthodox theologians of present-day America of whom Reinhold Niebuhr is the most distinguished representative.

Wesley's social thinking (as that of the most zealous reformers of his time) moved entirely within the horizons of *laissez-faire* economics. Quite a different social doctrine was advanced only a little later by the Broad Church Anglicans, F. D. Maurice and Charles Kingsley, and this revolutionary vision found ready acceptance from elements within Methodism and from other radical Protestant bodies: it was Christian Socialism.

Christian Socialism, which had already been foreshadowed by some of the sectarian movements of the Commonwealth period, represented the coming to consciousness of something which had been latent in British Protestantism. As we have seen, democracy was a natural product of Protestant churchmanship and an example of the moral application of religious convictions. But democracy, aiming at producing equality between citizens on the ethical level, through the use of the power of law to safeguard individual liberty and of representative government to provide just law-making, hardly touched the question of economic power and the injustice created by inequalities of wealth. In the great social upheaval we know today as the Industrial Revolution, the under-privileged had equality before the law but no voice in law-making; and society as a whole did not see the existence of economically-depressed classes as an issue involving justice. George Trevelyan writes of these under-privileged folk in Britain: 'Of the mass of unregarded humanity in the factories and mines, no one but the Nonconformist minister was their friend.'[12]

[12] *English Social History* (Illus. edn., 1943), IV, 19.

The Christian Socialists believed that the good society must have a concern for all its citizens which went beyond individual philanthropy and ensure that they are not denied the right to achieve the dignity of persons by being made the helpless victims of power, whether that power be political or economic. In this they were appealing to a principle already basic to the democratic *credo*: the individual is never expendable.

Christian socialism was not primarily an economic doctrine at all, but a moral *protest* in both the positive and negative senses of that word. The conditions of labour which Kingsley and his fellow Socialists denounced were indeed later recognized to be intolerable and were altered by legislation which extended democracy in the matter of the right to vote and also extended governmental control over the welfare of the people. The fact that this process was brought about by different parliamentary parties, and that no one nowadays would dream of repudiating it, makes it appear likely that we ought to sever the word *socialism* from its present associations, and use it in the same general sense that we have given to *democracy*.

We obviously need such a word to describe the moral ideal of the State which has a regard for the well-being of its citizens in their economic as well as in their more specifically political liberties. We dispute the right of Communist countries to call their unrepresentative governments democracies, yet we are quite ready to hand over to them an equally valuable term which could be used to make specific our democratic conception of a justly ordered community of persons who freely join together to promote the economic betterment of the whole. *Socialism*, as a term, has no more necessary connexion with State control of the entire national economy than democracy has with mob-law. Karl Marx did not invent the word, and there is no reason why we should not dispute the right of the Marx-Leninists to call themselves *Socialists*. Probably, however, the word is too firmly wedded by now to Marxist or semi-Marxist theory to be detached from the sense which has grown around it, implying a political theory advocating State ownership of the State's chief industries. In that case, we shall have to fall back upon the already over-worked term *democracy*; insisting, indeed, that it shall include the notion of that degree of economic control necessary to ensure that the interests of no one section of its citizens function to the total neglect of the interests of others. At present, where *socialism* is thought of as being the polar opposite of *capitalism*, and democracy equated with the latter, great confusion arises. Such a pigeon-holing sets up a doctrinal way of thinking which bears little relation to reality.[13] Even if we cannot rescue the word *socialism* to make it stand for the positive ideal of national self-help, all democracies are actually committed to (in various degrees, according to the national temper of the moment much more than according to the alleged position of the party in power to the 'left' or the 'right' of centre), we ought not to allow it to lose all meaning and become nothing more than an abusive label.

If the work of the Christian Socialists was essentially to put forward the challenge of a consistently democratic goal of freedom with justice for all, it can then be seen to be a contribution toward completing the Protestant will to an adequate social morality. Before Marx, Charles Kingsley had accused religion of being an opiate of the people. Only, Kingsley saw that one kind of religion alone merited this title: the religion blind to moral issues. Religion which was true to itself and to its own values must take the lead in developing a social conscience. The Social Gospel movement of the early twentieth century took up the challenge laid down by the Christian Socialists; but that movement was in danger of absorbing its religious protest in its moral one and of identifying the Kingdom of God with a just social order *simpliciter*. This confusion of moral and religious interests is still current in the belief that the salvation of souls is more or less identical with psychological 'integration' of personality. Yet moralism, no less than pietism, is inconsistent with the Protestant protest. For the urge to social righteousness becomes external and legalistic unless it is founded on the command to personal righteousness which arises from the relationship of faith and transcends the ethical; the dialogue between man and his neighbour is given meaning by the dialogue between God and the individual.

Social morality and personal morality are really one, since all morality has a social context and, equally, springs from a personal appropriation of truth. If morality is to escape the blight of legalism, it must develop the individual conscience, where responsibility has its genesis, until this conscience becomes effective in society. A wholesome ethic is necessarily one which is open to the sphere of grace, just as tolerable social relations can continue only when they are governed by the 'unwritten law' created by mutual good-will.

[13] Reinhold Niebuhr, in an essay on 'The Anomaly of European Socialism (*Christian Realism and Political Problems*, pp. 43 ff.) develops this point in one particular context. He argues that 'democratic socialism' in the Old World has rid itself of one set of artificial dogmas by rejecting *laissez-faire* conservatism. But, by admitting the validity of the Marxian view of capitalism, these parties have provided themselves with another set of dogmas, equally at variance with the facts.

Since the time of Kingsley and Maurice progress in social morality throughout Western society has been great, and this achievement is not to be discounted because its gains have been wiped out over large areas of our world by anti-humanitarian, anti-moral, anti-Protestant, and anti-Christian forces. Totalitarian efforts to destroy moral conscience and to put in its place unquestioning obedience to a party faith makes the Protestant witness all the more necessary, if increasingly difficult. In face of the demonic cruelty which has once more broken out of the thin crust of civilization covering the sinful nature of unredeemed man, and in face of the threat to historical existence itself which looms over the future of a generation possessing the knowledge that gives power without the wisdom which produces good-will, to talk of moral progress seems to many to be an empty mockery. Against all despair, it must be the duty of Christians to hold out in faith the counsels of courage. Where the Spirit of God is, there will be the fruits of the spirit also.

CHAPTER TEN

PROTESTANTISM UNDER JUDGEMENT

I. INCOMPLETENESS AND FAILURE

LOOKING BACK over history, we find the record of Protestant follies and crimes so largely created by Protestantism's failure to live up to its own insights that we are tempted to adapt G. K. Chesterton's epigram on Christianity and say, 'Protestantism has not failed; it has never been tried'. In that case, of course, we would be admitting the entire futility of Protestantism. A historical movement which never entered history would be an absurdity. A more considered verdict might be, 'Protestantism has been tried—but not enough'. This view would suggest that what happened at the Reformation was the planting of a tree of promise, whose full maturity was then delayed by poor conditions of growth and lack of the right kind of care. The delayed fruits of the tree—the gradual appearance of toleration, social reform, and the like—become proof of its entire wholesomeness. And all that is required from us is to protect it from all those hostile forces that imperil its continued growth, and to wait patiently for its final achievement of intrinsic perfection.

This idea of a Protestantism, incomplete but ever moving on to completion, is a consoling but a wholly misleading one. It is not really made much better if we amend the metaphor of growth (suggesting inevitability) to one of moral conflict, and picture Protestantism battling for its existence against foes without and within. Even if we admit that all is not well with Protestantism, and that a renewal of its former confidence by a return to its former convictions is most necessary, we have not progressed very much farther in our analysis. The advice of Polonius to Laertes:

> *to thine own self be true,*
> *And it must follow, as the night the day,*
> *Thou canst not then be false to any man.*

is the authentic voice of complacency, self-ignorant and self-deceiving. Only the self which is true to God can escape falsehood; and no self, individual or corporate, can claim so much in its own right and for its own being. Protestantism has not only had faults and still has them. It has been, and still is, faulty to the degree that it retains faultiness even in the act of reforming itself. Therefore, a right analysis will certainly begin by saying that Protestantism is in the process of being made. It is not a completed product and it gains its inner strength by its willingness to remain incomplete and under the guidance of the Spirit. Yet the analysis will, most surely, go on from there to make clear that Protestantism also has put itself in opposition to the Spirit from its beginnings until now. It is a child of history. By saying 'Yes' or 'No', when faced with decisions concerning its own destiny and character, it has brought about those irreversible results which characterize all history; results which, when issuing from mistaken decisions, make all subsequent decisions a choice between two relative evils for the achieving of no more than a relative good. Nothing historical can escape falling under the condemnation of God, because all nature shares in creation's condition of sin—this is fundamental to Protestant belief. Therefore Protestants can never assume that Protestantism is the infallible cure for all spiritual ills, and that it is merely incomplete. They must recognize that always, at its best and its purest, it represents a failure to understand God's will for men.

The plight of the world today brings home to all those who are sympathetic to the values proclaimed by Protestantism how increasingly powerless Protestant witness is to help men to find an answer to their desperate problems. Or, to look at the same thing from the other end, traditional Protestant teaching seems to be increasingly meaningless to the man of today. Protestants cannot excuse themselves by saying that the root of the matter is that our modern age has wilfully turned its back on the Protestant way and will know no peace until it comes to itself, like the Prodigal Son, and returns to the home it has forsaken. They cannot say this, although undeniably the modern relapse into authoritarian irresponsibility and amoral collectivism shows a revolt against the Protestant-liberal ideals of freedom and the developed conscience; and although it can be argued, with some plausibility, that Protestantism cannot be held responsible for the modern situation having arisen. Certainly, Protestantism has always been a minority movement. The dominant ideologies having most influence in the West have been either Catholic or secular in inspiration. And when liberalism was most triumphant in the last century, so that the logic of Protestantism seemed to be penetrating society, both Marx and Newman were at the head of crusades pledged to destroy all that liberalism stood for. Yet it is idle to pretend that

Protestant teaching and practice has not had enormous influence over post-Reformation civilization, reaching far beyond the boundaries of Protestant confessional groups into the very structure of contemporary culture. Both what Protestants have believed, and what they have failed to believe, must be considered of vital importance by any historian of the West. During the past four hundred-odd years, the dynamic of Protestant outreach shaped the course of events to an overwhelming degree. And if we now stand, as some think, at the end of the Protestant Era, then it is profitless to look around for some one else to take the blame.

Protestants have every right to object, of course, when either Catholic, or secularist—or other party apologist—tries to deduce all the evils of the present from Protestant 'error'. Protestants did not, as it were, take over the world's destiny for a season. They did not start with a clean slate, nor were they ever given a free hand to mould the world to the pattern of their dreams. History refuses to supply us with a convenient laboratory where we can test our party doctrines in isolation from one another and prove that some are unquestionably good for humanity and others just as certainly injurious. In the last resort, the fact that history is the realm of unique occurrences, where no conditions are ever repeated exactly, forbids any final or completely objective analysis of the past. We live in history, and that is the same thing as saying that we must always live by faith, open to subjectivity. Thus, while many interpretations of history are obviously grotesque over-simplifications of available facts, and while most blatant party views of history are suspect, tending as they do to reduce everything to a game of Cops v. Robbers, there is no understanding of the world we live in without making a stand *for* and *against*. Just as it is the duty of a parliamentary opposition to criticize (and the duty of the party in office to accept criticism and at the same time to deny the opposition's ability to implement an adequate counter-policy), so every faith must take into account the accusations of its critics, and be prepared to show where those accusations fail to measure up to truth. Protestants will not deny responsibility for failure, if they are to be as honest as their understanding of the Protestant protest compels them to be. But they will be alert to the ambiguity of every 'appeal to history'.

It would be small consolation for Protestantism to secure a verdict of 'Not Guilty', before the bar of history, even were such a verdict possible. Still less can it fall back upon the verdict, 'Not Proven', which in the main is fairly easy to secure. Protestantism stands under the judgement of the Lord of history, and has to account for its failure to obey the command it receives in encountering Infinite Subjectivity. With men, to know all may well be to excuse all, if not indeed to forgive all. Not so with God, where moral categories are insufficient and where those whom He calls stand without rights, though with the plainest of duties ! As Protestantism is under judgement by way of dialogue, it must confess to failure and to no simple incompleteness in achievement.

II. PROTESTANT IDOLATRY

No one is immune from that perverted vision which sees the mote abroad and ignores the beam at home. Butler's *Hudibras* struck at more than its intended target of Puritan hypocrisy when it aimed its wit at those who

> *Compound for sins they are inclin'd to*
> *By damning those they have no mind to.*

(Charles II, who is said to have slept with a copy of *Hudibras* under his pillow, might have taken to himself the lines meant to apply to his despised and persecuted subjects.) The poet Butler, of course, found the Puritans easy game. Men who profess a desire to reform public morals are likely to be taunted with the cry of 'Pharisee!'—to the glee of all the Publicans around who have no intention of beating their breasts or bemoaning their sins. Nevertheless, though the charge of hypocrisy is seldom made in a disinterested spirit, it may be justified all the same. Protestants have a peculiar temptation to fall into Pharisaism, as people are apt to do who, like Elijah (1 Kings 19$_{10}$), are *very jealous* for God's glory and feel that they, unlike others, have not bowed the knee to Baal.

Protestant Pharisaism is generally equated with Protestant Puritanism. Certainly the moral aspect of Pharisaism is the most obvious, and the moral rigorism of the Puritans was always in danger of turning sour and spreading moral corruption. Though it was sometimes fanatical, humourless, and unlovely, Puritanism was much more successful in resisting this danger than it is usually given credit for. The perversions of Protestant moralism offer fertile ground for satire to grow on, but Burns's *Holy Willie's Prayer* and Messrs Stiggins and Chadband as portrayed by Charles Dickens are not in any way serious evidence to be brought against that moralism itself. The most penetrating satirists of Protestant society—a Henry Fielding or a Jane Austen—have accepted the broad basis of Protestant ethical values as a norm by which to judge deviations into hypocrisy.

The moral aspect of Protestant Pharisaism is perhaps the least important one, just because it is so easily exposed by Protestantism's own strong social conscience. There are other aspects of it much less open to ridicule's reforming power and much more far-reaching. Protestant Pharisaism, for instance, has been largely instrumental in creating the denominational situation today against which the ecumenical movement has only recently begun to make a decisive counter-offensive. Each *going-out* in search of a pure Church since the Reformation has been accompanied by an intransigent Pharisaism on the part of the parent-body, or by a self-willed Pharisaism on the part of the seceders—and usually by both. That loyalty to principles and concern for the 'beloved community' were the conscious motives behind sectarian quarrels makes the whole business the more tragic. A mixture of good and evil, a mingling of self-abrogation and lust for power, has always been characteristic of what Burke called 'the dissidence of dissent'. But then it is the nature of Pharisaism to bring about evil through mistaken loyalty to the good.

The sectarianism which dissociates itself from all other bodies because it believes that it is the sole repository of Christian truth is carrying on a Catholic theological attitude even when it is loudest in its claim to be Protestant and anti-Rome. But there is a type of Pharisaic denominationalism which is peculiarly Protestant. This is much less concerned with making exclusive claims than with asserting the rightness of an individual's religion, *just as it is*. There is no desire to change the beliefs of others; indeed, those who hold this kind of outlook usually profess a large tolerance and like to speak of the many paths winding up different sides of the hill which leads to the Heavenly City. Equally, there is no concern for Christian unity. Often there is sacrificial loyalty given to the local place of worship, because it is the visible embodiment of the individual's faith. But loyalty to the narrow limit of those things which (as William James pointed out) are really direct extensions of the self exhausts the limits of self-dedication. The vision of the Kingdom of God is also exhausted within the limits of an individual imagination. All Pharisaism, of course, is a form of idolatry—of not allowing God to be God, but of creating a God of our own choosing. Hence the Pharisee's willing devotion to a cause with which he identifies himself, his preoccupation with standards of goodness such as come within his range of consciousness, and his readiness to believe he does God service when he hates his brother. Catholic and Protestant idolatry differ chiefly in this, that Catholic idolatry has its idol in the external, objective sphere, while Protestant idolatry is inward. Catholicism, like secular totalitarianism, finds absolute authority and value in an institution. The invisible God is worshipped in a visible image, as if the image could wholly contain Him—basically a pagan idolatry.[1] Protestant idolatry places the centre within. It mimics the relationship of dialogue, but with God speaking only what the self wishes to hear, as if the self could exhibit His Word.

The most evident Catholic virtue is humility—the humility of unquestioning obedience. True, that humility may be put at the service of spiritual pride, so that, like the obedient soldier, it may sometimes be guilty of the worst crimes, simply by carrying out the will of a superior authority. But Catholic humility is personal and shines by its own light. By being expressed habitually, it can even become a second nature. It will show itself in self-forgetting service and in great devoutness in the personal religious life. Catholic pride, by contrast, is impersonal because it is objectified in the authority of the Church: it does not depend upon any individual aggressiveness, for it shows itself best in an entirely unselfconscious assumption that every other standpoint except the Catholic one is necessarily wrong. But Protestantism breeds individual and strongly personal pride. Catholic societies of the past have been very familiar with aristocratic and ecclesiastic arrogance: it was a pride born of position and arising from security in enjoying the 'power that corrupts'. Democratic Protestant societies are familiar with a different kind of pride which arises from security: it is a complacency based, not on position, but merely on being oneself. In secularized democratic life, 'self-expression' has completely taken the place of the service of God as the declared purpose of existence. The Protestant who knows no humility, or who has lost his understanding of religion altogether, will say, 'here stand I' as a loud boast instead of as a desperate confession.

Protestant Pharisaic pride, it should be noticed, is very different from frank self-love, which is merely moral and spiritual immaturity, and far from Pharisaical. The deified self is not at all 'natural man', with his simple animal wants and an unambiguous ambition to

---

[1] 'The ostentatious grandeur of Saint Peter's, Rome, with its proud flaunting of the "*Tu es Petrus*" in letters of gold high above the Table of the Lord, seems to be the perfect historical development of the boasting spirit of him who said: "Though all men should deny thee, yet will I not deny thee." . . . We cannot altogether avoid feeling that in the architecture of Saint Peter's a catholicity of paganism has been achieved.' Jenkins, *The Nature of Catholicity*, p. 85.

satisfy them, but rather the spiritual self who is symbolized in the Fall of the Angels, the demonic self who desires absolute power. One of the disguises of this ego-God is the fanatical conscience—a worse enemy to morality than fanatical amoralism, and to religion than any cult of 'Satanism'. Another is the possessive 'love' which seeks to prevent another individual finding his own dimension of dialogue. In the form of complacent self-satisfaction and contentment with one's own inadequate version of the claims of the spiritual life, its demonic character may seem to be negated. Nothing can seem less harmful to others, if destructive of self. But it is out of this negative spirit which refuses to allow the Spirit entrance that the actively demonic grows. An ideal of self-development uncontrolled by religious standards of what the end of development should be will not long be satisfied with the aims which liberalism proposes. Protestant idolatry does not usually defy God or persecute His messengers. It simply cultivates a convenient deafness which ignores what it does not want to hear. It corrupts inwardness, until dialogue is made impossible and man is shut in with himself. When subjectivity is destroyed, then personal and moral development is at an end, and the stage is set for a new external revolt of man against God and against his fellows; an effete Christianity is broken by the confident outrush of doctrinaire paganism.

III. PROTESTANTISM'S 'DISTRESSED AREAS'

The failure of Protestantism to interpret the whole Gospel and its Pharisaic tendency to avoid self-criticism is shown most clearly in two prominent features of the twentieth century. The first is the increasing drift of the masses away from Protestant faith. Although historic Protestantism found its main strength in its appeal to the middle classes, and so tended to trim its message to a class mentality, its following in the past was by no means restricted to a class basis. When Kierkegaard launched his 'attack upon Christendom', he was protesting against Christianity being turned into a bourgeois ideology—especially, as he said, in Protestantism, and especially in Denmark. But, although Kierkegaard held up to specific ridicule the middle-class conventional outlook triumphant in Denmark (a favourite name he had for his fellow-Danes was *geese*), it was the whole nation, from the court to the farm, that he attacked. Today the urban population which makes up the bulk of our technological civilization is becoming less and less influenced either by Protestant dogma or by Protestant categories of thought. Catholicism is also adversely affected by the defection of the proletariat from its traditional allegiance and its conversion to secular ideologies. But those who remain under the rule of the Church—at least so far as the Roman Church is concerned—are still convinced of the adequacy of their religion to meet their everyday needs, as few Protestants from the same social background are convinced. While Protestantism becomes less able to cope with the urban situation, so it becomes more characteristically suburban in character. Even as specialized a Protestant body as the Salvation Army shows this tendency; from being a missionary movement, it has turned into a substantial denomination, with inevitable change in outlook as well as in size.

The second feature of contemporary life is the way in which psychiatry has become a successful rival to religion. Either because neurosis is greatly on the increase in our highly sophisticated culture, or because we have grown self-consciously preoccupied over the matter of mental health, psychotherapy seems to offer a practical salvation for the individual which he regards of the highest—indeed, final—importance. This is certainly a consequence of Protestantism's failure to meet the demands of modern living. Psychiatrists testify to the very small number of practising Roman Catholics who come into their consulting-rooms.

These two apparently distinct developments are undoubtedly closely related, for they show alike how Protestantism has proved inadequate to meet the needs of modern man.[2] The Protestant protest seems irrelevant to many, and even those who are prepared to accept it find that it fails to provide what they feel compelled to seek. In the years of the Depression between the Wars, there were districts which were called in Britain *Distressed Areas*. These were centres of acute unemployment and distress which served to show the real extent of an economic collapse which was not so abundantly evident in other places. The growth of mass secularism and the enormous prestige of psychoanalysis point in the same way to regions of life which Protestantism has consistently failed to cultivate: it is the region behind consciousness. Protestantism's distressed areas are found where those whose educational background has not been sufficient to accept Protestant intellectualism succumb to the attraction of some emotionally consoling myth, or where the intellectually disciplined find that their conscious beliefs are unable to deal with their emotional problems.

[2] Much the same argument has been advanced in Tillich's *The Protestant Era*, particularly in the essay, 'The End of the Protestant Era?' which is Chapter 15 in that work.

Protestantism has developed consciousness through its emphasis on personality in the individual. The Protestant is made sensitive to the need for personal decision, and this sensitivity follows from the theological foundations of Protestant faith in dialogue. Now the possibility of dialogue is not dependent upon a developed individual consciousness. It is probably present at the lowest level of religious and social organization. (Otto's category of the *holy* can only be justified by recognizing that it represents intuited I-Thou relationship at the threshold of consciousness; for, unless a subjective feeling of awe is capable of rising into a personal relationship between worshipper and the Worshipped, then Otto's *mysterium tremendum et fascinans* remains no more than a complex emotion.) Yet to depend upon dialogue for the major direction of one's values demands a very great extension of consciousness. Without this capacity for self-knowledge and reflection, the dimension of subjectivity must remain a mystery hedged about by superstitious fancies. In order that what is beyond the intellect may be interpreted, the call to dialogue is also a call to intellectual clarification. In Protestantism, as we have seen, this leads to a high value being placed upon education in general and upon theology in particular.

Protestant intellectualism thus has its basis in the need to develop individual consciousness, so that the dimension of dialogue may be properly approached and disentangled from primitive beliefs and habits. Primitive thinking regards the world as the abode of magical powers, capricious and yet also under law.[3] Rational thinking attempts to subject the whole universe to law—the act of *comprehension* is at once *understanding* and *imprisoning within one's grasp*, as etymology reminds us. Protestantism calls on reason to deliver us from thinking in magical categories, but it also puts boundaries upon reason to deliver us from the bondage of the universal reign of law to which rational theory would bind us[4] and makes us face the need for

[3] In Tillich's three-fold sociological scheme—theonomy, autonomy, and heteronomy—theonomy is an ideal never completely realized (see p. 146, *supra*). Yet Tillich speaks of the theonomy existing in primitive society. Actually, at a primitive level, theonomy must always be mixed with a large measure of heteronomy, though this heteronomy is not a self-conscious imposition by a legislative group but the traditional law of the community unconsciously accepted by the individual. That this primitive theonomy is a mixed state is shown by Tillich's insistence that the way to theonomy is by way of developing autonomy even though autonomy, by itself, breaks the unity theonomy demands.

[4] Again, Kant gives a theoretical statement of Protestant belief in his *Critique of Pure Reason*, where he says that ideas necessarily, by following their own nature, lead to illusion. Practical reason, recognizing the categorical imperative of duty, as well as the empirical world, where alone the understanding can profitably employ itself, has to restrain a purely theoretical rationalism.

personal responsibility. But the call to live beyond the law is even more demanding than the call to live consciously, putting away the irrational. In practice, the lives of all of us are largely determined either by external law consciously acknowledged, or by internal compulsions which we cannot, for the most part, explain. The positive law (the law of the land) is much less important in the place it occupies for us than either the laws we obey unthinkingly, the unconscious or semi-conscious laws of habit and social conformity and inherited beliefs, or than the hidden springs of action within the self, which appear to us to be a law to themselves, outside our control. Protestant subjectivity demands of us, in fact, to be conscious of every solicitation that prompts us to action, from whatever source it may come; to scrutinize all values we hold; to become aware of our responsibilities; and to implement these last by personal decision.

It is obvious that the Protestant way of dialogue makes great demands upon the conscious self. The severity of these demands is likely to prove intolerable unless dialogue is fully developed in order to supply the ground upon which personal responsibility can rest. Responsibility means inevitably a measure of isolation for the self, which in times of stress is hard to bear. Protestantism, for fear of encouraging moral immaturity, has largely failed to cater for the very real need for giving support to the self in its day-to-day perplexities. Disraeli remarked dryly in *Lothair*, 'A Protestant, if he wants aid or advice on any matter, can only go to his solicitor'. Today Disraeli would probably note that the Protestant could also go to a psychiatrist.

When dialogue fails, when the individual is left isolated from God and from his fellows, then man is left suspended in lonely self-awareness, haunted by an empty echo of dialogue commanding him to be responsible, urging him to duty and pointing him to the goal of perfection, without furnishing that grace which would enable him to fulfil his responsibility. This has both psychological and sociological consequences. In the psychological realm it appears as the maladjustment of the personality at its various levels. And in the sociological realm it appears as the decay of an established ideology, a cultural 'failure of nerve' which produces social disorder leading to the emergence of new social patterns based on rival ideologies. These happenings represent the revolt of the unconscious against consciousness which is not provided with resources to deal with what it does not understand or is not willing to admit. Recent history appears to drive home the conclusion that this is exactly the situation that has arisen. Protestantism's distressed areas point to a radical weakness in the whole Protestant economy of the individual which, unless corrected, must lead to the disintegration of Protestantism. Present symptoms indicate that disintegration has, in part, begun.

IV. RATIONALISM AND IRRATIONALISM

Protestantism's distressed areas have been produced by Protestant intellectualism. This may seem surprising when one of the chief charges against Protestantism from the Catholic side is that it encourages an irrational faith. But Protestant history shows that the situation has been too complex to be written off by a simple judgement of that kind. The drive towards a developed consciousness and the call to dialogue, which we have just considered, are both integral to Protestantism and together they create a tension: the one tends to rationalism, and the other to a limitation of reason.

This tension becomes obvious when we turn to an historical study of theology. In the Middle Ages, a rationalist tradition of theology, which regarded the true interpretation of the Gospel to be its correct doctrinal statement in propositional form, was dominant in spite of counter-tendencies: conspicuously, the strong elements of a theology of dialogue running from Augustine through Anselm to Bonaventure, and also the anti-rationalistic, pragmatic outlook of Occam. Breaking through rationalism to assert the primacy of dialogue was the real accomplishment of Luther's theology, and this essential insight was fundamental in Calvinism also. In this task both Reformers were very conscious of their debt to Augustine. But rationalism was brought back again by the Lutheran scholastics and by Calvin's own bent to legalistic thinking. Besides the traditional rationalism of theology, Protestantism was influenced strongly, both by attraction and by repulsion, by the intellectual currents of the Renaissance. The Renaissance was in some respects a reaction from the rationalism of the Middle Ages, learning from Occam and Roger Bacon to look to tangible facts rather than to abstract thinking for an understanding of the universe. But it had its strongly rationalistic bias also, which was evident in Descartes and was carried over into the Enlightenment.

Renaissance rationalism united an empirical and pragmatic interest with strenuous opposition to all subjectivity, and, where Protestantism was most strongly influenced by this intellectual current, the result was what we know today as *liberal Protestantism.* (The modern tradition of Biblical scholarship, for instance, goes back in unbroken line to the early Renaissance Hebrew and Greek scholars and is an authentic product of liberal rationalism, which, strongly discouraged by Rome, bore fruit in Protestantism.) Liberal Protestantism was almost as fierce an adversary of superstitition as was anti-clerical atheistic humanism. This brought great moral advance, but it also endangered a right understanding of dialogue, for dialogue cannot be interpreted in rational terms. Sometimes liberal rationalism was successfully united with a theology of dialogue. There were the nineteenth-century Biblical scholars, such as Robertson Smith, who, against the representatives of traditional Protestant orthodoxy, maintained that scientific Biblical criticism was fully compatible with the Protestant protest—a stand which led to the eventual conversion of the main Protestant denominations to so-called 'modernism'. At other times liberal Protestantism tended to surrender unconditionally to empirical-rational modes of thought, losing its distinctively confessional character. In reaction, traditionalists were driven back upon a legalistic standard of orthodoxy, producing the militantly 'fundamentalist' wing of Protestantism and—more recently—the neo-orthodox school of dialectical theology, which has a far better claim to represent essential Protestantism, stressing as it does the need for returning to the insights of the Reformers.

Earlier than the Biblical controversy, however, movements within Protestantism had tried to counter Protestant intellectualism by appealing to specifically religious feelings. These were the pietistic and evangelical-revivalist movements. Unamuno, leaning on Ritschl, has claimed that pietism represents a Catholic survival within Protestantism[5] and, undeniably, there are very close historical links between Protestant pietism and the practice of the contemplative life within Catholicism. But Protestant pietism was also, and perhaps chiefly, a protest against Protestant rationalism, and its weakness as well as its strength was typically Protestant. Its strength was that it insisted on the primacy of the religious sphere over the moral and the intellectual. Its weakness was that it tended to concentrate on a conscious wooing of emotion, because of its negative protest against intellectualism. This emotion was directed specifically to one area of life alone (the subjective *feeling* of faith) instead of helping to build up a total understanding of all life (the dimension of subjectivity), so that the unconscious levels of feeling were starved. Thus a dualism within Protestantism was perpetuated. Protestant religion became identified either with something to be explained intellectually, and so

[5] *The Tragic Sense of Life*, pp. 294-5.

liable to merge into a barren rationalism, or else with something to be felt but not by any means to be rationally justified, and so likely to evaporate into mere religious sentiment; unless, by taking refuge in legalism, it fell back upon some former theological orthodoxy. Although the authentic Protestant protest rooted in dialogue was never wholly lost, it could not succeed in bringing the unlimited grace discovered in dialogue to the whole area of life under the strain of this dualism. Consciousness was as overburdened in the pietistic as in the intellectualistic Protestant approach. The latter built upon moral effort, social awareness, and brotherly concern; the former upon conviction of sin, experience of conversion, and assurance of salvation.

The economy of the self cannot rest in continual demands, unless there is an equal flow of resources. It is not enough for these resources to satisfy the mind or the feelings, for they have to satisfy life itself. Like the attitude of mind which thinks the problem of unemployment is simply a matter of the willingness of people to work, Protestantism is too apt to blame the decay of faith upon wilful rejection of the claims of religion, and to think that this can be countered by greater zeal in evangelism rather than in overhauling the Protestant presentation of the Gospel. The distressed areas are left to turn to whatever ideology makes a bid for their support. While the humanistic-liberal branch of Protestantism was arguing that modern man would never again be deceived by authoritarian dogma, and the Evangelical-individualistic branch was arguing that Christianity was failing because it had deserted the fundamental call to spiritual salvation and was preaching the Kingdom of God on earth, Marxism was winning the unthinking and the 'intellectuals' alike by a unity of inflexible dogma and social Utopianism.

One of the truths which both liberal Protestantism and fundamentalist Protestantism have failed to grasp is that neither argument nor refusal to argue, reasonableness or the obstinacy which rejects logic, has much power to move men. The fundamentalists have indeed realized better than the liberals—and the extreme sects better still—that the way to prevent reason from dissolving dogma is to keep reason busy at defending dogma. No system is so crazy that it cannot be rationalized; and the more complex the rationalization, the greater the appeal both to the intellectually minded (who fear subjectivity, the sign of a rationalism which has failed to conquer the world) and to the unintellectual (who think of knowledge as a species of power and like to think they have such a talisman on their side).

Hume spoke for dogmatism as well as for scepticism when he said that reason is, and ought only to be, the slave of the passions. It is comparatively easy to show that orthodox Marxism is intellectually dubious, but it is not easy to dislodge the hold of orthodox Marxism over a believer, either on the grounds of his not having read *Das Capital*, or, if he has read it, of his not having understood it. Unamuno has argued that Catholicism is essentially *against* reason, and he speaks of Catholic theology as a compromise with 'the enemy'— a marriage between the irrational and the human intellect. But, even were his diagnosis correct, a 'compromise' which goes far to disarm the enemy is the wisest of strategies. Catholicism, so much more effectively than Protestantism, has been able to appeal alike to the intellectual and to the unthinking.

In the contemporary situation, Catholicism might be thought to have a greater opportunity to win, where Protestantism has failed, than an ideology such as Marxism. Conceptually far more profound, emotionally at least as potent, it can point to a long tradition that seems an impregnable guarantee that it is likely to outlive all modern rivals. Yet Catholicism's tradition is also a weakness. In blaming Protestantism for the present crisis of Western civilization it resembles a parliamentary opposition which tries to climb back to power on the plea, 'Look what a mess the government has made of things'. In such circumstances, voters usually remember that the present opposition was formerly defeated on the same issue, so that it can hardly fill the role of St George against the dragon. Better the devil they know than the devil they once knew only too well. Where, as in Eastern Europe, Communism has triumphed over a formerly dominant Catholic tradition, the will to break completely with the past has probably been more compelling than the lure of the Marxist Utopia. The present policy of Rome to declare Communism to be the root of all evil may yet turn out to be a mistaken one. Men who have grasped the values of toleration and individual freedom know well enough that it is the denial of these, under any party label, which is ultimately intolerable; and that it is the will to dialogue, instead of the liquidation of the heretic, which is the basis of social righteousness. Protestantism has shown the way to these values inadequately, failing for the most part to appeal to the unity of head and heart, and leaving men insecure and isolated in a freedom which has very little meaning for them. But an understanding of dialogue, however fragmentary, cannot readily be erased once it has been written in a life.

V. SACRAMENTAL DIALOGUE

The poverty of Protestantism's appeal to man's total being is exhibited in its inadequate attitude to the sacramental dimension of experience. Historically, Protestantism has been opposed to Catholic 'sacramentalism', and this negative protest has led to an undervaluation of sacraments as such, although Protestant theology's internal controversies over the nature and efficacy of the sacraments show that at least the subject has not been robbed of all meaning.

A sacrament has been defined by O. C. Quick in the following terms: 'A sacrament is any spatio-temporal reality which by its occupation of space or time expresses to us God's will and purpose and enables us the better to co-operate with them'.[6] According to such a definition, Protestantism has certainly a very definite place for sacramental worship, which goes beyond the traditional Protestant sacraments of Baptism and the Lord's Supper. Protestant worship is universally centred on the proclamation of the Word: that is, as we have seen, its apostolic charter (1 Cor. 1_{21}, Titus 1_3).[7] And, with a few partial exceptions such as the Society of Friends, this has led to preaching (that is, a personal appeal to those gathered for worship to hear God's Word to them, individually and corporately) being a central act of worship, mostly in the form of an exposition of a biblical text. The preacher, by mediating the eternal Word in human words is exercising a sacramental function. Although the *spatio-temporal reality* of the preacher and his message does not bring about its effect purely by occupying space and time, but also conveys intelligible meaning, yet the man and his words are of themselves 'signs' in their own right.

Unless the sacramental nature of preaching within Protestantism is appreciated, the heart of the Protestant protest in regard to the relation of the Gospel to the Church—and so to mankind as a whole—cannot be understood. Catholics who accuse Protestantism of a Manichean attitude to creation, leading to the pursuit of a false spirituality that despises the sensible world, fail to take into consideration the Protestant view of what proclaiming the Gospel means. *The preaching of the Word* is an embodiment in space and time of the

---

[6] *The Christian Sacraments* (1927), p. 104. A further definition of what a *Christian* sacrament means does not appreciably alter the first. It states: 'A sacrament is a ritual act, using a certain form and matter, which both represents some universal relation of human life to God through Christ, and also, in thus representing all life, makes life worthy to be thus represented' (p. 108).

[7] See Chapter 3, *supra*.

Eternal Word of God, and thus constitutes an extension of the earthly ministry of the Incarnate Word. To the Protestant mind, the continuity of the Church lies essentially in the continuity of the Word which is preached. The words of the preacher become the material means by which God's Word is mediated to men.

Yet, at the same time, the Catholic critics of Protestantism, though mistaken in their belief that Protestantism is Manichean, are right in sensing that there is a strong Protestant resistance to sacramentalism as such which goes beyond a rejection of the specifically Catholic understanding of the sacramental. It is true that orthodox Protestantism in its historic definition of where the Church is to be found adds 'and the sacraments rightly administered' to 'where the Word is rightly preached'. But the fact that some Protestant sects such as the Salvation Army, which do not depart far from traditional orthodoxy in other respects, find it possible to dispense with the two dominical sacraments altogether, while many others which retain the sacraments do not appear to cherish them particularly, points to something too important to overlook. It would appear that Protestantism altogether has a bias towards making verbal communication—the most personal and the least tangible of human activities—into its typical sacrament, and shows a certain reluctance to appropriate other more concrete symbols. This reluctance has been evident from the days of the Reformation. Although Calvin's theology had declared the unity of Word and Sacrament, Calvin himself could not persuade Geneva to make the regular Sunday worship a Communion Service.

Opposition to Catholic sacramentalism accounts for part of this Protestant resistence to the concrete sacrament, if only for part. The Catholic view tends towards replacing a genuinely sacramental conception of the spiritual *expressed* through the material by a pagan and magical notion of the material *transformed* into the spiritual, so that the sacramental sign becomes a sacred object. It was not for nothing that, at the Reformation, the Mass became the prime issue between Catholic and Protestant. The Mass, in its aspect of a sacrifice offered to God, typified Catholic egocentric theology as opposed to Protestant theocentricity which regarded the Lord's Supper as the gift of God to man; while the Catholic doctrine of Transubstantiation implied a quasi-mechanical view of the interaction of the natural and the supernatural.

Behind this suspicion of Catholic sacramentalism lies the whole personalist tradition of dialogue. Protests against the making of

images, which form so notable a part of the prophetic literature of
the Bible as well as appearing in the Decalogue, are very closely
related to the biblical idea of God. They spring from a desire to
avoid a superstitious and unworthy view of the relation of the God-
head to the material world. When the Christian Church of the eighth
century, after a severe internal struggle, finally sanctioned the ven-
eration of images and thus reversed the Biblical protest, one of the
conspicuous elements of modern Catholicism was established. The
Catholic view is that the stimulus to religious feeling provided by the
use of concrete aids to worship offsets the danger of lapsing into
idolatry—which in any case can be taken care of by properly defining
the right use of an image. Protestants have rejected this view on the
grounds that theological definition is likely to have little influence
upon practical devotion and that the definitions themselves did not
effectively banish the constant threat to Christian faith of pagan
ways of thought.[8] To the Protestant mind a sacramental object,
wrongly regarded, may belong to the same world of reference as a
pagan idol.[9] And so it has happened that to safeguard against a misuse of the Sacraments has been one of the leading motives of Protestant theology and Church order. Calvin, who insisted continually
that the Spirit worked through sacramental objects as well as through
the personal response of faith, also insisted—looking back here, as so
often, to Augustine—that the spoken word must be joined to the ritual
act if worship was to be true to the Gospel proclaimed by Christ.

But another consideration underlies Protestant resistance to sacramentalism. It is the fear that an unrestricted reliance upon a sacramental approach to communion with God may abolish the way of
dialogue in favour of seeking to know God only as an immanent
Spirit, pervading nature and the soul, and in the last resort indistin-
guishable from the latter.

This second understanding of sacramentalism has been advocated
in recent times by Nicolas Berdyaev. He agrees that Protestantism
has been right in repudiating magical views of the mystery of God's
dealings with His world. With the Protestant, he repudiates the
Catholic (Roman and Orthodox) belief that external authority can
control grace and alone mediates it sacramentally. With the Protest-

---

[8] For an historical examination of this question see Edwyn Bevan: *Holy Images:
An Inquiry into Idolatry and Image-worship in Ancient Paganism and in Christianity*
(1940).
   [9] 'All paganism consists in this, that God is related to man directly, as the
obviously extraordinary to the astonished observer.' Kierkegaard, *Concluding Unscientific Postscript*, p. 219.

ant, he denies the Catholic charge that any other view divides spirit from matter. But, finding Protestantism hostile to *mysticism*, he argues for the recognition of the Incarnation as a mystical expression of the divine element in man. In his *Spirit and Reality* he writes:

Spirit—the Holy Spirit—is incarnated in human life, but it assumes the form of a *whole humanity* rather than of authority. This is, indeed, the pivotal idea of my book. That is the only justification of anthropomorphism as a theosophy, for God is like a whole humanity rather than like nature, society or concept.[10]

Here is a sacramental view which comes near to identifying the Infinite Word and the finite creature. It escapes from legalism, but at the cost of by-passing the Gospel of repentance and faith. Protestants would say that God is no more like *Man* than he is like *Nature*, nor can humanity become a sacramental expression of the Spirit until it is redeemed and sanctified by God's free grace. Protestantism here would find common ground with Catholicism against Berdyaev in asserting that the Holy Spirit is incarnate only in the *ecclesia*, the people of God, and will be incarnate in a *whole humanity* only when His purpose is complete and God is all in all (1 Cor. 15$_{28}$); though it would not admit a legalized interpretation of the *ecclesia* which limits the Church to membership of one institution as Catholicism does. Sacramentalism of the kind advocated by Berdyaev has always appeared to Protestantism to challenge the uniqueness of the Incarnation of Christ and the redemption achieved by Christ's Cross, taking away value from the protest of faith, which then becomes just one example among many of the ways of the Spirit incarnate in human history.

While Protestantism is bound to raise a negative protest against the distortion of the Gospel found in these two conceptions of sacramentalism (the first denying the subjectivity of faith, and the second denying the need for obedience to faith), it has not been equally wise in rejecting both outright. Of course, there can be no surrender to the Grand Inquisitor who claims the right to delimit the sphere where the Creator enters His creation and thus to control also the supply of sacramental grace. But men refuse God's own gracious condescension to them if they belittle the sacramental signs by which He has chosen to speak to them through His incarnate Word in Christ and in the Church. We cannot think that the human spirit and God's Holy Spirit are one and the same. But when we

[10] p. 167 (1946 edn.); Berdyaev's italics.

deny that there is any sacrament which is not illuminated directly by the historic Incarnation of the Word, we limit the action of the Creating Word which speaks in the universe, and so not allow God to be God. Although God's work of reconciling the world to Himself can only be seen fully in Jesus Christ, and although all nature and humanity carries the marks of the bondage of the Fall, we shut ourselves off from effective spheres of grace if we fail to find in nature and mankind alike the sacramental workings of the Spirit.[11]

Protestant unwillingness to believe that the universe can be sacramental, and its seeking for the Divine Word almost solely in the personal response to the spoken word, has been chiefly responsible for bringing into existence the distressed areas of the self which we have already considered. Belief that our response to God must at all times be a personal and conscious response has impoverished Protestant witness and led to the decline of evangelical zeal. The 'way of the rejection of images' is a fruitful method of personal development, but it cannot be followed in the ordinary pilgrim way of the Christian life to the exclusion of its contrary, the 'way of the affirmation of images'. As well as the experience of individual salvation and of personal participation in the redeemed Community, we must admit a place for what Paul Tillich has named the Gestalt of Grace.[12] An assurance that Providence is nowhere absent but everywhere working for the redemption of all nature, so that no sphere of human experience is incapable of providing sacramental means by which the Spirit can be given, should lift the believer beyond mere immanency to the place where the Word of the Gospel is heard in thankful acceptance. Protestantism has still to learn that dialogue is not limited to conscious decisions to serve and love God and our neighbour. There is also a dialogue which extends to our relationship with our total environment, an unspoken communion with all which manifests visibly the love of God for His creation and His divine activity restoring it, so that it may show forth His glory.

---

[11] O. C. Quick reminds us that Incarnation applies to the completed Universe of God's purpose as well as to the earthly life of Christ (op. cit., p. 102). Unfortunately, Quick does not develop the question of how the 'different manners and degrees' in which, he says, the Universe at present mirrors the Christ (p. 104) are to be recognized. Catholic theology, because it holds that God's grace is active through the natural order, finds no difficulty in admitting a general sacramentalism in addition to the Church's guardianship of supernatural grace.

[12] This conception is developed in 'The Formative Power of Protestantism' (Chapter 14, *The Protestant Era*). Tillich quotes Jung's saying that the history of Protestantism is a history of continuous *iconoclasm*—a destruction of images (ibid., Author's Introduction, p. xxiii).

VI. ART'S SACRAMENTAL FUNCTION

The religions of the world have always employed art to impress themselves upon the societies where their influence was at work. Art has aided worship, but it has also shown a tendency to break away from the service of religion to assert its own values and exist in its own rights. This liaison with religion—and also its uncertainty—is because art has a sacramental function. The artist, *qua* artist, is a sacramentalist using the medium of his art as the form and matter through which supreme value is manifested both for himself and for all who can 'read' his work with comprehension. Art is necessarily to be grasped in subjectivity—which means that it is never merely subjective. As opposed to religious sacramentalism, the sacramentalism of art is not limited to the expression of particular beliefs, but seeks that universal Spirit of which Berdyaev spoke. That is why it can serve any religion whatever, or become a religion on its own account.

That the artist is concerned with Spirit is obscured for us by the common assumption that the artist is a copyist who busies himself with reproducing nature. In reality (as the example of music makes clear, and the art of the dance clearer still), art unfolds the self-awareness of Spirit through spatio-temporal forms which nature provides[13]. This self-awareness is, in the last resort, Spirit incarnate in a *whole humanity* which, as Berdyaev divined, is involved in the inner logic of a general sacramentalism. In Greek mythology, the nine Muses were daughters of Zeus and Memory, signifying a union between the Divine and human consciousness. To the modern view all the fine arts come under the province of imagination. The few artists who have tried to work out a consistent philosophy of the imagination have realized that their individual subjective visions were partial expressions of a universally valid realm of reality. The subjectivity of mankind's imaginative existence was the passport to a world of ultimate truth. Keats wrote in a much-quoted letter, 'I am certain of nothing but the holiness of the heart's affections, and the truth of the imagination. . . . The soul is a world of itself, and has enough to do in its own home'. William Blake inscribed on his engraving of the *Laocoon Group*, 'The Eternal Body of Man is The Imagination, that is God himself/The Divine Body/ישוע, Jesus: we

---

[13] ' "Holding the mirror up to nature" is a highly misleading description either of art or of aesthetic enjoyment itself unless one puts the emphasis on the "holding" rather than on the "mirror".' R. B. Perry, *Realms of Value*, p. 326.

are his Members. It manifests itself in his Works of Art (In Eternity All is vision)'.

The *whole humanity* (or Eternal Body of Man) which the artist seeks through his inspiration to express in works of art is the full range of the human spirit, both conscious and unconscious. In exploring the unconscious, modern depth psychology finds that art, like dreams, holds the key to unlock doors of the human psyche which are otherwise closed to consciousness. Art and dreams alike disclose the self through imagery; and this imagery, on being reduced to rational terms, provides the data for psychological theories of the unconscious. Thus it comes about that psychology is well able to appreciate general sacramentalism. This is especially true of Jung's psychology, which actually posits a 'collective unconscious', i.e. in its 'own home' the world of the soul displays the imaginative vision of a *whole humanity*.[14] When religion is described in purely psychological terms, it is also assumed that religious beliefs are imaginative pictures of the inner world of mankind: the 'revelations' of faith may be illusions, objectively speaking, but they are sacramental manifestations of great usefulness, being very potent symbolic statements of psychological truth. Religion is thus reduced to the status of a comprehensive art. It does for humanity at large what his art does for the individual artist. And its principal function is to make available an accepted vocabulary of imagery which brings the healing power of art to bear upon the common life of society. So psychotherapy uses art as a means of curing neurosis on a short-term basis, just as it encourages religious faith as a long-term policy for preventing neurosis.

Not many artists, however, seek the general sacramentalism of art consistently; artists such as Blake and Keats are exceptions in this respect.[15] Most subordinate their art to a religion or philosophy derived elsewhere, and establish a *modus vivendi* between their artistic conscience and the rest of their beliefs. The Church in the Catholic

[14] Blake's elaborate mythology can be translated almost exactly into the categories of Jung's psychology. The vision yielded by art is, according to this evidence, a symbolic representation of the psyche reached by imaginative intuition, which can be confirmed by rational analysis based on empirical findings. It is, of course, a question to be decided by psychologists how far such a system as the one advocated by Jung is built upon scientific hypotheses resting on empirically verifiable facts, and how far it is itself an imaginative symbolic structure.

[15] The Aesthetic Movement was born of a misunderstanding of the general sacramentalism of art. Art does not need any external credal values to support it. 'Art for Art's sake' is a creed, however, and demands that art shall express nothing. The result is that art is trivialized by being cut off from the fullness of living and becomes, as W. S. Gilbert's robust common sense perceived, a matter of uttering 'platitudes in stained-glass attitudes'.

tradition has consistently acted as a guardian of the social and cultural life of society, which, by putting itself under the Church's authority, has been assured of encouragement, support, guidance and (when need arises) rebuke from its patron and mentor. The artist has shared in this overall pattern of Catholic patronage of culture, which has varied in the freedom it has given to artistic expression, but which from its understanding of the sacramental nature of both the sacred and the secular, has on the whole valued and honoured art highly. In turn, the artist has shown his gratitude by placing his art at the disposal of Catholic faith. In the Middle Ages, Christian art of both Eastern and Western Catholicism was a cultural achievement parallel to the triumphs of other great religious cultures, and perhaps more remarkable than any other preceding it.

At the Reformation, Protestants turned against Catholic religious art as the transmitter of false religious values. This iconoclasm at first took a physical form, when images and shrines were destroyed because they were taken to be idolatrous. But much more permanent and far-reaching was the iconoclasm which tried to build up the interior personal consciousness of the people to be as far as possible independent of symbols. This resulted in a Protestant suspicion of art which has never been overcome. For the strictest Puritans visual art was *popery* and imaginative literature *lies*—a way of thinking very much in harmony with the rise of the scientific attitude.[16] Such outright rejection of art was by no means general, of course, and Protestants tended to be absorbed, so far as their artistic energies went, into the stream of Renaissance art which had an overwhelmingly secular character. But this meant that, instead of the growth of any specifically Protestant art, faith and art seemed more and more to be two aspects of life which did not mix, either for the individual believer who was an artist or for society at large.

If Protestantism can claim any one achievement in art for its own, it can claim the Church music of Bach. This is what Protestantism amounts to—Unamuno exclaims—*celestial music!* The Spanish phrase carries the same meaning as our *so much hot air*, and Unamuno goes on to contrast with Protestant music the close link between Catholic faith and the very concrete arts of painting and sculpture.[17]

---

16 Undoubtedly, Protestant anti-sacramentalism has been a factor in encouraging that outlook which divides reality into matters of fact empirically verifiable (*truth*) and emotion (*nonsense*). Positivism, in spite of its apparent willingness to dismiss ethics from the field of knowledge, is basically a moral faith which, like Puritanism, calls men to forsake vain superstitions and to live according to righteousness. Only, instead of the service of God, it proposes the service of technological progress.

17 *The Tragic Sense of Life*, p. 70.

Again, we see how Protestantism accepts sacramentalism when it is least 'material' and most closely associated with rational discourse. Church music is either joined with words directly, or by association implies them. The Church organ which leads the hymn-singing can be recognized by the worshipper as an extension of human praise. But both the Church organ and the choir set over against the congregation are creations of Catholic liturgical forms. As such, they were rejected by the more rigid Puritans; and Bach himself was censured in his day for hindering congregational worship by over-emphasizing musical expression.

Literature, the art which comes to terms with conceptual thought, is the other art which has been most congenial to Protestant consciousness. So long as the imaginative element was subordinated to the didactic, Puritanism was content to believe that the 'worldly' tendency of art had been neutralized, and (for example) allowed *The Pilgrim's Progress* to be a companion to the Bible. Protestant moralism and social concern have been conspicuously influential in the novel, and particularly in the British and American novel. Prose fiction is, after all, the only genuine post-Reformation literary invention. It is also noteworthy that, with the decline of socially unquestioned moral standards, the novel has so largely capitulated to the psychologists, presenting psychological case-histories rather than the record of moral conflicts. Protestantism's failure to speak to the deeper levels of the self is particularly evident in connexion with the artist, and not least so with the novelist. The most popular novels on the market are those which still continue in the Protestant-moralistic tradition (though with some show of adopting a 'modern' attitude to ethical standards). But very few writers who keep their integrity as artists also keep to Protestant beliefs; or, if they do so, they rarely show the fact in their works. Rather, they turn to Catholicism, like Hemingway; or revolt from their childhood faith and spend their lives vainly trying to find a substitute, like D. H. Lawrence; or they evolve for themselves an individualistic brand of humanism, like André Gide.

The tradition of Protestant humanism, which, in the past, to some extent countered Puritan suspicion of art and kept Protestantism in a living relationship to culture as a whole, lives on today in very meagre measure. And, although this poverty is largely the result of a wholesale breakdown of Renaissance humanism in the modern world which has left so many modern artists rootless and distressed (and incidentally led to a host of valuable experiments in new art forms), it has seriously weakened Protestant witness to the present generation. Protestantism seems to have no constructive share in contemporary culture.

VII. THE CHALLENGE OF CULTURE

Protestantism's failure to understand the sacramental nature of all that surrounds man, both in the world of things and in society, has affected for the worse its contribution to the arts and to culture in general. Yet it is also part of the essence of Protestantism that it cannot dictate cultural standards to society without violence to its conception of the Gospel. There has never been *Protestant art* as there has been *Catholic art*, and the post-Reformation culture cannot be labelled *Protestant* as we can justly label Medieval culture *Catholic*. If bourgeois liberalism can be regarded as a product of Protestantism (and the supposition is not unreasonable), liberal democratic culture may be considered to be Protestant in inspiration. To name it *Protestant* outright would be to overlook the fact that its secular framework can, and does, contain Catholic and Protestant, Christian and non-Christian elements.

Protestant culture is an almost impossible term because the Protestant protest is a witness given in subjectivity before it is externalized in allegiance to a party, and hence brought into the sphere of culture; it is offered as grace and not commanded as law.[18] Culture, although it is apparently spontaneous, is the result of law. Culture assumes a common set of external standards—a corpus of unwritten law—accepted as objectively valid for a given society. Just as a society is kept in being by the existence of positive law to which all its members owe allegiance, so a culture continues while society accepts one complex of standards to live by, and dissolves when new values, embodied in new institutions and expressed in new patterns of social behaviour, gain acceptance. This rule of law in culture is

[18] In *Christ and Culture* (1952), H. Richard Niebuhr examines the ways in which Christian theologians have tried to relate faith to culture. His study of the Catholic (Thomistic) synthesis of faith and culture is headed 'Christ above Culture' (Chapter IV), and Luther's contrast of love and law is put under the title 'Christ and Culture in Paradox' (Chapter V).
Catholicism believes that the law of culture can be made subject to the higher law of the Church. Protestantism is conscious that the legally based system of culture inevitably resists the Gospel because of its supra-legal character and thus that a fully Christian culture is (humanly speaking) impossible. In Tillich's language, Catholicism leads to heteronomy, while Protestantism knows that theonomy is the ideal, though, as ideal, it can never be completely realized. Luther, with his acute understanding of the opposition between grace and law, is relatively pessimistic over the possibility of culture being Christianized; Calvin, with his strong legalistic tendencies, relatively optimistic. Richard Niebuhr produces, as those who have seen the possibilities of a true theonomy, Augustine and F. D. Maurice. He lists them under the title, 'Christ the Transformer of Culture', Chapter VI.

seen in the way that a unity of *style* can be discovered in all the various productions of any one culture, as though men were never free but always in bondage to the *Zeitgeist*. Even in periods when individualism is encouraged, the free energy of genius is insufficient to break away altogether from accepted cultural patterns. Shakespeare is unmistakably an Elizabethan dramatist among others, though head and shoulders above the rest; and a painting by Picasso, belonging to no matter which of the artist's many 'periods', bears the stamp of the twentieth-century 'school of Paris'. Generally speaking, culture is too complex for its laws to be comprehensively plotted, and so made subject to control. But a large part of culture can be directed consciously. Even art, that recalcitrant element, can be kept within bounds. The celebrated saying of Alexander Fletcher of Saltoun, '*If a man were permitted to make all the ballads, he need not care who should make the laws of a nation*', indicated that song itself can be a vehicle for law; and censorship of the arts has always been a feature of authoritarian rule.[19] Custom, or tradition, is an essential ingredient of all culture, and, though called a *second nature*, custom is simply a law which is thought to be 'natural' because its compulsive force is not consciously related to an outside authority. Catholic culture was the product of an unceasing struggle on the part of the Church to be recognized as the supreme authority, and represented the very large success achieved by the Church in that struggle. Protestantism cannot produce any real parallel Protestant culture, because its history has been so different.

When Protestantism has tried to mould a distinctively Protestant culture, as in New England under Puritan rule or in Calvin's Geneva, it has done so by legalizing the Protestant protest, creating in consequence a theocracy in which every cultural value was set under the rule of religious law. This was inevitable because Protestantism did not recognize any independence of the natural over against the supernatural, as Catholicism did. Thus Protestant theocratic rule was, at least potentially, more oppressive than Catholic clericalism in that it set out to regulate man's entire existence. But it was also open to criticism in the light of the Protestant protest itself and so, unlike Catholic clericalism, never became a settled form of social

[19] In George Orwell's *Nineteen Eighty-Four*, only the 'proles' (the working class excluded from Party membership) ever sing. The Party members all live under a culture where every activity, including the use of language, is directed by Party policy. Orwell wished to emphasize the inhumanity of totalitarian rule, otherwise his Party members would be likely to sing also—though only Party songs, of course. Authoritarian rule always, in fact, encourages the illusion of spontaneity in obedience, and so art becomes an ideological weapon of great importance, and usefulness.

order. Switzerland and the United States grew to be pioneer examples of democratic States.

Where no complete separation between Church and State was
achieved in Protestant countries, a national Church could easily
become an echo of a secular and nationalistic culture. It was against
this State Christianity that Kierkegaard launched his 'attack upon
Christendom'. But Kierkegaard was not protesting against Erastian-
ism only. His slogan *Christianity does not exist* was directed, in the
last resort, against the assumption that any culture could claim to be
Christian. He regarded Christianity as 'a breach, the very deepest
and most incurable breach with this world'.[20] The precise way in
which the world got into the Church, whether by State patronage or
by toleration, was really immaterial. Kierkegaard rebelled against the
Lutheran accommodation of the life of faith to the life of bourgeois
society; and yet he was actually re-starting Luther's teaching about
the incompatibility between the way of love and the way of law. By
this standard, the more successfully religion permeates culture, the
less true it is to its essential witness.

Writing of the breakaway of the Greek Orthodox Churches from
the West and the subsequent decline in their external influence,
Ronald Knox has declared: 'They preferred to have their own way;
and he who has once made that choice will labour in vain to impress
his authority upon others'.[21] Perhaps, since the kingdoms of this world
and the glory of them are (at least on a short-term basis) in the gift of
Satan (Matt. 4$_{8-9}$), a truer judgement is that of Elie Halévy; 'No
Church, however, can be successful except by coming to terms with
the Devil'.[22]

Catholic dualism finds no difficulty in being both of the world and
not of the world. The Church exists to impress its authority upon all
who live by natural law; and so it is successful in ruling over culture.
The Church also calls those who can respond to the counsels of perfection to renounce life in the natural order; and so it shows the relative vanity of culture. Protestantism, while it sees the attraction of the
cultural ideal of 'Mother Church'—fount of law as well as of grace—
sees also the demonic element present in all cultural authority, both
secular and ecclesiastical. It is forced to live in tension between the
idea of a Christianized culture and the idea of a Christianity which is
at war with culture ; and thus it is continually tempted to resolve the

[20] 'The Fatherland,' Friday, January 12, 1855, *Kierkegaard's Attack Upon
Christendom,* translated by Walter Lowrie (1946), p. 17.
[21] *The Belief of Catholics,* p. 143.
[22] *A History of the English People in 1815* (Pelican Books edn., 1937), II, 114.

tension by capitulating to the one idea at the expense of the other. In our own day the Protestant neo-orthodoxy of Barth and Brunner has reacted sharply from the humanism of liberal Protestantism which sometimes spoke as though the Kingdom of God were to be identified with a culture achieving the liberal ideal. But the danger then arises of not relating the Gospel of Christ to men in their cultural environment, and of preaching a purely 'religious' evangel which calls men to salvation but ignores the Word of God in the midst of history. Against the neo-orthodox reaction, Tillich has advocated a theology which shall be apologetic as well as dogmatic, relating the Gospel to modern man's existential 'situation'.[23] Yet apologetic theology, whether of the second-century Apologists, of Aquinas, Schleiermacher, Oman, or Tillich, is forced to take the categories of contemporary culture as the ones by which faith must be judged, and so it is always inclined to try to remove the *offence* of the Gospel in order to make it acceptable to culture. It wants to rule over culture by the authority of reason, producing religion's credentials as having been rationally examined and found convincing, and urging the necessity for faith to undergird the structure of culture.[24] The anti-rationalistic note which has been persistent in Protestant theology is a sign that Protestantism has never finally lost a sense of the tension between culture and faith.

Culture remains a perpetual challenge to faith because, although no Christian humanism can ever build the Kingdom of Heaven upon earth, and no apologetic theology can ever prove Christianity to be the final word of truth spoken to humanity, yet faith cannot be found apart from man's life in society and cannot be communicated in society apart from reasoned discourse. Personal life is not bounded by social life, nor is communication limited to logical argument and scientific demonstration. The poet and the prophet, the lover and the mystic—these refute those who imagine the social dimension of life

---

[23] Neither Barth nor Brunner, of course, neglects the practical aspect of Christianity. But Tillich rightly objects to the arbitrary method of Barth in 'attempting to derive every statement directly from the ultimate truth—for instance, deriving the duty of making war against Hitler from the resurrection of the Christ' (*Systematic Theology*, I, p. 5). And Brunner has been driven into finding a place for natural theology in order to prescribe Christian principles for culture, to Barth's great disapproval.

[24] Compare the title of Schleiermacher's *Addresses on Religion to its Cultured Despisers*. Tillich's theology is carefully constructed to avoid the usual defects of apologetic systems. Yet even Tillich is anxious to bring faith within the rational rule and subject it to reason's law. For example, he contends that all Christian paradox is agreeable to 'logical rationality', i.e. above reason but not contradictory to it (*Systematic Theology*, I, p. 57). This seems to imply some kind of 'two story' view of reason and revelation, like that of Thomism.

to be all-important. Yet personal existence (and the experience it brings transcending the social dimension and its categories) is rooted in society and must, in some way or other, come to terms with it. When a faith has been rejected by culture, then we are compelled to say that this faith has 'failed', even though in saying so we are relying on a purely human view-point. It is from this human view-point that the Cross of Christ is claimed to have been a victory, when the continuing appeal of Christianity to mankind is invoked.

In this chapter we have been considering the relative failure of Protestantism to capture modern culture. But if Protestantism is at a disadvantage compared with Catholicism in the matter of making a marriage with culture, Catholicism's present position *vis à vis* culture is by no means assured; and this in spite of a very conspicuous brilliancy in modern Catholic apologetic literature, both philosophical and imaginative. In a study of some eminent French Roman Catholic poets and novelists Rayner Heppenstall remarks tartly,

Catholicism is certainly 'founded in the depths of existence', if we mean the existence of other people, either in the past or in a lower stage of intellectual perception than ourselves. It is fantastically rich in what Pareto called 'residues'.[25]

Whether or not this judgement is a fair one, it represents a widespread cultural outlook. We cannot always be successful in impressing our authority upon others; and all pacts with the Devil—however lofty our motives for entering into them—are provisional ones, destined to end abruptly. It would be futile for Protestants to prophesy about the future of Catholicism, which in the past has been so resourceful in adapting itself to changing patterns of culture. If Catholicism ultimately fails to perpetuate its characteristic tradition of 'Christian civilization', a Christian interpretation of culture will still be required. If it emerges from its struggle with Marxist and secularist ideologies stronger than before, Protestantism will still have its historic task to perform of protecting *against* what it considers to be Catholic mis-interpretation of the Gospel. In either case, Protestants will not be relieved of the task of self-criticism in the light of judgement of the Gospel upon its failure to bring Christ into contemporary culture.

What Paul wrote of himself can be applied to Protestantism's task of witnessing to the faith in history (which means cultural history):

[25] *The Double Image. Mutations of Christian mythology in the work of four French Catholic writers of today and yesterday* (1947), p. 74.

Let a man so account of us, as of the ministers of Christ, and stewards of the mysteries of God. Moreover it is required in stewards, that a man be found faithful. But with me it is a very small thing that I should be judged of you, or of man's judgement: yea, I judge not mine own self. For I know nothing by myself; yet am I not hereby justified: but he that judgeth me is the Lord (1 Cor. 4₁₋₄).

Protestantism finds much to call for repentance. Too often it has been an unfaithful steward. But it knows, too, that the God who judges is also the God who redeems.

CHAPTER ELEVEN

PROTESTANT VALUES: A SUMMING-UP

I. THE SUBJECTIVITY OF VALUE

THE PRESENT study began by looking at the kind of word *Pro-testantism* was and noting that the problem of understanding a word of this type lay in its being a focus for values. As a group name, *Protestantism* could be given meaning only in the process of subjecting it to personal judgement. At this stage, having reviewed different aspects of this group name, we are in a position to appreciate the better those values which the word has drawn about it and which demand our verdict. For, only as we feel that we are able to choose intelligently between being either pro-Protestant or anti-Protestant, can we be sure that we know something of the meaning of *Protestant* and *Protestantism*. To understand the words is to grasp the importance of Protestant values.

A choice made blindly on emotional grounds alone—a kind of reflex action prompted by the sound of a party name—cannot be called an 'intelligent' choice. Yet intelligent choice is not made purely on intellectual assent. It must be a movement of the whole self. Values will always elude us, unless we can make them our own to some degree. Only as we experience them personally and live by them can we admit them to be authentic values. If our only understanding of a value is that we are told some one else holds it in esteem, we shall always suspect it of being a false value, or another value altogether, mistakenly interpreted. For instance, a psychologist who is not prepared to admit that any religion has access to a true revelation of God will believe that all religious believers misread the psychological values contained in their religious dogmas. He will say that the believer values dogma because he imagines it to convey truths about the structure of reality as a whole, while he (the psychologist) knows that the truth of dogma is limited to the subjective world of the psyche. If pressed as to why he dismisses the objectivity of religious truth, the psychologist may say he does so on intellectual grounds: religion has been, to his satisfaction, proved to be mere wish-fulfilment, an illusion created by psychological forces.

If the religious believer argues back that such a 'proof' can easily be reversed, and religion proved true by contending that the rejection of religion is the result of psychological forces and itself a blatant form of wish-fulfilment, the psychologist is likely to shrug his shoulders and remark that the latter suggestion is very improbable. He may further urge that religion's claim to be true is based on sheer assumption, while the myth-building powers of the psyche have been scientifically demonstrated. In other words, he will fall back upon those values which he is prepared to live by.

It follows that no one will be convinced of the existence of values which he does not accept as valid in his own experience. No one will be convinced, simply on the basis of etymology or history, that Protestantism is more than a negative movement, unless he also accepts some aspect of the Protestant protest as being *true*. The Catholic who sees in Protestant theology nothing more than heresy must argue that Protestantism is a caricature of Catholic truth; that what is good in it is the residue of Catholic truth it contains; and that what makes it distinctively Protestant is 'error' and for that reason valueless (except in so far as error, being necessarily parasitic upon truth, draws attention to positive value in the act of denying it). An appeal to reason, in such a case, establishes nothing, for reasoning as a discursive process depends upon a perception of values which is prior to ratiocination. We must be agreed first upon what we are reasoning *about*. And, although argument may help to clarify definition, it can never establish the truth of definitions. Plato perceived this when he said that only the philosopher who has knowledge of the eternal Forms can employ dialectic so as to arrive at truth, while the Sophist by a show of dialectical ingenuity merely perverts the truth. But how do we know the Philospher from the Sophist? Plato's answer is largely a moral one. The philosophical spirit is drawn to pure wisdom, and the sophistical spirit is motivated by self-seeking. If Plato's criterion is indecisive (for how do we distinguish the disinterested lovers of truth from the hypocrites?), it at least brings out the fact that any purely intellectual test is futile. Ronald Knox says that 'simple minds can easily be seduced by the sophistries of plausible error'.[1] But error is not plausible if it cannot seduce acute minds just as easily. And, in fact, the greatest philosophers do not agree. John Byrom's witty lines on the different points of view of Jacobites and Hanoverians is relevant to more than the particular dispute he had in mind:

[1] *The Belief of Catholics*, p. 242.

God bless the King, I mean the Faith's Defender;
God bless—no harm in blessing—the Pretender;
But who Pretender is, or who is King,
God bless us all—that's quite another thing.

Every one has to decide for himself which value is royal and which is not, and the standard of legitimacy is always open to question.

II. DIALOGUE—AN ANTI-RATIONALISTIC VALUE

The history of Protestantism shows how the way of dialogue has gradually asserted itself as a pre-eminent value, spreading out from theology to include all aspects of Protestant witness; Luther's insight into the nature of faith has had revolutionary consequences. Its most decisive result in changing man's understanding of the world has been its effective challenge to rationalism, an event which is only in our own day coming to be fully appreciated and is still widely misunderstood.

To ancient and modern opponents of Protestantism the placing of revelation beyond reason has been the supreme error of the movement. Behind this charge there has, no doubt, lurked the thought that man's cultural achievements have been realized by the use of reason, and that to sanction irrationalism is to make breaches in the wall of civilization and risk the destruction of all that has been gained. (Probably a fear of the irrational within the self—the Freudian *id*— of which each individual is uneasily aware has contributed to build up a picture of 'the barbarian at the gates' with reason, like Horatius, alone barring the way.) This pattern of thinking is very evident in Hooker's case against the Puritans, as presented by Peter Munz;

The Puritans, by excluding reason, allowed authority only to faith and thus to an irrational factor. Hooker as a Christian neither would or could deny the authority of faith; but he saw that if human society was to be saved from chaos, faith had to be synthesized with reason. . . . Although, he said, the spirit leads us to truth and goodness, its workings are so privy and secret, that we stand on a plainer ground when we use reason as the criterion as to whether our inspiration is from God or not.[2]

Here are all the chief assumptions of the rationalist-theologian; faith an ally of irrationalism, culture in jeopardy from unreason, and reason the inspector required to certify faith's credentials.

For the thorough-going rationalist, men meet only through their mutual participation in the conceptual process. That is, they do not meet at all as *men* but simply as walking arguments. So Hooker

[2] *The Place of Hooker in the History of Thought*, pp. 40-1.

maintained: 'There is as yet no way known how to dispute or to determine of things disputed without the use of natural reason'.[3] It was exactly this contention that those challenged who believed in faith as dialogue. The way of dialogue makes use of reason and finds it an indispensable instrument of communication; but it is not confined to reason, far less to reason*ing*—and never to *natural reason*, if by this is meant a gift from God which makes man 'practically independent, even of God himself'.[4] Dialogue rejects the claim of reason to rule as the sole law of man's encounter with man. As God gives His grace and speaks to us, so in the same spirit (which is His gift) we can speak to our neighbour; and the more evident the grace, the clearer the speaking. When we fail to understand one another we may argue, but we do not trust in logic to bring us to truth. We find harmony in a mutual acceptance of values.

As experience proves, disputes are more often than not settled before reasoning begins at all. The psychological aspect of this common experience has always been recognized—Æsop put it succinctly in the fable of the Wolf and the Lamb before ever *rationalization* became a technical term in psychology. But to keep the recognition of this fact on the plane of psychology is to ignore its real importance. It is easy enough to blame other people for letting their prejudices dictate their conclusions and resolve that we ourselves will follow reason wherever it leads; but it gets us nowhere, except perhaps to that place where pride goes before a fall. What we need to see is that all arguments are rationalizations, yet that rationalizations differ, not simply in being sometimes more intellectually convincing than at other times (though that may be important too), but because of the values which they exist to promote. There is today a widespread appreciation of the view, championed by R. G. Collingwood, that philosophy is concerned first and foremost with the presuppositions of thought and only secondarily with the systems built upon these presuppositions. From this standpoint, philosophic systems are rationalizations of beliefs held prior to reason. Collingwood's thesis is basically a philosophical version of the Protestant theological contention that faith in revelation is the prime datum of the Christian life.[5] Men first make their stand, in subjectivity, and then try to find

---

[3] Munz, ibid., p. 40.

[4] ibid., p. 62. The phrase is Munz's, stating the case for Hooker's rationalism.

[5] I do not claim, of course, that Collingwood's philosophy as a whole is philosophic Protestantism in the same way that Kant's philosophy is. Indeed, Collingwood's thought, diverse and changing as it was, cannot easily be tied down to any one label. There is a good deal of Kantianism in Collingwood, however, and Kant was the first philosopher to draw attention to the place of presupposition in thinking.

out the implications of that stand. Reason has its part in this process, but it is the part of a servant and not of a judge.

But if reason is not to rule, the rationalist sees the destruction of moral standards and the ruin of culture as an inevitable outcome. Did not the sceptic Hume wish to reduce reason to the status of a servant of the passions? Now Protestants are unable to share the pre-suppositions of those who, like Hume, would deduce morality from an empirical science of human nature. They believe that empiricists and pragmatists import covertly those absolute values which they deny on principle. But, in so far as the empirical attitude is more humble in its desire to let the created order speak for itself than is the rationalistic attitude in its confidence that it can dictate *a priori* rules to nature, Protestantism has been able to make common cause to a very large extent with the former. The pragmatic temper which has been so conspicuously evident in American thought has been influenced to no small degree by Protestant values, as can be seen in the ethical convictions cherished by William James and by his *faith in faith*, even though the authority of faith meant nothing to him. More recently, K. R. Popper, who with great moral fervour has attacked rationalistic theories of the State[6] because of their inhumanity, and who puts his trust in nominalism, finds some kinship with Barth, whom he quotes several times with approval. Yet the Barthian theology is a violent protest against a Protestantism unduly infected by a pragmatic temper which has exalted 'practical' Christianity at the expense of the authority of revelation; and Popper would be unlikely to follow Barth here.

Luther's theology itself was made possible by the challenge to Thomist rationalism in the current nominalism in which he was trained, but it was not nominalist. In the same way, confronted by the rationalistic claim to rule the world by the power of conceptual thought and by the empirico-pragmatic claim to manage the world by the power of trial-and-error, Protestantism finds the latter much nearer to the needs of dialogue, but lacking any positive foundation. If rationalists imagine values to be objective and indubitable, given in the immutable nature of man, empiricists think that values will emerge as the varying needs of men are progressively assessed by induction; and that these values will be really objective and indubit-

[6] In *The Open Society and Its Enemies*. This book has become the centre of much dispute, has been called 'ideological', and has prompted several 'replies'. Popper claims to be attacking irrationalism in the name of reason, but he continually appeals to the righteousness of the views which he champions and to the wickedness of opposing views.

able, because they are based on facts, not on dogmas. Protestants recognize that values are always dogmatic. On the other hand, they agree with the empiricists that dogma is not capable of objective proof. Therefore, against two fronts, they contend for the subjectivity of values.

III. AUTHORITARIAN, EMPIRICIST, AND ROMANTIC VALUES

The close alliance between rationalism and authoritarianism has often been noted. That the partnership is based upon the fact that both operate within the context of legalism is not so often appreciated. Reason, in its analytic aspect, is an instrument which can be used very effectively by the will to doubt, but in its synthetic aspect it attempts to subject all experience to the laws of the intellect. Because this latter process can show a fair measure of success, rationalism comes into being and assumes that there is nothing outside these laws.[7] Authoritarianism, living by the law which it lays down as its personal *fiat*, is greatly reinforced if it can counter doubt by showing that reason indubitably establishes this same law.[8] Both authoritarianism and rationalism represent an attempt by the human spirit to achieve objectivity. Man escapes from uncertainty, from the need for faith and grace, into a universe where law reigns supreme. Man finds that his own spirit is the centre of resistance to law, including reason's law. He can neither explain his existence nor justify it. Therefore if he does not, like Paul, reach beyond law to grace, he must regard the spirit as something to be controlled externally by all the powers of law. Spirit is the irrational element which would throw off the yoke of rational rule, and the disobedient element which rebels against lawful authority.

Culture is the product of law. It represents a partial, yet real, victory of reason and authority over the forces which resist these bringers of law. Of course, culture is a creation of the human spirit; it is made by men. But it is the creation of the human spirit put under authority; and in so far as this authority is not freely accepted, the spirit is made, like Samson at the mill in Gaza, to work blindly by those who have subdued him.[9] The rationalist says that spirit is free

---

[7] The *malleability* of the world of experience, the way it seems to accommodate itself to our presuppositions, however conflicting, gives the possibility of contradictory philosophies and theologies existing side by side in every age without one gaining a victory over the rest. See Paul Roubiczek, *Thinking in Opposites* (1952), pp. 14, 232.

[8] See pp. 219–20, *supra*.

[9] The contrast between these two types of authority is the contrast between Tillich's *autonomy* and *heteronomy*. Note that Tillich's names for these cultural

only when it obeys reason, and the authoritarian says that spirit is free only when it is subject to due authority. When both combine to hold their Samson so as to prevent him pulling down the palace of culture about their ears, then the authority of reason is identified with the dogmas of accredited authority. Authority becomes established in tradition, and traditional values are taken to be final. The institutions of culture—law, politics, education, art, religion, and the rest—are the repositories of these values and represent in tangible form the rule of law directing the whole.

Empirical and pragmatic thinkers criticize the static cultural ideal of the rationalist-authoritarians. They point out how conflicting dogmatic claims cancel one another out and how the rational laws so confidently appealed to turn out to be relative and not absolute. When their opponents retort that without fixed standards society will dissolve, and that by abandoning these they are committing cultural suicide, they deny both the premise and the conclusion of this argument. There are no better standards to go by than those reached by trial and error. To the extent that tradition has proved itself beneficial it deserves to be retained. But the values recognized by tradition are not sacrosanct and need to be rejected when they no longer satisfy. Only an opinionated fool will jettison the wisdom of mankind up to date to make the world square with his private opinion about it. If reasoning seems to lead to sceptical conclusions, so much the worse for reasoning; and so much the more need for finding out, by careful investigation of the facts, what we can do to mould the world nearer to our heart's desire.

By *the facts* the empiricist means primarily those features of the universe around man which can be investigated experimentally and made subject to his control. The empiricist's case is built upon the assumption that, while nature is bound by law, in his essential being man is a free spirit beyond all law.[10] Hence the chief task of culture is social engineering, i.e. constructing an environment which shall be adapted to all the needs of man's spirit and allowing it full scope for

types are founded on *nomos*-law. That is why the third of Tillich's terms, *theonomy*, can never be more than approximately realized. If God's Word was nothing more than law, then a culture might perfectly embody God's law, and thus fully deserve to be called *theonomous*. But because grace, not law, is the heart of the Christian revelation, a culture remains an inadequate expression for man's response to God, and *theonomy* is always incomplete.

[10] This is true even of those who imagine that scientific determinism extends to man also. For such people, theory and practice are opposed—see John Macmurray, *The Boundaries of Science: A Study in the Philosophy of Psychology* (1939). J. V. Langmead Casserley, in *Morals and Man in the Social Sciences*, argues throughout that making man part of nature makes nonsense of the scientific attitude.

self-expression. He never contemplates the possibility that the spirit of man ought to be subject to any law higher than itself. When it shows any defect, this is the result of being distorted by environment. Some extreme anti-rationalists are inclined to judge, as Freud did, that culture itself is inimical to man's spirit, but most assume that culture brings the possibility of the fullest development to spirit, because in cultural life man realizes his highest potentialities.[11]

Protestantism must agree with the empirical outlook to the extent that it regards culture as the opportunity for creative endeavour instead of the arena which displays the omnipotence of law. It agrees that experience rather than a priori rules must discover those cultural values which are sound. It agrees that standards of good and evil are to so great an extent relative that we must test them as we go along. And in the empirical waiting on facts it sees an opportunity for dialogue to emerge. (The place of sympathy in Hume's ethics, for example, shows how psychological analysis, when thorough enough, brings into view dimensions of personal relationships which might otherwise be neglected, even if these dimensions are inadequately estimated.) But Protestantism finds the empirical analysis of man as inadequate as the rationalist-authoritarian one. Man is not made for law, and authoritarian culture stifles his spirit. But neither is man made for unconditional freedom, and spirit freed from law without being made subject to grace will turn into destructive evil.

While the empiricists who value tradition realize that the laws curbing free expression of spirit are very necessary in an imperfect culture in the course of developing towards freedom, there are those who see in law as such—and in traditional law in particular—the chief impediment to the spirit's self-realization. For such Romantic thinkers as Rousseau, Blake, and Nietzsche, the vital principle in man is not only spirit but the Holy Spirit, and to deny or curb that spirit is blasphemy against life. The Romantic protest is directed against rationalism, but equally against all standards based on prudential or utilitarian principles, and its chief object of attack is moral virtue conceived in terms of social well-being. Romanticism cares nothing at all for culture, for it makes life its final value, and it is quite prepared to lose its life in order to live it to the full. Romanticism finds tyranny wherever spirit submits to anything outside itself. In addition to reason, individual self-consciousness comes to be regarded as outside spirit, which is thought of as existing in a whole

[11] Erich Fromm's Man for Himself: An Enquiry into the Psychology of Ethics (1949), is a typical exposition of this view.

humanity represented by an ethic or other 'natural' group. So what the Romantic calls freedom spells serfdom for the individual possessing a moral conscience or the capacity for doubt, or who happens for any reason to be considered outside the group where spirit dwells.

Romanticism is a protest, a faith in the spirit of man. As such it is a judgement on the lack of faith found in the secularist, humanistic culture against which it revolts. Our empirical-pragmatic Western world has produced within itself the two Romantic creeds of Fascism and Communism[12] which, if powerful enough, could yet destroy it. However, when Catholicism sees the movement into irrationalism as a consequence of abandoning a Catholic rational-authoritarian culture, Protestantism dissents. For, if the demonic element in the human spirit is released so as to threaten culture when spirit is deified, authoritarian culture distorts spirit so as to give rise to demonic traits in that culture which eventually destroy it. Neither rule by the law *within* man (the vital law of his being as a breathing, feeling, aspiring part of nature) or by the law *above* man (the rational law which commands him to live according to a pattern imposed on nature) can banish the demonic in man's spirit and permit him to live at peace with nature and himself. Law cannot be the answer to sin. Thus no culture can fully and finally succeed. The rationalist's dream of perfect order and the Romantic's dream of unlimited self-expression through creative energy are continually contradicted by the rise and decay of cultures. But if sin does not fall before law, immorality is checked by it, and the wise use of psychological drives within the self is encouraged by the rules it provides. Therefore, though Protestantism does not demand authority to create a Christian culture, it is committed to giving support to a morally sensitive and tolerant culture which leaves room for faith without binding tradition to creed. It knows well enough that cultural values are rooted in religious values and will not indefinitely continue without any roots, but it knows also that the roots of faith are kept alive by dialogue and not by religious authority.

[12] It may seem strange to class Marxist-Communism, which is so highly rationalistic, as Romantic. Communism is a highly complex creed (which accounts for its very wide appeal), but its Romantic elements are very prominent. This can be seen in Hegelianism, from which Marxism derives. Hegel's *Spirit* is a combination of rationalism's *intellect* and a vitalistic *life force,* and produces a political theory supporting authoritarian nationalism. The Marxist proletariat is a natural group which will emerge triumphant as the result of the cosmic process. Communist appeal to nationalistic sentiment is very similar to that of Fascism, as is its political use of the Party to control the individual.

IV. FORM AND SPIRIT

Protestantism clashes with Catholicism over the cultural question because Protestantism denies what Catholicism affirms: that some values are objective. Even if some Catholics are willing to admit that Catholic interpretation of natural law has been too rigid in the past because of an undue rationalism ignoring the relativities of existence,[13] no Catholic could admit that revelation does not establish beyond all possible doubt certain fixed standards which establish the norms for Christian faith. Protestant subjectivity and Catholic objectivity have created widely diverging beliefs about the values represented by the institutions connected with the Christian religion. The Catholic case has been put with great clarity (and in an extremely charitable spirit) by A. G. Hebert in *The Form of the Church* (1944). Written as an Anglo-Catholic answer to Daniel T. Jenkins's statement of the Protestant doctrine of the Church in *The Nature of Catholicity*, this book is based on the theme that Protestantism one-sidedly asserts Christianity to be a faith lived in the Spirit, when it is also and just as essentially an institutionalized tradition existing continuously from the Incarnation. The Incarnate Christ, the Word of God, is the *Form of God* and thus also the *Form of the Church*: 'If the Spirit is necessary, so is the Form; if the Form is necessary, so is the Spirit'.[14]

According to Hebert, there are four 'essential forms' making up the Church Catholic. These are Sacraments, Creed, Apostolate, and Scripture. They derive directly from Christ, the Form, and from them are derived other subordinate forms, such as the various liturgies of the Church, which are of human origin.[15] These two orders of forms are said to correspond to the difference between *natural law* and *positive law*;[16] and, although the Church is 'founded on personal relations, and is not a system constituted by law', its structure cannot be supposed to be indefinite or subject to alteration.[17] The necessity for this enduring formal element in Christianity leads to the creation of 'appropriate' ecclesiastical forms to enshrine the

---

[13] J. V. Langmead Casserley criticizes the traditional Catholic doctrine of natural law, though he would retain the concept of natural law to explain 'universal conditions of social health and stability' (*Morals and Man in the Social Sciences*, pp. 61 ff.). This would seem to say no more than that, if you seek a particular end, you must seek the appropriate means to bring it about; whereas the concept of natural law surely must mean, if it is to mean anything, that certain definite ends are necessarily to be chosen and pursued by certain definite means.

[14] Hebert, op. cit., p. 16.   [15] ibid., pp. 36 ff.
[16] ibid., p. 37.   [17] ibid., p. 41.

essential forms; hence the need for fixed orders and ritual in the practical life of the Church.[18]

In spite of the statement that the Church is not created by law, Protestants must view with apprehension a doctrine of the Church worked out against a background of legalism. But the heart of Hebert's argument is plainly in the identification of Christ with Form. Here a Protestant must say, 'No'. The eternal Christ is the Word of God. The incarnate Christ was the Image of God and the Pattern for His followers. Certainly a *word* is a *form*, considered externally. But a word is not only, or essentially, a form; it is the means whereby dialogue is initiated. An image and a pattern are *forms* in a more restricted sense. Yet neither of these are forms which are final, or carry meaning in themselves. They are forms which have an instrumental use. An image directs us to the reality *imaged*—to the content not given in the image itself; and a pattern directs us to another content to be produced with the help of the pattern which shall resemble, not the pattern itself, but that reality on which the pattern is *patterned*. When the New Testament speaks of Jesus as the Image and the Pattern (or Example) (2 Cor. 4_4, Heb. 1_3, 1 Tim. 1_{16}), it is not telling us who Jesus is and why He is Lord. It is telling us what Jesus, who is Lord, *does*. The metaphors cannot be pressed into providing us with a definition of His Sonship.

God is Father, Word, and Spirit. But He cannot be called the Form without violence to language, for form cannot confront men in personal relationship. Form is an 'it' which cannot be apprehended as a 'thou'.[19] The New Testament speaks of Christ in His pre-existence possessing 'the form of God', and in His earthly ministry as taking 'the form of a servant' (Phil. 2_{6-7}). Similarly, the Word is *formed* in the believer through faith and by brotherly concern for the salvation of others (Gal. 4_{19}). The form taken by the Word varies according to the work to be done by the Word, and the form exists for the sake of the Word. There is no thought here of Form being itself God's Self-revelation. Just as it is idolatry to wor-

---

[18] *The Form of the Church*, p. 82.

[19] Citing Plato's Forms and Aristotle's God as Pure Form, Hebert argues that Christian theology 'makes a true synthesis of elements which in the Greek philosophers lie in scattered fragments' (p. 20). But Christian theology may well have to protest *against* the findings of philosophy—surely here, if anywhere. If the nature of God is given in philosophy, revelation becomes superfluous. The God of the Bible is known through His acts and by a proper name, i.e. by that which eludes being caught in the net of form. Pascal's *God of Abraham, Isaac and Jacob, not the God of philosophers and scholars*, and Barth's *wholly other* witness to a God who transcends all forms. Otherwise the taking of human form by the Word in the Incarnation is not a paradox.

ship an image, so it is vain to imagine that form can achieve anything in its own power. Those who are *conformed* to the image of God's Son (Rom. 8$_{29}$) are those who are *transformed* by the renewing of their minds (Rom. 12$_2$). And those so transformed, having the mind of Christ, are those who have received the gift of the Spirit (1 Cor. 2$_{16}$).

Theologically, there would seem little justification for putting Form over against Spirit as an equal and distinct element in the Christian revelation. Protestants will certainly not easily be convinced that failure to do so indicates a failure to appreciate the Incarnation. What they believe the Incarnation to proclaim is that form can be God's chosen channel for bringing the gift of 'life in the Spirit'—a very different thing from God being Himself Form. This means that no Christian can be indifferent to form, not because form has itself a final value, but because it has instrumental value. The Church has its forms and the life of faith is not to be lived apart from them. But is lived through the gift of the Spirit manifested in them, they having no power of their own.

If we consider the Bible, externally it is a form of words. Hebert grants that the Bible without the Spirit is a mere form, but insists that *as a form* it is essential to the Church. Protestantism (outside Protestant fundamentalism) protests that, as a form the Bible is no better than any other form. Unless men hear the word of God in it, it is an object which, like all created things, may become an idol, a form of man's disobedience. Here, in a most direct way, unless the Spirit gives life, the letter brings death (2 Cor. 3$_6$). It is the same with creeds, the sacraments, or Church order. These forms are not good of themselves, and when the Spirit is absent from them are but occasions of stumbling and incitements to idolatry.

The Protestant way of speaking would not be of *essential* forms but of *given* forms. What is essential is that the Word of God is heard and men engrafted into Christ, and God alone can make this possible. But we cannot hear the Word apart from the forms God has given us and in which He makes His Word available to us. The Sacraments of Baptism and the Lord's Supper are bequeathed to the Church as forms instituted by Christ. The Bible is God's gift to us through His activity in the Church. The Creeds and the Apostolic Ministry may be similar gifts, though here most Protestants are not convinced by Catholic arguments for believing these to be Divine institutions and regard them rather as the creation of men concerned for the good ordering of the Church. About these last there is always room for further dialogue. It may be that Catholicism has here preserved something which Christ intended for His Church and which Protestantism in its reforming zeal has too rashly discarded or too slightly valued. But what Protestants cannot consent to is a legalism which binds the Word to forms in the absence of the Spirit, though they gladly admit that, when the Spirit is given, the Church finds the Word through the forms which are His gift. What matters is whether the form is valued because the Word is heard by means of the form, or whether the form is considered to have an intrinsic value and its presence believed in some sense to guarantee the authenticity of the Word. Here Protestant and Catholic divide, with a 'No' and a 'Yes' denying and affirming different beliefs. These differing beliefs concern the mode of God's dealings with men, and hence the meaning of the Incarnation. They thus involve the whole understanding of Christian faith and not simply the doctrine of the Church.

V. THE RE-FORMATION OF THE CHURCH

Yet, if the whole of theology is involved in any one theological issue (as Protestants believe), the doctrine of the Church is perhaps the best place at which to start to understand differences between Christians. We can see theological differences when they are thrown into relief by a background of conflicting ecclesiastical traditions. Hence the importance of the ecumenical movement today.

Undoubtedly, the relation of form and Spirit is a crucial one for Church union, for every Church is a form and divided Christendom is divided over the conception of how the Spirit of Christ is related to the formal existence of specific churchly organizations. The Reformation was a revolution because it revolutionized theology. But its most conspicuous revolutionary feature was that it revolutionized the conception of the Church, and turned the world upside down in so doing. It opposed something totally different from the traditionally accepted Catholic standard of what the Church was. When Protestants are accused of jumping straight from the Reformation to the New Testament and ignoring the intervening years, this is true mainly of the Protestant understanding of the Church. The Reformers drew heavily from the theology of those intervening years, but in their attack upon Christendom as they found it, they were challenging a very long tradition. At the same time, the revolutionary idea was also an idea of reformation. The Reformers did not simply attack the Church. They were concerned to rebuild it. The Church had to be re-formed in obedience to Christ, and this by no once-for-all event but continually. No form, by itself, could contain the Spirit and compel the Spirit's presence.

The historical result of this process was the fragmentation of Protestantism. Each attempt to reinterpret the mind of Christ led to a new form of Church life springing into existence. The principal causes of this multiplication of forms were two: the search for a form of pure doctrine and the search for the exact form of the New Testament Church. Credal orthodoxy had been the foundation of Catholic Christendom. Sectarian Protestantism, indefinitely multiplying itself in a quest for an orthodoxy to end all other orthodoxies, was the *reductio ad absurdum* of the formalist ideal. But Catholic credal orthodoxy had been backed up by Catholic tradition; and the more tangible forms of the Church served to authenticate the more immaterial ones. Every man could set himself up as his own Pope in the realm of faith, but to become recognized as the Bishop of Rome was a harder matter. Therefore Protestants who, under the spell of formalistic legalism, demanded proof of the identity of the one true Church turned to the Bible as the Infallible Book and to a Church order supposed to duplicate precisely the order of the primitive Church.

This outlook, a legacy of Catholic principles,[20] was in fact a claim to possess the *essential forms* of the Church. Any stand upon forms must inevitably demand uniformity, since an essential form is one which stands over all other forms and determines their form. Thus the distinction between essential and non-essential forms tends to be disregarded by formalist legalism, and any form at all may be judged to be the standard of authenticity. The Catholic must believe all the doctrines of the Catholic faith, no matter how many alterations are made to the corpus of Catholic articles of belief, and Protestant denominations have been founded on very trivial peculiarities in belief or practice. Although orthodoxies of every complexion tried to ignore the fact, the revolution brought about by the Reformation made it necessary to re-examine Christian theology at the deepest level, taking the doctrine of the Church as an indication of the problems involved. A new world began when, as Charles Williams has said: 'From being a threat heresy had become a continuous event'.[21]

The ecumenical movement is an attempt to deal with this new world. It is an expression of a will to re-form the Church. Yet, if we take for granted a formalist definition of the Church, the task will

---

[20] See Chapter 8, Section 6, *supra*.
[21] *The Descent of the Dove*, p. 178.

seem to be a hopeless one from the start; and because of this many Catholics (not by any means only Roman Catholics) belittle the significance of the movement. If it were only a programme designed to discuss the re-union of existing denominational bodies, this scepticism might be justified, but happily the movement which has led to the formation of the World Council of Churches has a wider range. Protestants may not be deceived when they see in it the beginnings of a new Reformation.

In *The Form of the Church*[22] Hebert has outlined the issues which ecumenicity has to face and has stressed the need to begin with the theological question of unity instead of with the practical question of re-union: unless the Churches build their Unity on the Risen Christ, they can hope only for a 'comprehensive' organization containing within it parties which co-exist without real contact. He admits that 'comprehensiveness' partly describes the condition of the Anglican communion at the present—'a largely formal and external unity'.[23] And he envisages the time when unity will be restored to the Church by universal acceptance of the essential forms of the Church. He argues that unity, in fact, exists now wherever these forms exist, though that unity is broken because of the imperfection of the Churches. When these recognize the areas of their lack of faithfulness to Christ, then wholeness will be restored together with the full expression of those partial truths which now our separate denominations unevenly emphasize in isolation from one another.

For the irenical spirit of this expression of Catholic faith all Protestants must be profoundly grateful. They will be grateful too for its insistence that unity and not union is our problem. But they may not be so sure that the proposed solution of the problem is on the right track. If they believe that Christians know the truth of the Gospel always in subjectivity, they will not be convinced easily that the doctrine of the Church is the one exception. The forms of the Church are given, so Protestants believe, in faith and in no other way. If Christians can know objectively that unity positively exists where Hebert's four essential forms are present, and defectively exists where any of these are absent, then form and Spirit are divided. For apparently the unity of the Church can be seen in the form of the Church even where the Spirit is absent, rather as we see the unity of a table in its having four legs and judge it to be imperfect

---

[22] Chapter 5, 'Unity'; also the chapters following, 'Holiness', 'Catholicity', and 'Apostolicity'.
[23] ibid., p. 99.

if one leg is missing. Hebert's rejection of the Roman claim that part of the essential form of the Church is that it is grounded in the unity provided by the See of Rome is based on his belief that Rome does not distinguish between what in the Church is due to human authority and what to God.[24] He probably recognizes that Protestants will not accept his own delimitation of essential from non-essential forms on the same basis. The question then arises as to whether we must just be content to recognize that Christians are divided on what constitutes the Church, and agree to differ; or whether we can go further in making clear the theological reasons for our differences.

Protestants can at least state unambiguously that they do not merely dissent from the Catholic view of the Church because they accept some forms of the Church, while Catholics accept others. They protest that forms are no part of the Church at all without the Spirit, and that whatever forms are *given* must always be known through the Spirit. That the Bible is a form of the Church is believed by Protestants because without the Bible we cannot find Christ the Lord of the Church. This is not because the form of the Bible gives us the Church's Christ, but because through the Bible we are incorporated by the Spirit in the Church's faith. The Sacraments are forms by which also we find Christ, because the Spirit uses these forms to bring us the Real Presence of Christ. These forms have no efficacy in themselves. The canon of the Bible, as Tillich reminds us, is never finally closed.[25] The historic Church has given us the Bible in the form with which we are familiar, but it has not objectively delimited its form. It has not the power to do so, for the Spirit is not bound by man's judgement, nor can any ecclesiastical tradition declare that *here* and not *there* is God's Word to be found. And, though no 'individual judgement' has a right to reject the tradition of Christian witness egotistically, yet no tradition, however venerable, is free from correction by the Spirit meeting believers in subjectivity. The Sacraments are given us by dominical command. Yet Christ Himself has laid down no Mosaic law in which the Spirit is bounded by an essential form. The Society of Friends, in refusing to observe the sacraments has fulfilled in the Spirit what they have disobeyed in the letter, for no Protestant denomination has so well preserved the sacramental understanding of worship and humility before the mystery of the Incarnation.

Creed and Ministry, the two remaining forms of Hebert's four, are not only disputed matters between Protestant and Catholic, but

---

[24] ibid., p. 102–3. [25] *Systematic Theology*, I, 51.

also, to a lesser degree, between Protestant bodies (as they are, of course, between the different branches of Catholicism). Creed, in its narrower sense as a form of theological statement is dependent upon its wider sense as Christian protest. Ministry depends upon the other three forms.

In connexion with the Ministry and its function we can see how, in the last resort, the Protestant contention that *protest* determines everything would seem to be true. Do non-episcopal ministries *'mean the same thing* as ours?' asks Hebert, and answers decisively, 'they do not'.[26] If he is right—and surely he is—we are brought back, beyond the question of forms in the Church, to the question of interpreting the Gospel as a whole. The attempt to re-form the Church (which involves scrutinizing the meaning of our ecclesiastical practices and finding how we can justify our being divided from other Christians) confronts us with the need for retesting our total response to the grace which is mediated to us through Jesus Christ. The hope of final agreement with Christians of other traditions, long separated from our own, may seem slight; while other Church Unions already achieved may restore our hope. But we should not build upon the fluctuations of hopes and fears within us, but rather pray for that hope which is God's gift, along with faith and love. The Church is God's Church. What men have deformed, He will re-form through a renewal of His Spirit.

VI. UNITY AND DIALOGUE

If unity depends upon agreement about the forms of unity, then the communions of divided Christendom must reach full theological unanimity concerning these forms before they can effectively co-operate at any level or consider organic union. Or else an attempt must be made to achieve union on a 'comprehensive' basis, where the forms are accepted without any agreement about why they are considered necessary. But if Christ Himself is considered to be the Church's unity, there is no need to agree upon every aspect of the interpretation of that unity to know that, across our divisions, there is already a measure of unity achieved.

This is not just a sentimental attitude which pretends that 'we all really believe the same things after all', for it starts with a clear perception that we do not believe the same things in the least and that our differences extend from non-theological party prejudices to head-on-conflict about the basic presuppositions of theological thought.

[26] op. cit., p. 120. Italics in the text.

But it also starts with a belief in the value of dialogue and in the creative possibilities which dialogue opens. From our side, as Protestants, we can claim to have found a way—the Protestant way— by which, in spite of opposition, we can meet in love, knowing that Christ's will for us is more important than our party programmes. It is a claim we can make because the Protestant way is not only a Protestant way and does not belong exclusively to 'our side'. Nor have we found it for ourselves, but we acknowledge that it belongs to God's self-revelation.

Dialogue can reach across all barriers, ecclesiastical and theological. A Roman Catholic writer, E. I. Watkin, can look back in history and say:

> Catholics remember only too well the evil aspect of Puritanism, its unlovely fanaticism, its iconoclasm, its persecution of their religion. These memories widen an inevitable separation of creed into a gulf of misunderstanding and hostility. It is time to turn our gaze to the good aspect of that Puritan movement, its strong and earnest and tender devotion, its personal love of Jesus. This love of our common Lord is a unity behind our differences.[27]

Some differences between conflicting parties can be removed by discussion at the intellectual level. But there must first be the will to seek reconciliation. The sympathy which can look through party principles and find the dimension of subjectivity a meeting-place for beliefs which objectively diverge sharply is essential for this. It is also of the highest theological importance. Without an understanding of love there can be no understanding of divine grace; and this understanding can only be on the level of subjectivity.

Of course, unity on the ground of the possibility of dialogue is not yet unity among the people of God, that unity with which the Church is called to confront the world and to find fullness of life in Christ. The theological spade-work still to be done before that unity is achieved is intimidating. But we are called to carry through this search for unity by the Lord in whom all are one. The call to repentance and newness of life is a call to every individual and to the whole Church. We cannot hear the one call without hearing the other. The possibility of dialogue with our neighbour begins in Him, as it is from Him and through Him. Our faith is the answer—not our own— to His grace. The Protestant protest will be made perfect when it is no longer 'Protestant', but merged in the wider protest of a Catholic Church no longer 'Catholic'.

[27] *Poets and Mystics* (1953), p. 69.

INDEX OF SUBJECTS

INDEX OF NAMES